FRAMED!

FRAMED!

LABOR AND THE CORPORATE MEDIA

CHRISTOPHER R. MARTIN

ILR PRESS an imprint of
CORNELL UNIVERSITY PRESS

ITHACA AND LONDON

First published 2004 by Cornell University Press
First printing, Cornell Paperbacks, 2004

Printed in the United States of America

Library of Congress Cataloging-in-Publication Data

Martin, Christopher R.
  Framed! : labor and the corporate media / Christopher R. Martin.
    p. cm.
Includes bibliographical references and index.
  ISBN 0-8014-4198-6 (cloth : alk. paper)—ISBN 0-8104-8887-7 (pbk. :
alk. paper)
  1. Labor unions and mass media—United States. 2. Mass
media—Objectivity. I. Title
  P96.T72U66 2004
  331.88'0973—dc21

                                  2003012870

Cornell University Press strives to use environmentally responsible suppliers and materials to the fullest extent possible in the publishing of its books. Such materials include
vegetable-based, low-VOC inks and acid-free papers that are recycled, totally chlorine-
free, or partly composed of nonwood fibers. For further information, visit our website at
www.cornellpress.cornell.edu.

Cloth printing   10 9 8 7 6 5 4 3 2 1
Paperback printing   10 9 8 7 6 5 4 3 2 1

To Bettina, Olivia, and Sabine

CONTENTS

PREFACE

I have a confession: I was a College Republican who cheered approval of Reagan's firing of the nation's striking air traffic controllers in 1981. I thought that labor unions were corrupt, belligerent organizations that protected lazy, unproductive workers and caused products to be more expensive. I believed that economic matters were the prerogative of savvy entrepreneurs and executives, who—unfettered by unions and regulation—would create a robust economy with benefits that would trickle down to all of us.

My views in the 1980s, however, did not reflect a well-developed sense of ideology but rather my acceptance of the common sense of the day. I watched the network news on a regular basis and read a daily newspaper and national newsweekly magazines. And that is what I knew about labor unions.

The transformation to the person who wrote this book was gradual, and one in which the mainstream news media offered little help. The people who educated me along the way are those I wish to thank.

My first lessons about labor were the lived experiences of my own family. After a divorce, my brave, intelligent mother raised three sons and one daughter mostly on her own. I began to see that despite her competence, she was paid far less than her male colleagues at work and received far fewer opportunities for advancement. Her treatment as an "office gal" by her employers had a big effect on the kinds of wages she would earn trying to sustain her family.

Two older brothers also taught me something about work. Collectively, they have labored through a long list of jobs. Plastics manufacturing, department store catalogue phone bank, hotel maintenance, produce truck delivery, swimming pool installation, nursing home custodian, and food prep at various McDonald's restaurants are just a few of the jobs they've held. They quit most of the bad jobs and were laid off of some of the better ones. Their hard work and optimism demonstrates the indomitable spirit and dignity of American workers. But, for their dignity, they suffer the all-too-common indignities of work in the United States. In middle age, they still struggle to pay for health care and have accumulated little in pension savings from their jobs. They deserve better. My sister and her husband also struggle with health care coverage. He is self-employed, and after she resigned from her full-time teaching job to have children, they've had to contend with paying out of pocket for steep health insurance premiums. They, too, deserve better.

If you don't know much about labor unions, or if your main information source about them is the mainstream news media, it's easy to blame unions (or the Japanese, or recent immigrants, or some other scapegoat) for every bad working situation. I was fortunate to have outstanding mentors at the University of Michigan to help me begin to understand the politics of work that affect myself, my family, and millions of other middle-class Americans and why the news media frame labor unions as part of the problem rather than a potential solution. I am deeply indebted to Jimmie L. Reeves, Richard Campbell, Hayg Oshagan, and Howard Kimeldorf for their expert guidance in my research there. Reeves and Campbell also imparted a valuable piece of advice that still motivates me: No matter whether you win or lose, you should always fight for the right things.

Living in Michigan in the first half of the 1990s made me a witness to several important labor events. Foremost was General Motors' shutdown of its Willow Run Assembly Plant. Presidential candidates George H. W. Bush, H. Ross Perot, and Bill Clinton debated in Michigan and paid homage to the four thousand displaced workers, but they never offered a decent economic strategy to prevent such tragedies. In Detroit, the two major newspapers—the *News* and *Free Press*—conspired to break their workers' unions by locking them out. At the same time, touring Michigan and the Midwest were the "Road Warriors" from Decatur, Illinois—locked out or striking workers from the A. E. Staley Corporation, Caterpillar, and

Bridgestone/Firestone—who were trying to raise funds and labor support for union members who were truly under siege in that small industrial city. I also witnessed and participated in a labor event that was at least as important to me and my coworkers. At the University of Michigan in Ann Arbor, the administration attempted to cut health care coverage to graduate assistants, who taught 40 percent of the classes at the university. As a department steward, I joined the Graduate Employee Organization in carrying pickets and shared in the celebration when we won.

This book is the culmination of more than ten years' worth of research and writing on labor and the news. I am grateful to several entities for financial support along the way. At the University of Michigan, the Horace H. Rackham School of Graduate Studies assisted me through a One-Term Dissertation Fellowship and a Rackham Dissertation Grant for the rental of network news videotapes from the Vanderbilt Television News Archive. At the University of Northern Iowa (UNI), I received support from two UNI Faculty Summer Fellowships and a Project Grant from the Graduate College of UNI.

At UNI, in the surrounding community, and around the globe, I have been blessed by good friends and colleagues who have offered their guidance and wisdom, including Mark Grey, Mary Grey, Konrad Sadkowski, Alicja Boruta-Sadkowski, Lou Fenech, Christine Fenech, Kamyar Enshayan, Laura Jackson, Greg Bruess, Isabela Varela, Renata Sack, Loree Rackstraw, Ronnie Bankston, Laura Terlip, Victoria DeFrancisco, Anelia Dimitrova, Leonard Curtis, David O'Shields, Jim Lubker, Walter Sanders, Jonathan Chenoweth, Kathleen Sihler, Ralph Beliveau, Nicholas Taggart, Kyle Keith, Michael Epstein, Lamia Karim, Anny Rey, and Ralph Gladitz. Family members in Ohio, Massachusetts, and beyond also offered moral support and, often, inspiration. Thanks to Barbara Martin, Michael Martin, Bernice Martin, Phillip Martin, Jennifer Candor, Rob Candor, Julius Gy. Fabos, Edith Fabos, Anita Fabos, Adrian Fabos, Laszlo Hevizi, and Nora Gal.

Charles R. Conrad, Corey Dolgon, Eric Rothenbuhler, and Dina Gavrilos all read parts of what became this book, and I appreciate their formative advice. Jefferson Cowie and William Solomon were both incredibly thoughtful reviewers of the complete manuscript. I can only hope to live up to their high expectations. Fran Benson, editorial director of ILR Press at Cornell University Press, and Melissa Oravec, editorial assistant, have been delightful to work with, and I give them many thanks. Ange Romeo-Hall, manuscript editor, and Cathi Reinfelder, copy editor, also helped to improve this book in innumerable ways.

Part of Chapter 4 was previously published in Christopher R. Martin and Hayg Oshagan, "Disciplining the Workforce: The News Media Frame a General Motors Plant Closing," *Communication Research* 24, no. 6 (1997): 669–97. Part of Chapter 7 was previously published in Christopher R. Martin, "The 1997 UPS Strike: Framing the Story for Popular Consumption," *Journal of Communication Inquiry* 27, no. 2 (2003): 190–210. Both journals are published by Sage Publications.

The two greatest gifts during the research and writing were the births of daughters Olivia (1998) and Sabine (2001). Their existence and unconditional love gave me the best reason for finishing this book: I want them to avoid their father's horrible mistake of uncritically accepting the commonsense news of the day with all of its incumbent pitfalls.

Finally, my deepest thanks, love, and admiration goes to Bettina Fabos. In this project, and in all things, my best work has been inspired and sustained by her intellect, love, time, humor, and passion.

FRAMED!

HOW LABOR GETS FRAMED

Just prior to the dramatic interpretation of the National Anthem for Super Bowl XXIX on January 29, 1995, by Kathie Lee Gifford (who, incidentally, would have her own line of sportswear at Wal-Mart publicly linked to Honduran sweatshop labor a year later), ABC paused for one of the television broadcast's frequent commercial breaks. The first commercial of the intermission, a thirty-second spot costing approximately $1 million to air before tens of millions of viewers, peddled Pizza Hut pizzas and—simultaneously—epitomized the news media's coverage of contemporary labor relations in the United States.

The commercial presented a stereotypical labor-management standoff as it quickly cut back and forth between the two parties. Outside of chain-link factory gates, a group of industrial workers holding picket signs huddle around a steel barrel fire to keep warm in a snowy wind. Two or three stories above, in a quiet, warm, executive conference room, white-collar executives complain *"We can't accept these demands,"* and *"This is outrageous!"* Below, the workers brace themselves against the wind and agree that *"We can stay out as long as we need to."*

Back in the conference room, a balding male executive looks up from his stack of papers and says, *"Listen, they gotta eat, right?"* A more patient male executive thinks out loud: *"There's got to be some kind of common ground here."* As the workers down below vow *"They're not gonna break us,"* up above an executive bemoans *"I thought they were our friends."* The intro-

The worker nods and "toasts" the executive with a pizza slice. Labor and management find common ground as consumers of pizza.

"Sometimes, something as simple as a hot pizza can bring people together." The beneficent executive looks down from above.

spective executive gets an idea as he looks down upon the striking workers in the cold. *"Yeh . . . our friends."* Through the window, we see the executive hang up the telephone.

During an era when unionized industrial workers in the United States have seen their jobs shipped overseas and have been forced to work more for less wage and benefit compensation lest they be replaced by nonunion workers, the groundwork for the resolution of this labor-management dispute is remarkably simple. A Pizza Hut delivery van pulls up to the factory gates, eliciting worker cheers, and the commercial's narrator tells us: *"Sometimes, something as simple as a hot pizza can bring people together. Like a Pizza Hut one-topping pan pizza. Large. Two for thirteen bucks."* The workers take time between bites to wonder who ordered the pizza. One male worker in baseball hat, hooded sweatshirt, and green army-style coat looks up to the thoughtful executive standing at the window. The executive returns the gaze, and smiles and nods to communicate his gift of one-topping pan pizzas. The worker nods and "toasts" the executive with a pizza slice.

In this pleasant thirty-second story of class conflict resolution, Pizza Hut suggests that most labor-management conflicts are not based on substantial issues, but instead on simple misunderstandings between equals and friends. The message to the huge Super Bowl audience is that labor peace can be "bought" with the right kind of consumer product, in this case Pizza Hut pan pizzas. The commercial's common ground between labor and management is not found through negotiations. Instead, understanding occurs only in the sphere of consumption.

Of course, advertising isn't the "real world," one might say. But, in the "real" world reported in the national corporate news media, stories concerning the labor movement are played out in the same consumer sphere. The mainstream news media, divisions of major corporations themselves, are usually savvy enough to avoid covering labor relations with a blatant business perspective. Instead, the news media find a "common ground" narrative between labor and management positions by reporting on labor relations from a consumer perspective.

Although this consumer point of view functions as a strategy to be journalistically "objective," it isn't an objective or value-free position. Any perspective has consequences. The news media's consumer point of view on the labor movement conflict has the effect of submerging issues of citizenship, political activity, and class relations and of elevating issues of consumption and the myth of a class-free America. Instead of facilitating a *public sphere*, the democratic ideal that Jürgen Habermas has defined as a forum where the public can engage in discovery and rational-critical debate,[1] the news media have fostered a *consumer sphere*, in which public discourse and action is defined in terms of appropriate consumer behavior. Thus, the news media cover strikes, lockouts, shutdowns, and protests largely based on the relevance of the conflict to the interests of the consumer—that is, the impact of the conflict on such things as the price, quality, and availability of consumable goods and services and on the consumer economy at large.[2] With this focus on commodities, the commercial mainstream news—like the advertising that supports it—obscures the laborers behind those branded commodities and the myriad of conditions in which they work. The ultimate outcome of the news media's consumer-oriented framing of labor stories is that the news is often severely critical of labor's actions and enthusiastically supportive of capital's actions.

A brief analysis of two national newspapers' coverage of the 1993 American Airlines flight attendant strike illustrates how the news media frame labor issues for the viewpoint of the consumer. The framing begins with the lead (first) paragraphs of *USA Today*'s and the *New York Times*' front-page stories announcing a strike by American Airlines' 21,000 flight attendants on November 19, 1993. Both leads focus on the dispute's consumer impact. The *USA Today* story elevated the commonplace problem of lost luggage into strike-specific traveler catastrophe:

> Paul Dean, 38, of Silver Spring, Md., didn't get to Dallas on American Airlines Thursday.
>
> But his luggage did.
>
> It was left on a jet that was empty of fliers because American Airlines didn't have flight attendants to fly with it. "This is a disaster," Dean said, as he watched the jet push back from the gate at Washington's National Airport.[3]

The *New York Times* took a less dramatic approach, but framed the story as primarily a consumer disaster: "American Airlines' flight attendants went on strike yesterday morning, disrupting service for tens of thousands of passengers in the United States and overseas."[4]

To be fair, both newspapers covered other angles of the five-day strike in their period of coverage.[5] For example, the two newspapers reported on the egregiously low salary (starting at less than $15,000 and averaging about $23,000 annually) of the American Airlines' flight attendants. But the debate over low pay was always tempered with the argument that American needed to downsize, control labor costs, and increase profitability. The newspapers subsequently treated labor cost increases as inflationary and directly related to airfare increases and the consumer's interest.

How could have the news media coverage of the strike been elevated from the pedestrian issues of the consumer sphere into the broader concerns of the public sphere? One way would have been to fully develop the issue of class inequities between the low-paid flight attendants and the executives of American Airlines. In this way, readers could evaluate the need for AMR, American Airlines' parent company, to achieve "cost control" and extract profits through greater discipline of its flight attendant labor force.

Robert Crandall, then-chairman/CEO of AMR, had already found some ways to cut extravagance at his corporation; it was, for example, Crandall's own decision to remove olives from its customers' in-flight salads, saving AMR $40,000 a year.[6] But, while Crandall adeptly pared down others' salaries and salads in hard times, Crandall's own compensation soared during the second half of the 1980s, even as AMR lost money under his direction. Crandall's annual base salary of $381,000 in 1985, with a matching bonus, rose to $600,000 by 1990, with another hefty bonus. Crandall also received a restricted AMR stock grant worth a minimum of $11.8 million in 1988, with a guarantee of reimbursement for any drop in his stock's value. As business professor and compensation consultant Graef Crystal noted, Crandall's compensation package "seems to float free of such mundane matters as the company's performance."[7]

Meanwhile, American's flight attendants, 85 percent of whom are women, noted during the negotiations that they had lived through a 40 percent decline in real wages since making concessions to AMR management in 1983.[8] While the *New York Times* and *USA Today* freely debated the value of flight attendants' labor, not one story questioned compensation of Crandall and other high-flying AMR executives as a possible labor cost problem (only one story even mentioned Crandall's compensation) or debated the impact of management's performance or salary on airfare prices. Other mainstream media outlets produced strikingly similar coverage of the flight attendant walkout and avoided expanding the issue of "controlling labor costs" to the level of executive compensation. To discuss executive-level compensation would, of course, have introduced social inequality as a major issue of the strike. Instead, the news media framed the American Airlines flight attendant strike of 1993 as a story of consumer inconvenience and expense, precluding the development of critical debate of class and compensation issues in the airline industry. In this and other instances, the news media use "impact on the consumer" as the organizing theme in deciding which labor stories they tell and how they tell them.

Five Dominant Frames of Labor News

When the news media cover labor, they don't do so by communicating "neutral" facts but by telling us stories about labor, especially stories that shape and reflect our culture's commonsense ideas about labor, management, and capital.[9] Like any good narrative, news stories can be engaging, and the way in which the story is told can encourage the news audience to understand and experience the story in a certain way. Media historian James Carey explains that "[N]ews is not information but drama. It does not describe the world but portrays an arena of dramatic forces and action; it exists solely in historical time, and it invites our participation on the basis of our assuming, often vicariously, social roles within it."[10]

Thus, the narrative story form in news gives individual events and circumstances meaning. The particular structure of a story is its frame. As W. Lance Bennett and Murray Edelman explain, "the who, what, where, why, how, and when . . . give acts and events a narrative *frame*. A choice among alternative settings or among origins of a political development also determines who are virtuous, who are threats to the good life, and which courses of action are effective solutions."[11] Similarly, Todd Gitlin has called media frames "persistent patterns of cognition, interpretation, and presentation, of selection, emphasis, and exclusion, by which symbol-handlers routinely organize discourse, whether verbal or visual."[12] The act of framing is largely an act of common sense on the journalist's part. Unfortunately, common sense leads back to the familiar and traditional, and it often cuts off creative thinking and imagination in news coverage.

Peter Golding and Graham Murdock suggest that there are two general ways in which cultural forms, such as news, work as mechanisms regulating public discourse. First, the form itself limits the range of discourses possible, from solely official discourses to the articulation of counterdiscourses. As previously noted, news tends to operate within the parameters of a consumer sphere, addressing its audience as consumers. Second, discourses within the form can be treated in various ways, from being arranged in a "clearly marked hierarchy of credibility which urges the audience to prefer one [discourse] over the others" to "a more even-handed and indeterminate way which leaves the audience more open to choice."[13] Thus, news can regulate discourse on issues through the amount of coverage provided and the kinds of portrayals in the coverage.

Ralph Miliband concurs with the notion that the media regulate public discourse. He notes that the mass media have the power to "foster a climate of conformity . . . by the presentation of views which fall outside the consensus as curious heresies, or, even more effectively, by treating them as irrelevant eccentricities, which serious and reasonable people may dismiss as of no consequence."[14] Jimmie Reeves and Richard Campbell describe this journalistic function as "policing" the boundaries of reason and nonsense, or the normal and abnormal: "In the ongoing representation of authority and the visualization of deviancy, the well-informed journalist mediates two symbolic horizons of common sense . . . on one horizon the journalist bridges the knowledge gap between 'expertness and the lack of it'; on the other, the journalist guards the frontier between 'normalcy and the lack of it,' between 'reasonable people' and 'deviant nonsense.' "[15]

We might then expect similar policing of the boundaries of common sense in news stories of labor relations, where stories are framed to suggest who are the virtuous and threatening actors, what are the most effective solutions to labor disputes, and whose interests are paramount.

Five frames dominated the news media coverage of major labor stories in the 1990s, in effect, setting such boundaries. These frames are consistent with the generalizations and stereotypes noted by earlier media research, but go further in explaining the "commonsense" consumer-oriented ideological environment in which the U.S. corporate mass media structure news stories about labor unions:

1. *The consumer is king.* Because the consumer and his or her consump-

tion is fundamental to the U.S. economy and culture, treating the individual consumer as a hallowed entity is the unstated assumption of all news. Likewise, this is a consumers' democracy. Americans are told they are blessed with an abundance of choices and can "vote" with their pocketbooks. But, caveat emptor to the consumer: In this news frame, the consumer is valued when acting individually and a menace when acting collectively on behalf of a social purpose (see Frame #5 below). As economist Juliet Schor explains, "Ours is an ideology of non-interference—the view that one should be able to buy what one likes, where one likes, and as much as one likes, with nary a glance from the government, neighbors, ministers, or political parties. Consumption is perhaps the clearest example of individual behavior which our society takes to be almost wholly personal, completely outside the purview of social concern and policy."[16]

2. *The process of production is none of the public's business.* The role of the consumer is to decide whether or not to buy a product or service, and not to inquire about the production process. Yet, aside from a few government labeling laws, it is nearly impossible to know anything about the means of production of a product or service. In fact, it is often a main function of advertising and public relations to avoid discussing the actual collective process of production (which would entail the stories of workers and their conditions) and instead create a substitute meaning that typically has little or nothing to do with material production.[17] The news treads lightly on the topic of production because to undermine advertising/PR's myths and images of production would be to undermine the work of their sponsors.

3. *The economy is driven by great business leaders and entrepreneurs.* This news frame is the flip side of the hidden production process. Why bother talking about the workers, the news seems to say, when the embodiment of production can be portrayed by individual CEOs and entrepreneurs? The heroic CEO and entrepreneur were staples of journalism in the 1990s, an era that witnessed an explosion of growth in business reporting. Yet more business journalism was not necessarily better journalism, as the news more often glorified the developing information economy with sycophantic features on the new "Culture Trust" and celebrated the ultra-wealthy's outrageous fortunes so excitedly that a writer for the *Columbia Journalism Review* dubbed the genre "wealth porn."[18] A corollary of this frame is that anyone with the gumption can become a superrich entrepreneur/CEO, too—the myth of the self-made man. This view asserts that

those in power are there because, according to the business cliché, they work harder and smarter—thus denying any advantages to being born into the right social class or having access to cultural capital.

Of course, business leaders became a tarnished lot in the corporate management scandals of 2002. At first, the Bush administration and the news media largely protected the business executive image by blaming "a few bad apples" for the problems.[19] But stories of corporate malfeasance extended beyond Enron, Arthur Anderson, Tyco, Adelphia, and Worldcom to include dozens of companies with the mildly named problem of "accounting irregularities" and executives who gave themselves enormous loans from the corporate till or cashed in millions in stock options before their companies slid into ruin. Nevertheless, the great business leaders and entrepreneurs frame persisted, and the news media seemed eager to consign the scandals to distant memories. For example, in a year-end assessment of business in 2002, the *New York Times* began by noting the "downcast year" but made a seamless transition back to the same familiar frame by celebrating about a dozen executives "who made 2002 a winning year," many of them profiting from stock options.[20]

4. *The workplace is a meritocracy.* This frame derives from an individualist vision that doesn't include unions. It basically suggests that "you get what you deserve" in the workplace. Similar to the corollary of Frame #3 above, the myth here is that good people rise to the top and are compensated likewise. Those who aren't rising to the top probably aren't working hard or smart enough. Moreover, working is like consumption—an individual choice. If people don't like their job, they should get another. This kind of frame, of course, deflects any responsibility for the workplace by the employer and preempts collective action, as noted in Frame #5 below.

5. *Collective economic action is bad.* The notion here, developed historically in the corporate assault against unions and liberalism,[21] is that collective action by workers, communities, and even consumers will upset the well-functioning, democratic U.S. consumer economy and the decisions of great business leaders and entrepreneurs. The news media disapprove of collective action—including strikes, slowdowns, boycotts, and protests—with a number of standard canards: It is inflationary, un-American, protectionist, naïve, causes bureaucratic red tape, disrupts consumer demand and behavior, foments fear and violence, etc. The frame carries an interesting underlying assumption: that economic intervention

by citizens should happen only at the individual level (e.g., tell your boss to "take this job and shove it" if you are dissatisfied, or "vote with your pocketbook" if you don't like something). Of course, individual action preempts collective action, which is more democratic and potent. But, politics outside the reigning corporate-political structure is largely disdained, if not usually ignored, by the press.

These five dominant frames resulted in news coverage throughout the 1990s that was often severely critical of labor's actions and enthusiastically supportive of capital's actions. With such framing, the news media's stories have continually undercut a legitimate social institution—labor unions—that might serve as a useful remedy to millions of U.S. workers who want independent representation in their workplace for collective bargaining and dispute resolution, and a voice in the economy.[22] Of course, one could argue that labor unions, especially in the second half of the twentieth century, have often failed to adequately communicate their case to the mass media. Even the American Federation of Labor and Congress of Industrial Organizations (AFL-CIO), the nation's largest labor union, charged in 1985 that "efforts should be made to better publicize organized labor's accomplishments," "union spokespersons need training in media techniques," and "efforts must be made at every level to better inform reporters about unions and trade unionism."[23]

But the dominant news frames back labor into a tight corner. Especially in the 1990s, even with the best public relations, labor was left with little possibility for framing its story in a way that would both represent its mission and somehow fit into the typical consumer frames of coverage. However (as we will see later in the book), with advanced planning, collective action, and a widespread and consistent public message, it is possible for labor unions to engage these same consumer frames to define the news story to their benefit, publicizing issues in ways that are difficult for a corporate, consumer-oriented press to ignore and that are salient to both consumers *and* citizens.

Earlier Research on News Media Coverage of Labor

Perhaps the most important characteristic of mainstream coverage of labor is that the media are often not covering labor at all. Jonathan Tasini's

1990 study of more than one thousand network news broadcasts (approximately 22,000 minutes) found that only slightly more than 1 percent of the airtime (265 minutes) was devoted to covering U.S. unions. A strike by Eastern Airlines employees accounted for 72 percent of all union airtime, leaving just a few minutes for all other union issues. In the print media, the labor beat has almost disappeared, Tasini reports, as editors at medium-sized and large U.S. newspapers devote less money and space to labor reporting, while business news thrives.[24]

Although labor is seldom in the news, there are typical ways in which labor news is described. Michael Parenti catalogued seven generalizations about the way the news media portray labor:

1. The larger struggle between capital and labor is ignored, making it possible to present labor struggles as senseless conflicts that could be solved if only the union would be willing to negotiate in good faith.
2. Company "offers" are emphasized, while company takebacks, employee grievances, and issues such as job security, health insurance, and safety are underplayed or ignored. As a result, workers appear irrational, greedy, and self-destructive.
3. While "fat" labor wages are reported, management compensation usually is not. Especially when workers are asked to make concessions, no coverage is typically given to management salaries, bonuses, and other perquisites.
4. The problems a strike has on the economy and public convenience are emphasized to the detriment of in-depth coverage on the cause(s) of the strike. Striking workers are thus portrayed as indifferent to the interests of the public's well-being.
5. Reports fail to consider the impact on the workers if they were to give up the strike and accept management's terms.
6. Instances of union solidarity and broader public support are rarely covered, eliminating the class dimension of a strike.
7. Governmental agencies are cast as neutral entities upholding the public interest, yet the president, courts, and police often act to force workers back into production, protect corporate property, or guard strikebreakers.[25]

William Puette found that mass media stereotypes portray labor unions as "protect[ing] and encourag[ing] unproductive, usually fat, lazy and insubordinate workers" and "institutionaliz[ing] conflict . . . dredg[ing] up conflict where there would otherwise be perfect harmony."[26] Although such stereotypes create popular images of labor inefficiencies, unionized establishments are often more productive than nonunion establishments.[27] In addition, the fact is that less than 2 percent of all contract talks result in strikes.[28]

Empirical research of labor coverage in the news is scarce. The small number of existing studies all seem to support Parenti's and Puette's lists of news generalizations and stereotypes. The main issues of analysis have been the frequency of coverage, and—if coverage is given—the nature of portrayals. As noted earlier, the frequency of labor news in mainstream news outlets is increasingly rare. All across America, newspapers have replaced traditional labor beats with more general workplace beats. By 2002, there were fewer than five labor beat reporters left at U.S. daily newspapers.[29] Workplace stories now most often appear in newspaper business sections, which implicitly embrace business interests, and are most often written by staff business reporters who are occasionally assigned to cover labor issues.[30] Coverage in magazines and the broadcast media is even less regular. William Serrin, former labor reporter for the *New York Times*, decried the state of labor journalism: "Much of the labor movement and much of the United States—including the nation's newsrooms—believed in the 1980s and 1990s that nothing was going on in labor. The truth was, everything was going on in labor . . . in truth, industrial America, the labor movement, and the lives of America's working people were being turned upside down. It was just that almost no one could see this . . ."[31]

In the cases when labor issues *are* covered (most likely strikes),[32] labor has often been characterized in a number of negative ways. One of the earliest studies of such news coverage, a 1945 content analysis of American radio news stories on labor, found that unions are usually portrayed as being the "wrong" party in workplace disputes.[33] The radio stories typically quoted prominent government officials, political leaders, business executives, and even union members to construct the management's "side" of the story. Only labor leaders were used to provide quotes supporting the labor position, suggesting that the union had few advocates beyond its own leadership.

Other studies note that in coverage of labor-management disputes, quotes and interviews are most typically from management representatives, occasionally from union representatives, and least likely from regular workers.[34] Citing workers might seem to be redundant when union representatives are already quoted. But, when workers undertake strikes that aren't endorsed by union leadership (wildcat strikes) or when workers disagree with their union leadership and form opposition groups within the union (such as the New Directions caucus in the United Automobile Workers [UAW]), quoting rank-and-file workers is especially important. The visual language of news reports is also damaging to labor's image, studies suggest. Television news interviews typically portray management representatives speaking directly to the camera, in the calm, rational environment of business offices. Conversely, workers are depicted in the often chaotic, noisy environment of a street picket line and are rarely interviewed face to face.[35]

Studies on the linguistic interpretation of labor-management conflicts again support the analysis of Parenti, Puette, and others. For example, the extensive Machinists Union Media Monitoring Project of television entertainment and news broadcasts in 1980 and 1981 found that "television typically casts unions as violent, degrading, and obstructive."[36] Although class structure is more pronounced in Britain than in the United States, media coverage of labor-management conflict is often similar. Three major studies by the Glasgow University Media Group on British television's coverage of industrial news consistently demonstrate poor coverage of labor issues.[37] The Media Group found that events reflecting negatively on management, such as industrial accidents, were "systematically underreported," whereas labor's reasons for striking were reported irregularly or not at all. The British studies also show that the credibility of labor's position is always in question in the description of industrial conflict:

> [I]ndustrial reporting relies on the assumption that industrial disputes are about "trouble"—trouble for us as customers, commuters and members of the public, trouble for the managers of industry, trouble for the nation; but never trouble for the workers involved. In the detailed examination of the vocabulary used we have demonstrated that in disputes the traditional *offers* of management are inevitably countered by the *demands* of workers—to the point where the nouns and verbs describing management actions are generally positive while the matching vocabulary for worker's actions is negative.[38]

Not all agree that business is favorably covered in the news. Some studies suggest that the news media is biased against business, although none go so far as to conclude that the news media is biased in favor of labor or a socialist economy. A Freedom Forum survey of business executives, business reporters, and editors suggests that business executives believe the news media is dangerous, mean-spirited, and arrogant. Yet, Warren Phillips, former Dow Jones chairman and a former executive editor of the *Wall Street Journal*, notes that business executives have particular expectations of the press. "The majority of business leaders are really looking for cheerleaders, just like the majority of government people are mostly looking for people to support their policies in government."[39]

In *The Media Elite*, S. Robert Lichter, Stanley Rothman, and Linda Lichter offer another survey comparing business executives and the news media. In their view, an elite, liberal East Coast media strongly influences the general tone of America's national news coverage. This elite group is generally in favor of liberal social positions, which are out of step with surveyed business leaders' opinions. Thus, these authors conclude, the media is biased against business. But, their conclusion of an antibusiness bias is certainly problematic, not least because they also find that the media elite are broadly supportive of America's capitalist system. Large majorities of the elite newspeople in their survey responded that they believe "people with more ability should earn more," "private enterprise is fair to workers," and "less regulation of business is good for the U.S."[40] Thus, the elite media worker's liberalism apparently doesn't extend to the concerns of labor.

Lichter, Rothman, and Lichter also reported that the elite media respondents would, in ranking seven groups based on who should have social influence, place labor at the bottom of the list.[41] The news watchdog organization FAIR (Fairness and Accuracy in Reporting) came to a similar conclusion in 1998 when they found that on a wide variety of economic issues—including the expansion of the North American Free Trade Agreement (NAFTA), taxing the wealthy, concern over corporate concentration of power, and government-guaranteed medical care—the press was to the right of the public's views.[42]

For business, then, the issue of complaint is rarely over frequency of coverage (indeed, business enjoys extensive media coverage), but instead the nature of portrayals. Perhaps most relevant to this book is that these complaints of antibusiness bias in the press do not mean corresponding allegations of a prolabor bias. For labor, the problem of news coverage has always been a problem of both frequency and portrayal. A comparison of two coal strikes, one in the United States and one in the Soviet Union, demonstrates the frustrating situation for U.S. workers attempting to communicate their situation in the news media.

In 1989, 1,700 United Mine Workers (UMW) struck the Pittston Coal Group plants in Virginia, West Virginia, and Kentucky to protest the company's efforts to take back pension and health benefits and to subcontract work to nonunion laborers.[43] At one point in the eleven-month strike, nearly one hundred workers and a United Methodist minister took over a Pittston coal-processing plant for four days. Not since the heralded 1937 sit-down strike by autoworkers at the General Motors plant in Flint, Michigan, had striking workers occupied a major U.S. production facility.[44] Yet, national media coverage of the strike was slight and generally unfavorable. Within nine months from the beginning of UMW's strike against Pittston, the three major television networks had supplied a total of just 22 minutes and 40 seconds of coverage. During the same summer, miners in the Soviet Union were also on strike. In this case, however, the miners had garnered extensive and enthusiastic network coverage by these same three U.S. networks in just a few days. As Tasini notes, "the strikers, who were portrayed by the media as a shining symbol of the democratic challenge to the Soviet government, were showered by the network nightly newscasts with 37 minutes and 20 seconds of positive coverage during nine straight days from July 17 to July 25."[45]

Similar was the news media's treatment of the Professional Air Traffic Controller Organization (PATCO) strike in 1981 and the labor actions by the Lech Walesa–led Solidarity union in Poland during the same early years of the Reagan administration. Labor scholar Art Shostak notes that both Reagan and major news outlets "uniformly vilified" the PATCO air traffic controller's union for its national strike over stressful work conditions and compensation.[46] Reagan responded by quickly firing 11,345 striking air controllers and blacklisting them from all government jobs. Solidarity, the emergent labor union in communist Poland, was conversely treated with great esteem in the news media. According to Edward S. Herman and Noam Chomsky, "protest over political prisoners and the violation of the rights of trade unions in Poland was seen by the

Reagan administration and business elites in 1981 as a noble cause, and, not coincidentally, as an opportunity to score political points. Many media leaders and syndicated columnists felt the same way."[47]

Interestingly, no one decided to make any political points in 1999 when McDonald's—heralded for bringing U.S.–style capitalism and expensive fast food to Russia in 1990—violated Russian law by failing to recognize its workers' union and pressured employees into signing antiunion declarations. McDonald's established its first Russian restaurant in Pushkin Square in 1990, and by 1999 operated forty-seven outlets in mostly the Moscow area, employing almost seven thousand workers. Yet there was no popular sentiment (and no mainstream news reports) in the United States to cast the Russian workers as noble democrats as they battled America's favorite icon of consumerism over unsafe working conditions, low wages, and employee harassment.[48]

The contrast in most news coverage between American and foreign labor unions begs the fundamental questions of this book: Why is class-based debate missing from the public forum of the mainstream national news? Are the broad economic and democratic interests of working-class citizens intentionally distorted, actively ignored, benignly forsaken, or habitually recast by the press?[49] Or, is it true that, in the words of philosopher Thomas McCarthy, "the press and broadcast media serve less as organs of public information and debate than as technologies for managing consensus and promoting consumer culture"?[50]

Overview: A Decade of Labor News

The corporate news media's framing of labor becomes even more evident in the following chapters, which critically analyze coverage of five major labor events from the 1990s: the 1991–94 shutdown of the General Motors Willow Run Assembly Plant in Ypsilanti Township, Michigan; the American Airlines flight attendant strike of 1993; the 1994–95 Major League Baseball strike; the 1997 United Parcel Service (UPS) strike; and the 1999 protests against the World Trade Organization's (WTO) Ministerial Conference in Seattle. These five events offer a range of circumstances for comparison.

In many ways, the Willow Run case represents the most typical face of labor as it is covered by the media. It involved relatively low media coverage (just 22 stories in *USA Today*, 31 stories in the *New York Times*, and 15 network [ABC, CBS, NBC] news packages[51] in 2½ years), low direct consumer impact, well-paid blue-collar workers, competitive bidding between two unions and cities (Arlington, Texas, and Ypsilanti, Michigan) to keep a plant open, and America's largest corporation, General Motors.

In contrast, the flight attendant strike was a service industry strike with a short but intense period of media coverage (33 stories in *USA Today*, 30 stories in the *New York Times*, and 16 network news packages in less than 3 full months), high consumer impact, low-paid and mostly female service workers, and the well-known company American Airlines. The baseball strike provides a case with massive news media coverage (more than 1,500 reports combined from *USA Today* and the *New York Times*, and more than 100 network news packages, in less than a full year—easily the most-covered labor event of the past decade and perhaps of all time), high consumer impact, the unusual situation of mostly enormously wealthy athletes/workers, and the hallowed, quasi-public institution of Major League Baseball.

The UPS strike of August 1997 is now commonly cited as labor's greatest success of the 1990s, where 185,000 Teamsters (members of the International Brotherhood of Teamsters union) brought the nation's largest parcel delivery service to a standstill and won most of their demands, despite the fact that millions of consumers were inconvenienced. The strike was one of the top stories of 1997, with 77 *USA Today* reports, 139 *New York Times* stories, and 70 network news packages from July through August 1997. But, perhaps the most unique feature of the strike is that by the account of the news media's own surveys, the striking workers gained a majority of the nation's support. Still riding on the crest of the UPS victory, labor groups in 1999 united with environmentalists, human rights organizations, and a host of other interest groups totaling 50,000 people strong to protest at the World Trade Organization's meeting in Seattle. It was the last big labor news story of the decade, with 31 *USA Today* stories, 72 *New York Times* articles, and 33 news packages on the big three television networks from October through December 1999.

Each of these events was one of the most closely followed stories of the decade, as measured by the nonprofit Pew Research Center's monthly

News Interest Index nationwide surveys, which ask people how closely they follow certain news stories. The UPS strike was the fifth most closely followed story (in terms of "very closely" responses) of all news stories in 1997, and was the most closely followed labor story of the entire decade, with 76 percent of respondents following it closely—a combined 36 percent "very closely" and 40 percent "fairly closely."[52] The General Motors plant closings were the sixth most closely followed story of 1992, and the second largest labor story of the 1990s, with 73 percent following it closely—a combined 35 percent "very closely" and 38 percent "fairly closely."

The nation's attention to the news of the WTO protests of late November–early December 1999 was more comparable to typical news stories. (The Pew Center notes that "the typical story tested by the Center is followed very closely by just one in four respondents.") Just 18 percent of the nationwide survey respondents followed the story "very closely," with 30 percent following it "fairly closely" for a total of 48 percent following it "closely." The Major League Baseball strike story has similar levels of attention, but had great endurance as a news story. It was the only labor news story of the decade to chart on three of the Pew Center's monthly surveys, with 34 percent of the respondents following it closely in September 1994 (13 percent "very closely"; 21 percent "fairly closely"), 35 percent following it closely in October 1994 (15 percent "very closely"; 20 percent "fairly closely"), and 38 percent following it closely in February 1995 (12 percent "very closely"; 26 percent "fairly closely"). The brief American Airlines flight attendant strike of November 1993 was not included in the list of stories that the Pew Center asked respondents about in its December 1993 monthly survey, but the strike nevertheless was a significant story with front-page reports and several network news packages, especially as it idled a major airline right before the heavy Thanksgiving travel period.

Thus, it is safe to conclude that these five labor events were among the top stories about labor in the 1990s. These are stories that mattered, stories that told millions of Americans how to make sense of the labor movement. Given that most Americans did not belong to labor unions in the 1990s, that the nation's spaces are increasingly privatized and gated (a design strategy that protects the upper classes from social intermingling with the economic have-nots), and that other media such as entertainment television and film rarely address labor issues,[53] the news remains one of the few sites for any stories about labor and the working class. Unfortunately, the news about news coverage of labor is not all good.

In Chapter 2, I discuss the state of U.S. workers and labor unions at the end of the twentieth century, and the structural and historical reasons for the decline of labor. Chapter 3 links the state of labor to the news media and explores the rise of a consumerist ethos in American journalism. One of the main ways in which the consumerist ethos plays out is in the recurring news narrative of union-caused inflation, which stokes consumer fears and disdain for labor unions. The myth of union-caused inflation is but one of the logical corollaries to the five dominant frames of news stories about labor.

Chapters 4, 5, and 6 cover the Willow Run shutdown, the American Airlines flight attendant strike, and the Major League Baseball strike case studies, respectively. Chapter 7 looks at the trajectory of labor and the news from the late 1990s—with brief case studies of the UPS strike and the WTO protests—into the twenty-first century. The chapter concludes with a discussion of the future of labor in the news and of how labor might best deal with behemoth media corporations and their news divisions that cover unions with such limiting frames.

LABOR AT THE MILLENNIUM

Throughout the 1990s, and into the beginning of the twenty-first century, relations between workers and their employers in the United States were seemingly peaceful. Indeed, the number of major strikes or lockouts in the 1980s and 1990s declined dramatically from work-stoppage levels in the previous decades. President Ronald Reagan's firing of striking air traffic controllers in 1981 had a great chilling effect on major strikes. Each year since the late 1940s, there were regularly more than 100 major stoppages, as labor organizations flexed their muscles to jump-start contract bargaining impasses. Since 1981, however, major strikes in the United States have numbered far less than 100 each year. This decline indicates the hesitation and inability of labor unions to effectively use strikes, the decreasing numbers of workers belonging to unions, and the increasing propensity of unions to avoid debate by signing longer labor contracts with management. In 1998, for example, there were only 34 major work stoppages, idling just 378,000 workers—a far cry from an average of 352 major work stoppages a year in the 1950s, which affected more than 1.5 million workers annually.[1]

A glance at a sampling of economic headlines from the 1990s would seem to indicate U.S. workers had little reason to complain. By mid-1999, the United States was still riding on an economic expansion lasting more than eight years, the longest peacetime period of sustained growth in U.S. history. Unemployment hovered below 4.5 percent, inflation was minimal, the minimum wage had been raised from $3.35 in 1989 to $5.15 in 1997, and the stock market soared to almost unimaginable heights. "This is a rising tide that is lifting all boats," President Bill Clinton proclaimed in 1999.[2]

But, the façade of seemingly peaceful worker-management relations and glowing economic reports in the 1990s masked a troubling economic trend: a socioeconomic order that continued workplace inequalities for women and racial minorities, that undermined the comfortable position of white middle-class "mainstream" Americans, that ignored a significant population still in poverty, and that exacerbated the gap between society's richest and poorest. Contrary to what President Clinton had decreed, labor researchers Richard B. Freeman and Joel Rogers explained that "The 'rising tide lifts all boats' effect of economic growth—the belief that growth benefits all and reduces poverty—ceased to work in the past two decades. It lifted the yachts but sank the dinghies."[3]

Sinking in a "Rising Tide"

The shortcomings of the economic expansion were evident on several fronts. First, although there were some gains in employment and earnings for women and racial minorities, serious inequities remained. In fact, the record ten-year U.S. economic expansion—which officially lasted from March 1991 to March 2001, according to the National Bureau of Economic Research—had little positive effect on the gender gap in wages. In 1979, full-time female wage and salary workers earned 62.5 percent of what their male counterparts earned. That gap steadily narrowed through the 1980s, to 74.8 percent by 1991, year one of the decade-long boom. Women's earnings improved to 77.1 percent of men's by 1993, but all progress on the wage gap faltered through the remainder of the decade. The gender gap in wages stood at 76.0 percent in 2000, the last full year of the expansion.[4]

Unemployment levels were low for all groups by 1999, but a racial divide persisted. The unemployment rate for whites, age sixteen and older, was just 3.7 percent for the year, while those of Hispanic origin (who could be classified as both black or white) experienced a 6.4 percentage rate of unemployment. Blacks experienced an unemployment rate of 8.0 percent, more than double the rate of whites.[5]

The failure of economic gains to have much positive impact on the middle class was perhaps the most surprising element of the expansion of the 1990s.[6] In fact, it was only until 1999, several years into the recovery, that median wage returned to its 1979 level.[7] (Contrary to the common wisdom that the new economy was based on highly paid information technology workers, most new jobs were in the low-wage service sector.) Benefits such as health care and employer pension contributions grew at an even slower rate, and even experienced a *reduction* for the average worker in the late 1990s. Families didn't do much better. As researchers from the Economic Policy Institute noted, "Between 1989 and 1999, the inflation-adjusted income of the median, or typical, family grew just 0.6% per year—slightly higher than the 0.4% average growth rate of the 1980s and well below the 2.6–2.8% average rate from 1947 to 1973."[8]

Most families maintained their positions or realized minor gains only by working more hours on the job. Despite a significant growth rate in the U.S. economy's productive capacity in the 1990s, the spouses of the typical married-couple family worked a combined 247 more hours—over six weeks of extra time—per year in 1998, compared to 1989.[9] The extra hours, of course, mean that families have less time to spend with each other.

In a decade when France reduced their official work week to 35 hours, and workers in other comparable countries such as Japan, Canada, Germany, and the United Kingdom were able to decrease their work time as well, U.S. workers put in more and more hours. According to a 2001 International Labor Organization study, U.S. laborers worked an average of 1,978 hours in 2000, an increase of nearly an entire work week from 1,942 hours in 1990. Australian, Canadian, Japanese, and Mexican workers all put in about 100 hours (about 2.5 weeks) less work per year, and Germans worked almost 500 hours (about 12.5 weeks) less than Americans. U.S. workers led all nations in productivity, measured in terms of value added per person employed. At the same time, though, French and Belgian laborers, who worked fewer hours, had higher productivity in terms of value added per hour worked.[10]

Thus, after decades of struggle to reduce the hours of the work week, U.S. workers put in more hours of work each year than the workers of any other advanced economy in the world. Economist Juliet Schor found that Americans worked more hours and got less paid time off than they did in the late 1960s, creating a situation where "the average employed person is now on the job . . . the equivalent of an extra month a year."[11] But, ever-longer work hours did not eliminate the most disturbing trend of the 1990s: an increasingly two-tiered U.S. society, with a growing gap in income and wealth between the richest Americans and those in the middle- and low-income tiers. More regressive tax policies, cutbacks on social welfare programs, and the changing economic regime resulted in an alarming situation for individuals and families who might have expected to share in the wealth of the longest economic boom of the post–World War II era.

Despite the famous bull stock market of the 1990s, the typical middle-class household hardly shared in the wealth. In fact, as the Economic Policy Institute notes, "The ownership of stocks is particularly unequal. The top 1% of stock owners hold almost half (47.7%) of all stocks, by value, while the bottom 80% own *just 4.1% of total stock holdings*."[12] So, while the average wealth (the value of assets minus debts) of the elite top 1 percent of households grew by more than $1 million between 1989 and 1998, the vast majority of households did not do so well. During the same period, the median U.S. household's wealth grew at a 0.4 percent annual rate, less than half the 1.6 percent growth rate for 1962–83, and less than the 1.1 percent rate for 1983–89. Thus, it's not surprising that the distribution of wealth in the U.S. remains very unequal after the 1990s, with the richest 1 percent of households holding 38 percent of national wealth and the bottom 80 percent of households holding just 17 percent. Even with improvements in wealth at the lowest economic tiers, the poorest 20 percent of households still left the 1990s with negative net worth.[13]

Moreover, as workers' wages and salaries moved sluggishly in the 1990s, chief executive officer (CEO) pay continued to rise unfettered, nearly doubling between 1989 and 1999, and jumping to 107 times the pay of the average worker—a more than fivefold increase over 1962, when the median CEO pay was 20 times more than the typical worker. While the average worker's pay stagnated, the median CEO's real wage grew 62.7 percent between 1989 and 1999. Although economies became increasingly global in the 1990s, the salaries of U.S. CEOs remained otherworldly, at levels 2.5 times more than their foreign counterparts. As the economic elite in the United States grew ever richer during the record economic expansion of the 1990s, poverty rates were slow to improve. In fact, only in 1999 did the poverty rate fall to 11.8 percent, about the level of 1979.[14]

The secret behind the relatively poor compensation of U.S. workers, even as they worked more hours than ever before and had the highest level of per-worker productivity in the world, is that for the first time since World War II, the division of total corporate income between workers and owners of capital tilted sharply in favor of capital in the 1990s. As the Economic Policy Institute noted, "In 1999, owners of capital received 20.5% of the income paid out by the corporate sector, up from 18.2% in 1989. This 2.3 percentage-point rise in the 'profit share' was more than four times larger than the 0.5 percentage-point increase between 1979 and 1989."[15]

Thus, the reality of the U.S. economic recovery is that the vast majority of Americans didn't fully share in the benefits. Instead, poverty and income stagnation continued for the working classes, and the richest groups continued to compound their wealth. As early as 1994, the Dunlop Commission on the Future of Worker-Management Relations posited that "a healthy society cannot long continue along the path the U.S. is moving, with rising bifurcation of the labor market."[16] In the similar words of then-Clinton administration Labor Secretary Robert Reich (a member of the Dunlop Commission), "a society divided between the haves and have-nots, or between the well-educated and the poorly educated, that becomes sharply divided over time, cannot be [a] prosperous or a stable society."[17]

With increasing economic inequality among classes, continuing inequalities among workers, stagnant or declining wages and benefits, the greatest work load of any advanced economy, and little progress on poverty—all of this with the world's highest rates of worker productivity and in a decade that was billed as the best of economic times—the conditions would seem ripe for a nationwide examination and discussion of the one institution that has historically worked to remedy these problems for the American worker—labor unions. Why, then, isn't this happening?

Finding the Strength to Swim

In part, the absence of this discussion is linked to the decline of organized labor membership in the United States. In the first half of the twentieth century, U.S. workers frequently banded together in labor unions to address gross economic disparities and unacceptable workplace conditions. In the last quarter of the century, the declining strength of organized labor has paralleled the declining fortunes of U.S. workers. Indeed, membership in labor unions has dropped from a peak of 34.7 percent of the workforce in 1954 to only 13.5 percent in 2000.[18] (Broken down further, 37.5 percent of government workers belonged to unions, while only 9.0 percent of private sector employees were members.) Union membership in the nonagricultural workforce hasn't been this low since the period prior to the approval of the National Labor Relations (Wagner) Act of 1935, which guaranteed the right of U.S. workers to organize and collectively bargain with employers.[19] As the Dunlop Commission noted, "the decline of unions, who historically reduce earnings differentials within establishments and bring the earnings of production workers closer to that of supervisory workers, has contributed to the rise in inequality." This decline of unions and collective bargaining "has created an arena for employee-management relations in which most employees have no independent organization to discuss issues with management."[20]

As we shall see, a fair and credible discussion of labor relations also seems to be missing in large part from the national news media. Judging from the way in which the news media address their readers/listeners/viewers as consumers, one would never guess that most of these people are also workers. And, although these workers are predominantly not members of labor unions, the vast majority of workers—according to Richard B. Freeman and Joel Rogers in their groundbreaking 1999 book *What Workers Want*—"want more of a say/influence/representation/participation/voice (call it what you will) at the workplace than they now have." In fact, Freeman and Rogers note, "Overall, 45 percent of employees want a strongly independent workplace organization (which only unions provide in the current system), 43 percent want an organization with more limited independence from management, and the remaining [12 percent of] workers want a workplace in which management alone rules."[21]

It is naïve to expect the mainstream corporate news media to promote labor union agendas. Yet, it is a failure of the news media to report on the broad range of existing labor relations issues and conflicts, including workers' desires for new ways to organize the workplace. Mired in consumer narratives, the news media forsake a public debate on workplace environments, standards of living, and the unprecedented income and wealth gap—all stories that revolve around one of the most common elements of U.S. citizens' lives: work.

How do we account for the decline of organized labor's membership and its related ability as an economic and political force in the United States over the last decades of the twentieth century? A number of economic and political factors have been cited. The reasons generally fall into two categories: *structural* factors, which include deindustrialization, globalization, and flexible production, and *historical* factors, which include antiunion legislation, employer resistance, shifting union ideology, and changes in popular attitudes toward unions.

Structural Changes in the U.S. Economy

It has not escaped labor analysts that the decline of labor has roughly corresponded with the decline of basic industry in the United States. Political economists Barry Bluestone and Bennett Harrison note that industrialists collected substantial annual profits during the peak years of U.S. industrial might, from 1945 to the early 1970s.[22] During this postwar period, the United States was the undisputed economic leader of the world, with a thriving "Fordist" economy based on mass production and mass consumption (so named after industrialist Henry Ford, who in 1914 began to pay his workers $5 a day—enough to mass consume the mass produced automobiles). Given the healthy profits of the era, David Harvey notes, corporations "grudgingly accepted union power, particularly when the unions undertook to control their membership and collaborate with management in plans to raise productivity in return for wage gains that stimulated effective demand in the way that [Henry] Ford had originally envisaged."[23] Thus, for the price of regular collective bargaining, big business could count on organized labor to deliver a disciplined (i.e., nonstriking) labor market for industry's needs in the Fordist economy.

A third party to this "social contract" between big business and organized labor was the federal government, which aided mass production through investment in public infrastructure, such as transportation and communications, and by providing a social safety net of unemployment compensation, welfare programs, and social security to alleviate deep poverty and stabilize mass consumption. The government also promulgated the laws and governmental bureaucracy that served as the framework for the postwar industry-union relationship.

Of course, the Fordist mass production/mass consumption boom years were not boom years for everyone. The socioeconomic order after World War II benefited a core labor market, mostly white, middle-class men. The "other" Americans—including most women, racial minorities, urban teenagers, and the lower-class elderly—were never fully admitted to the mainstream of the Fordist labor market. The social conflicts and civil rights movements of the 1950s and afterward stand as symptomatic crises associated with these persistent exclusions in U.S. society.[24]

The Fordist economy and social contracts between industry, unions, and government held up as long as the economy continued to expand. But, in the early 1970s, the expensive Vietnam War finally ended and the OPEC (Organization of Petroleum Exporting Countries) oil cartel delivered a shocking blow beginning in 1973 when it cut production drastically and raised world-wide prices. The postwar boom seemed to be running out of gas. According to Mike Davis "the upper levels of demand led by 'automobilization' and household mechanization were being reached by the late 1970s."[25] As consumer demand moved toward saturation, the average annual rate of corporate profits began to decline, from a healthy 15.5 percent on investments in the early 1960s to 12.7 percent by the end of that decade. Profits continued to slip, to 10.1 percent in the early 1970s, and below 10 percent after 1975.[26] The economic stagflation of slow growth, high unemployment, and high inflation that struck the United States also affected other advanced capitalist nations but to a lesser degree.

Many business leaders have argued that the economic world has changed and that unions are a relic of the past. Additionally, they suggest, although unions did help to relieve some miserable working conditions in the past, the tenacious grip of the unions in the postboom economic downturn served only to stifle innovation, fuel inflation, and hurt U.S. competitiveness. Political scientist Charles F. Sabel and economist Michael J. Piore analyzed the two main responses of businesses to the economic crisis, neither of which have been particularly hospitable to unions.[27] The first strategy attempts to boost profit margins by shifting the capital created through domestic mass production to speculative and global investments. The second strategy, which Piore and Sabel embrace as the more promising route to prosperity, is an economic model of "flexible specialization."

Moving Capital from Mass Production

In an attempt to maintain or restore the high levels of profit that were typical in the 1950s and 1960s, a number of U.S. companies in the 1970s and 1980s diverted capital from reinvestment in existing productive capacity (e.g., plants and equipment) into what they hoped would be more immediately profitable ventures: other production locations, speculative deals, mergers and acquisitions, and foreign investment. Bluestone and Harrison refer to this technique as "managerial capitalism," for the main goal was not to reinvest to save the primary industry of the corporation but instead to find an administrative "quick fix" to protect or enhance the bottom line and stock price. Accordingly, a number of corporations emerged with unusual product line mixes, such as Mobil Oil's acquisition of Montgomery Ward. Several major corporations, such as Gulf and Western, ITT, Litton Industries, Northwest Industries, Textron, and United Technologies, had no primary business at all.[28] The negative effect of the merger and acquisition frenzy of the 1970s and 1980s (which still continues) is that existing primary industries often serve as "cash cows." Corporations "milk" the profits out of their older divisions—often running them out of business—by forsaking scheduled reinvestment and diverting the funds to finance more speculative transactions. The final result of this shifting of capital is deindustrialization, particularly in heavily unionized basic industries such as automobiles, steel, rubber, glass, electronics, and shipbuilding.[29]

Another strategy employing capital mobility is the globalization of production. By shifting production to less-developed countries, or by purchasing (outsourcing) product components or services from suppliers in other regions (e.g., the less unionized southern or western United States) or other nations, labor savings may be achieved in many cases. Structural changes that have made global transportation and communication reasonably inexpensive for businesses make this kind of capital mobility possible. For U.S. union members, the shift of capital from the "cash cow" plants into foreign production facilities can be devastating. For example, General Motors (GM) diverted investment from many aging U.S. production facilities in the 1970s, '80s, and '90s to build a network of *maquiladoras* (low-wage, foreign-owned assembly plants that export back to the parent company) in Mexico, along the Mexico–U.S. border. By 2000, Delphi Automotive Systems, the former GM division that became an independent publicly held company in 1999, was the largest private employer in Mexico, with 75,000 employees and 53 plants.[30]

Ironically, as many U.S. businesses during the 1970s and 1980s argued for tighter restrictions against imports, it was American business capital that was largely responsible for the increase in imports. Kim Moody, citing a congressional report, notes that by 1970, "close to three-quarters of total US exports and upwards of one-half of all imports [were] transactions between the domestic and foreign subsidiaries of the same [U.S. and foreign] multinational conglomerate corporations."[31] American private assets abroad, usually invested in foreign subsidiaries or in partnerships with foreign firms, grew at an enormous rate: from $19 billion in 1950, to $49.2 billion in 1960, to $118.8 billion in 1970. By 1980, U.S. private foreign investment totaled $579 billion, a gain of 335 percent in a single decade.[32] Thus, in search of more lucrative investments, the United States experienced an enormous outflow of capital, undermining the relatively closed Fordist system of mass production and mass consumption.

The Idea of Flexibility

In their 1984 book, *The Second Industrial Divide: Possibilities for Prosperity*, Piore and Sabel endorsed an alternative to mass production called "flexible specialization." They describe *flexible specialization* as "a strategy of permanent innovation: accommodation to ceaseless change, rather than an effort to control it. This strategy is based on flexible—multi-use—equipment; skilled workers; and the creation, through politics, of an industrial community that restricts the forms of competition to those favoring innovation. For these reasons, the spread of flexible specialization amounts to a revival of craft forms of production that were emarginated at the first industrial divide."[33] The authors cite small high-technology manufacturing firms in central and northwest Italy as exemplars of this economic model, as they integrated computer-controlled equipment to improve efficiencies in such processes as firing ceramics and casting metals.

Applied to the realities of the U.S. workplace, flexible specialization (similar to David Harvey's term, "flexible accumulation") loses some of its northern Italian luster. Piore and Sabel cite GM's experiments with flexible work rules in its nonunion southern U.S. factories as an encouraging approximation of a flexible accumulation system. The record of some other U.S. examples of flexible specialization cited by Piore and Sabel in

1984—Wang Laboratories, Digital Equipment, and Atari, all now defunct—suggests that flexible specialization is no panacea.[34]

Perhaps the most prominent example of an experiment in flexibility in a traditionally unionized work setting in the United States is GM's Saturn unit. Billed as "a different kind of car company," GM set up their assembly plant in Spring Hill, Tennessee—far from labor's stronghold in Detroit—and attempted to re-create labor-management relations as a cooperative partnership of equals, with shop-floor decisions made by flexible, informal teams. As GM notes in its corporate history, the agreement Saturn signed in 1985 with the United Automobile Workers (UAW) at the plant was "a revolutionary agreement so simple it fits in a shirt pocket instead of a three-inch-thick binder," suggesting that traditional union work rules unnecessarily complicate workplace relations.[35] But, by 1999, the UAW members at Saturn voted to remove from office the group of union representatives who had worked closely with management since the original pact in 1985. The reason? The rhetoric of flexibility and cooperation had begun to ring hollow, and "many workers had come to see the partnership as benefiting only management and the hundreds of full-time appointed union reps who help run the Saturn system."[36]

Structural changes in the U.S. (and global) economy led to business demands for flexibility, but it ultimately became clear to unions that flexibility was typically deployed to require only the workforce to be flexible, diminishing unionism's wage and work rule gains. According to Harvey, "Faced with strong market volatility, heightened competition, and narrowing profit margins, employers have taken advantage of weakened union power and the pools of surplus (unemployed or underemployed) labourers to push for much more flexible work regimes and labour contracts."[37] Even Piore and Sabel conceded that "it seems likely . . . that the spread of flexible accumulation in the United States would weaken the labor movement—unless some widely acceptable flexible, unionized system of shop-floor control suddenly emerges from one of the innumerable industrial-relations experiments now under way in American plants."[38]

Can much of the decline of organized labor in the United States be attributed to these structural changes in the economic realm? Michael Goldfield argues that structural changes in the sectors of labor (e.g., highly unionized basic industries) do not necessarily lead to an overall decline in labor. Goldfield explains that "the fact that a high-density sector [e.g., highly unionized New York] is losing its constituency while a low-density sector [e.g., less unionized Mississippi] is increasing in number is not prima facie evidence of a sufficient cause for a decline in total unions density or membership."[39] Thus, while an economic shift may affect certain industries, union organizing in regions and work sectors with increasing laborers can more than offset the difference. Goldfield suggests, then, that historical difficulties in *organizing* may be a culprit in the decline of unions.

Historical Changes in U.S. Culture

American labor's promising position immediately after World War II was largely due to the passage of the National Labor Relations (Wagner) Act in 1935, which established the legal infrastructure for labor unions to exist and collectively bargain with industry.[40] The Wagner Act attempted to balance what it described as "the inequality of bargaining power between employees who do not possess full freedom of association or actual liberty of contract, and employers who are organized in the corporate or other forms of ownership association." To remedy this disparity in bargaining power and help secure a more prosperous economy, the Act specified employee rights of association: "Employees shall have the right to self-organization, to form, join, or assist labor organizations, to bargain collectively through representatives of their own choosing, and to engage in concerted activities, for the purpose of collective bargaining or other mutual aid or protection."[41] According to Robert Zieger, the passage of the Wagner Act (and its favorable review by the U.S. Supreme Court in 1937) ended a period of violent confrontation in which "literally hundreds of workers had been killed and thousands injured in a long history of disputes stretching back into the nineteenth century."[42]

Somewhat surprisingly, then, labor's postwar decline came during a period of relative labor-industry peace and legally sanctioned unions. It was through the more subtle, overlapping factors of unfavorable legislation, employer resistance, labor's own growing conservatism, and changes in popular attitudes toward unions that labor's membership declined and its economic and political power began to unravel.

Unfavorable Legislation

Passage of the Wagner Act in 1935, which had evolved from labor provisions in President Roosevelt's National Recovery Administration (NRA), sealed labor's connection to Roosevelt and the Democratic Party. Although industry grudgingly accepted the existence of unions, it also immediately began efforts to amend labor law in its favor. Zieger notes that "throughout the late 1930s, employers, right-wing newspapers, and conservative legislators assailed the NLRB [National Labor Relations Board]. The new agency, they charged, stacked the deck in favor of unions. Communists dominated its staff, they asserted. The 'unfair labor practices' sections of the Wagner Act made employers sitting ducks for all sorts of union coercion."[43]

Labor's champion in the White House, Roosevelt, died in 1945. The legislative culmination of conservative antiunion efforts occurred shortly thereafter, with the Taft-Hartley Act of 1947. The Act's veto by Democratic President Truman was overridden by the Republican majority in Congress. Although Truman vetoed Taft-Hartley, making an official display of continuing Democratic sponsorship of labor's interests, his true support for labor was only mild at best.[44]

The provisions of the Taft-Hartley Act were devastating for the union movement's hopes of organizing beyond the industrial centers of the North, Midwest, and West Coast. By outlawing most secondary strikes, sitdowns, slowdowns, and wildcat strikes (i.e., strikes by rank-and-file members that occur during the course of a contract, *without* union leadership approval), labor's primary means of redress necessarily became the slow, legalistic challenges through the National Labor Relations Board or the courts. By permitting states to adopt laws that ban "union shops" (which require workers who are hired to become members of the union), most southern and western states subsequently adopted so-called right-to-work laws that created "open shops" where workers are not required to join a union, thus hindering union organizing and shop-floor cohesiveness.[45]

Finally, Taft-Hartley, in the political atmosphere of the day, required that union officers sign affidavits swearing that they were not Communists and that they were loyal to the U.S. government. The loyalty oaths, required for the union to obtain NLRB collective bargaining privileges, exploited the leftist origins of unions and increased the political tensions within the unions. Unionists turned against each other, with ultimate expulsion of leftists. The Landrum-Griffin Act of 1959 finished the work of the Taft-Hartley Act by further limiting secondary strikes and picketing rights and by opening union records to government investigators. Sociologist Howard Kimeldorf notes that "after driving out the organized left, the industrial union movement drifted unchecked to the right, abandoning independent political action before finally collapsing into the waiting arms of the Democratic Party."[46]

Although common wisdom has it that labor unions have always enjoyed special treatment from the Democratic Party, the experience of the past thirty years suggests otherwise. In the 1970s, the Democratic Party, increasingly abandoned by white southern voters and weakened by the breakup of the northern political machine, began to more actively woo suburban, educated middle-class voters as its new base. Kim Moody argues that the transformed Democratic Party that brought "New South moderate" Jimmy Carter to the White House in 1976 had little interest in labor: "The new Democratic constituency produced a generation of Democratic politicians with no loyalty to labor or other traditional groups that favored liberal economic policies. Indeed, much of this increasingly middle-class electorate had a material interest in the perpetuation of the near poverty of service workers, whose low wages subsidized the consumer preferences of the newly affluent. Redistributive income policies, like labor unions, were anathema to them."[47]

Moody reports that "labor's major legislative goals were defeated one after another" in 1977 and 1978, even with Democrats in control of the White House and Congress. Even the Federal Aviation Administration (FAA) plans that helped Reagan quickly break the 1981 PATCO strike were formed under the auspices of the Carter administration.[48] The Reagan-Bush administration's stand against the striking PATCO workers is well known. But, the administration's general policies (passed with a Democratic Congress) had an adverse effect on organized labor (and all working people) as well. The combination of increased capital mobility and sharp reductions in the government-supported social safety net created a situation in which industry gained the power to make " 'take it or leave it' propositions stick."[49]

To date, labor has failed to successfully push any major prounion legislation in the postwar era, a testament to labor's declining political clout.

The Clinton administration changed some of the Reagan administration's most egregious antilabor moves. For example, the probusiness NLRB of the Reagan-Bush era was replaced by members who vow to return balance to the board's enforcement and adjudication of labor law.[50] Unable to pass legislation preventing the hiring of replacement workers (scabs), Clinton signed Executive Order 12954 on March 8, 1995, to prohibit federal agencies from contracting with companies that use replacements for striking workers. Although a similar government ban in Canada has not resulted in more frequent or longer strikes there, Republican leaders in Congress later nullified Clinton's order.[51]

Yet, for most of Clinton's eight years in office, labor organizations required a great deal of time and effort to fight poorly conceived trade agreements, particularly the North American Free Trade Agreement (NAFTA), an initiative of President George Bush that the Clinton-Gore administration embraced with great enthusiasm. Approved in 1994, NAFTA resulted in a large outsourcing of U.S. industrial and textile production to miserable maquiladora factory towns just across the Mexican border and oppressive sweatshops in Central America—all places where U.S. companies and the host countries flagrantly violated workers' rights to organize due to NAFTA's weak labor rights enforcement provisions.[52]

Taylor Dark, in his 1999 book, *The Unions and the Democrats: An Enduring Alliance*, critiques the notion that unions have lost political power in recent decades, arguing that "there is no causal force requiring that declining union density should inevitably translate into declining union political power." At least in the realm of national politics, Dark asserts that labor unions are still "major but not dominant players in the Democratic Party" and that, like most political interest groups, labor has a mixed but not altogether poor record in national politics.[53] For example, Dark notes, although the Clinton-Gore administration abandoned labor when it supported NAFTA, the labor unions showed their political muscle when they were able to successfully rally Congress in 1997 and 1998 against Clinton's efforts to gain "fast-track" authority for future trade agreements (which would grant the President the power to negotiate international trade agreements that cannot later be debated and amended by Congress).[54]

Nevertheless, Dark agrees that "at some point, the unions have got to staunch the loss of membership. Eventually decline will decisively undermine union power, though the moment of crisis may not arrive for another decade or perhaps much longer."[55] Indeed, unions will fail as a popular movement if there is not a sufficient population within them. Moreover, it becomes easier to cast unions in general as a special political interest group if they lack a flourishing and democratic membership base to back up their political efforts.

Employer Resistance

As noted earlier, employer resistance has become much less violent than it was in the days when Henry Ford's "Service Department" of more than three thousand thugs regularly beat and intimidated employees to undermine unionization.[56] In the postwar era, employer resistance has taken three quieter, yet largely effective, forms. One method of resistance has been through the seemingly benign structural changes that industry has experienced. Economic developments such as those discussed above—increased capital mobility, outsourcing, globalization, and flexible specialization—are not only strategies for improving profit levels but can also be used to gain concessions from unions, destabilize them, or eliminate them entirely.[57]

A second employer resistance strategy has been increased probusiness lobbying. Industry was fairly unorganized as a lobbying force prior to World War II, and the NLRA was a bitter defeat. In the postwar period, though, business coordination scored several successes for capitalism and severely curtailed union power with the passage of the Taft-Hartley and Landrum-Griffin Acts, while preventing additional legislation that would reform law in favor of labor. Goldfield argues that "there has been a continuous, growing capitalist anti-union offensive, widening in both its forms of resistance and its sectoral importance, since at least the 1950s." Trade associations such as the National Association of Manufacturers, the National Retail Merchants Association, the American Hospital Association, and the National Public Employee Relations Association have all "developed vigorous anti-union programs," according to Goldfield.[58] Most effective has been the Business Roundtable, a high-powered business group founded in the early 1970s to lobby Washington with a precise business and economic agenda of corporate tax breaks, deregulation of the transportation, finance, and energy industries, and the repeal of labor legislation. (The Business Roundtable's agenda became the Reagan boilerplate in the 1980s.)[59] Since the mid-1980s, corporations have also spent millions of dollars on a new lobbying strategy that mimics the best grass-roots efforts of unions, civil rights organizations, and public interest groups. As investigative writer Ken Silverstein explains,

> Once a term that conjured up wholesome images of citizens sponta-neously mustering to protect their interests, "grassroots lobbying" is now an industry directed by enormously expensive [Washington] beltway con-sulting firms. The goal is to mime populist revolt. The phony grassrooters set up phone banks, manufacture letter-writing campaigns, arrange meet-ings between legislators and "white hat" community figures—preferably a religious leader or Little League coach—and rent "third party experts" to draft op-ed articles or testify before elected officials.[60]

Business groups have also utilized political action committees (PACs) to their advantage. Originally invented by organized labor in 1943, PACs serve as a conduit for contributing money to political candidates and par-ties. A change in the law in 1974 permitted corporations and business as-sociations to form PACs, which they did rapidly. By 1982, corporate PACs easily outstripped union PACs in campaign contributions, $84.9 million to $35 million. In the 1990s, PAC money was overshadowed by the gushing flow of so-called soft money campaign contributions, which went to na-tional political parties and totaled nearly $500 million by election year 2000. Although unions were a major force in these contributions, busi-nesses again had far greater assets to extend their influence; the securities industry alone contributed $72 million in soft money during the 1990s, more than the $59 million from all labor unions during the same period.[61]

Finally, businesses have resisted unions through more direct antiunion activities. By 1985, a reported "95 percent of employers actively resist unionization, and 75 percent of all employers hire so-called 'labor-management consultants' to guide their efforts to avoid unionization at an estimated cost of over $100,000,000 annually."[62] The May 1994 *Fact Finding Report* of the Dunlop Commission offered evidence of increasing corpo-rate antiunionism. The report charted the frequency of illegal firings when workers attempt to organize a union bargaining in a workplace: "In the early 1950s, approximately 600 workers were reinstated each year because of a discriminatory discharge during certification campaign. By the late 1980s, this number was near 2,000 a year. Adjusted for the number of certification elections and union voters, the incidence of illegal firing increased from one in every 20 elections affecting one in 700 union supporters [in the early 1950s] to one in every four elections victimizing 1 in 50 union supporters [in the late 1980s]."[63]

A 1999 analysis of NLRB election data found even greater frequency of firings, noting that "a third of the companies in the NLRB study illegally fired union supporters during elections . . . up from a mere 8 percent in the 1960s." Moreover, "half threatened to close facilities if the union won, and 91 percent required workers to meet one-on-one with supervisors on the issue."[64] Even if workers are able to successfully organize a bargaining unit, employers can fail to bargain in good faith and can bring in scab replacement workers in the event of a strike, often exhausting well-intentioned union member energies.[65] Loopholes in federal law make professional union busting a successful and profitable business.[66]

Shifting Union Ideology

Looking at the state of labor in the United States in the early 1990s, then AFL-CIO president Lane Kirkland saw a victory of sorts: "We've maintained our membership in the most extraordinary combination of adverse circumstances."[67] Looking at the same state of labor, Moody and several other leftist critics find not a valiant AFL-CIO defense but instead AFL-CIO inaction. Moody argued that, "the AFL-CIO's inability to respond effectively must be explained by the frozen ideological and institutional matrices of union leadership in the United States since the late 1940s and above all by the concept and practice of business unionism." *Business unionism*, as defined by Moody, is "a unionism that sees members primarily as consumers and limits itself to negotiating the price of labor."[68] Thus, the individualist approach of business unionism is the antithesis of a social unionism that seeks to build a labor movement.

The roots of business unionism trace back to the two original large labor organizations, the American Federation of Labor (AFL), which represented mostly trade unions (e.g., carpenters, plumbers, electricians), and the Congress of Industrial Organizations (CIO), which represented mostly industrial workers (e.g., steel and auto workers). There had long been a philosophical split between the two organizations. Formed in the 1880s, the AFL was a relatively conservative organization with often discriminatory practices; it was accustomed to organizing workers into local units by trade. But, with the huge influx of new union members under the NRA provisions and, later, the Wagner Act in 1935, the AFL was grossly under-prepared to organize unskilled industrial workers. Where would they fit into the AFL's organizational logic? The CIO was formed by breakaway AFL official John L. Lewis of the Mine Workers, who quickly began to organize industrial workers.[69]

Industrial unionism tended to be much more leftist and diverse. The CIO traditionally worked for social change and presented itself as a labor movement for all working people. It was one of the first institutions to support racial minorities and women in the workplace and to guarantee the same pay for the same work. Particularly in Detroit, there was a strong relationship between the CIO and the National Association for the Advancement of Colored People (NAACP). The CIO also drew on the experienced organizing skills of its Communist members, several of whom were top CIO officials.[70]

Although Communists were valuable contributors to the CIO movement, they were increasingly viewed as a liability. There had been persistent rumblings about Communists in labor from the Roman Catholic Church, Evangelical Protestants, and right-wing politicians and editors. Over the course of World War II, Communist union members were among the most adamant supporters of the wartime no-strike pledge and faster production rates, which angered some union members who felt that the Communist Party members were more concerned about the fate of the Nazi-invaded Soviet Union than the fate of the union.[71] In the postwar union power struggles, both the AFL and CIO acceded to increasing demands from within and without to purge Communists from the unions. In their efforts to rid themselves of Communism, unions also gave up most of their progressive socially oriented activities. Zieger notes that "since Communists were active in such progressive causes as civil rights, union organizing, and support for the unemployed, hostility toward them often spilled over to include anyone involved in those endeavors."[72] The resulting purges made most of the major unions strongly disciplined, undemocratic organizations focused on income maintenance for their members.

As it eliminated the more radical union members, the CIO also gave up efforts to form a U.S. labor party and allied itself more closely with the Democratic Party. This stronger alliance also compromised labor's radicalism. Labor had long planned on organizing the South, and in 1946 the CIO embarked on Operation Dixie to do so. Unfortunately, the effort failed; Goldfield attributes this to labor's hesitancy to offend conservative southern Democrats (who had been allied with Roosevelt), its lack of resolve to demand complete equality for blacks, and its preoccupation with purging Communists.[73]

Having eliminated their gulf of differences, the AFL and CIO merged in 1955, symbolically creating a new institution for business unionism. Organizationally, though, the resulting top-down style of business unionism was problematic to new organizing. If members looked to leadership for mobilization, they rarely got it from business unionists. Radical self-mobilizers historically have often been quashed by international union leadership, such as the case of Austin, Minnesota's Local P-9 of the United Food and Commercial Workers (UFCW) in their lone 1985–86 efforts to resist the UFCW-approved concessions to meat processor Hormel.[74]

Nevertheless, the failure of radicalism and the normalcy of business unionism in the United States is not all-pervasive. Howard Kimeldorf's study of the radical socialist International Longshoremen's and Warehousemen's Union (ILWU) of the West Coast, which has operated with great success since the 1930s even as the East Coast longshoremen's union has been a bastion of conservative business unionism, teaches a valuable lesson. Kimeldorf argues that "the ILWU offers proof that . . . alternatives to business unionism were not only possible but practical, and that socialist leadership remained a viable option well into the twentieth century for at least some American workers."[75]

Indeed, reformist movements in U.S. labor unions began to finally yield dividends in the 1990s. Reform candidate John J. Sweeney, who had led the Service Employees International Union (SEIU) to great growth during the 1980s while most other labor union were in decline, was elected president of the AFL-CIO in 1995. Sweeney's leadership called for reinvigorating unions by refocusing efforts on building social movements and by shifting away from increasingly ineffective attempts to influence policies via Washington lobbying and from unquestioned support of the Democratic Party. Sweeney and the AFL-CIO initiated the Union Summer program to instruct young activists and built a grassroots campaign on the theme that "America Needs a Raise."[76] The campaign spread union activism beyond the membership and eventually led to an increase in the minimum wage.

However, new leadership alone does not guarantee a more progressive or radical unionism. Under Sweeney's leadership, the AFL-CIO gave only limited support to workers involved in the 1993–95 A.E. Staley lockout in Decatur, Illinois and the 1995–98 Detroit Newspaper strike and lockout.[77] And after acknowledging that union members wanted the AFL-CIO to stop its ineffective "political lapdog" strategy of trying to win influence via relationships with the Democratic Party and its candidates, the AFL-CIO endorsed Vice President Al Gore on October 12, 1999, for the 2000 presidential election, more than a year in advance of election day. Just a few years earlier, Sweeney had argued that "restoring out independence will make us more effective than tethering ourselves to a political party."[78]

Union reformers with the Teamsters also experienced both joy and disappointment in the 1990s. Ron Carey, a candidate supported by the reform group Teamsters for a Democratic Union, was elected to lead the Teamsters in 1991. Carey helped to shepherd United Parcel Service (UPS) workers through a dramatic strike victory in 1997. But later that year, federal investigators nullified Carey's 1996 reelection to head the Teamsters due to illegal campaign fundraising conducted by his aides. The Teamsters later elected James P. Hoffa, son of the late Teamsters leader Jimmy Hoffa (whose name is commonly synonymous with union corruption). Reformers feared a turn away from their movement for greater democracy in the union.[79]

The most progressive grassroots workers' organizations of recent decades haven't necessarily been labor unions. In 1973, 9 to 5: The National Association of Working Women was established by a group of Boston clerical workers to highlight women's labor issues; it is now a grassroots national women's advocacy organization.[80] The National Labor Committee (NLC), supported mainly by religious organizations, is a human rights advocacy group established in 1981 that is dedicated to promoting and defending the rights of workers. One of the NLC's most famous accomplishments is bringing to light the Central American and Asian sweatshops that employed child labor to sew Kathie Lee Gifford–label clothing for Wal-Mart and apparel for Disney, the Gap, Liz Claiborne, Ralph Lauren, Ann Taylor, among other companies and labels. The NLC's work has

inspired United Students Against Sweatshops, a college campus movement in which students have pressured their universities (including
Duke, Michigan, Wisconsin, Georgetown, and Stanford) to ensure workers' rights for clothing produced bearing collegiate logos.[81] Finally, Jobs
with Justice is a human rights group established in 1987 that works in the
United States with community, religious, and labor groups for worker
rights and economic justice.

Changing Popular Attitudes

Public approval of labor unions has slipped since the era of the Wagner
Act. In 1936, public approval of labor unions stood at 72 percent; by 1985,
58 percent of the public approved.[82] Public support for labor unions is
complicated though, with a high percentage of Americans receptive to the
practical utility of unions, even as overall support waned. For example, in
a 1985 labor issues survey, 75 percent of respondents in a nationwide survey agreed that "unions in general improve the wages and working conditions of workers" and 80 percent agreed that "unions are needed so that
legitimate complaints of workers can be heard."[83]

Other popular attitudes, though, suggest a legacy of decades of business unionism and, perhaps, misconceptions. In the labor issues survey of
1985, 65 percent of nonunion workers thought that "unions force members to go along with decisions they don't like." Sixty-three percent of
nonunion workers believed that union leaders, and not union members,
decide whether or not to strike. Half of all workers agree that "most union
leaders no longer represent the workers in their union." In issues of business efficiency, 54 percent of nonunion workers believed that "unions will
increase the risk that companies will go out of business," while 57 percent
believed that "unions stifle individual initiative," and 52 percent believed
that "unions fight change."[84]

By 1999, some popular attitudes had shifted in favor of labor. A national
survey found that 52 percent of those polled thought it would be good for
the country if more workers had union representation, whereas only 22
percent said it would be bad.[85] But another survey found that when posed
with the question of voting for a union in a NLRB election at their workplace, only 32 percent of nonmanagerial/nonunionized workers would
vote to have a union. Conversely, 90 percent of workers who already belonged to a union would vote again to keep a union in their workplace,

suggesting a very high degree of satisfaction with union representation for those who had actually experienced it.[86]

So, why is it that most Americans seem to overwhelmingly accept the theoretical practicality of labor unions, yet largely reject unions as a valid response to their everyday workplace conditions? The next chapter attempts to answer this question by investigating the way in which labor unions are presented to the public by the news media.

THE CONSUMER MEDIA EMERGES

The most significant development in the news media in the 1990s was a story hardly told in the news: how U.S. news media businesses merged, bought out, and consolidated into an enormous industry controlled by a few global industry behemoths. By 2000, a dozen media conglomerates—AOL Time Warner, AT&T, Bertelsmann, Clear Channel, Disney, Gannett, General Electric, Microsoft, the News Corp., Sony, Viacom, and Vivendi Universal—controlled just about every media sector, including television, cable, newspapers, radio, film, music, magazines, books, and the Internet. One might ask: If the new economy is about diversity of information, why do just a few conglomerates have so much power to control the content and distribution of that information?

Clearly, enormous media outlets, which have the same kinds of profit goals as other large publicly traded corporations, have little reason to provide regular and fair coverage of labor unions. With such ownership patterns, broadcast and print reporters and editors become socialized into corporate work environments that advocate certain news values while discouraging reporting on other topics.

A study by the Pew Research Center and the *Columbia Journalism Review* in 2000 directly revealed such reportorial self-censorship, with 35 percent of journalists surveyed agreeing that "news that would hurt the financial interests of a news organization often or sometimes goes unreported." Moreover, about 20 percent of reporters surveyed said they "faced criticism or pressure from their bosses after producing or writing a piece that was seen as damaging to their company's financial interests."[1]

A survey of newspaper editors in the early 1990s revealed even more extensive pressure from advertisers to influence news content. Researchers Lawrence Soley and Robert Craig reported that "about 90 percent of editors have been pressured by advertisers because of the type and content carried by the paper. Seventy-seven percent said they were pressured to kill stories, and more than 90 percent of editors said advertisers withdrew advertising because of content disputes. More than one-third reported that advertisers succeeded in influencing the news at their papers. And more than half said there was pressure from within their newspapers to write stories to please advertisers."[2]

Of course, news coverage that serves the interests of capital—including advertisers and the commercial news media business itself—has been occurring long before the 1990s. Sociologist Warren Breed recognized in 1958 that the mainstream news media held certain values, such as capitalism, as unassailable, while they were disinclined to report anything that might question the public's faith in such institutions. "Perhaps the most striking fact is that the word 'class' is almost entirely absent from the media," since "class, being social inequality, is the very antithesis of the American creed."[3]

Even decades earlier, muckraking journalist Upton Sinclair, in his 1920 book *The Brass Check*, charged that large industrialists of the early twentieth century used newspapers to curry favorable public opinion for industry. Sinclair noted that "in great strikes, all the efforts of the employers are devoted to making it appear that strikers are violent." This was achieved, he suggested,

> by the wholesale method of elimination. There are some violent strikers, needless to say, and Capitalist Journalism follows this simple and elemental rule—if strikers are violent, they get on the wires, while if strikers are not violent, they stay off the wires; by which simple device it is brought about that nine-tenths of the telegraphic news you read about strikes is news of violence, and so in your brain-channels is irrevocably graven the idea-association: Strikes—violence! Violence—strikes![4]

In the 1990s, however, the news media became even less quasi-independent observers of labor-capital relations and more and more aligned with the interests of the largest and most powerful elite corporations in the United States and the world. The location of broadcast and cable television news departments such as ABC, CBS, NBC, and CNN and newspapers such as the *New York Times* and *USA Today* within enormous media (and industrial) conglomerates spurred an increasing conflict in the missions between the practice of journalism and the business of media corporations.

The Drive for Profits

It has always been true that news operations want to make money; profit is necessary to their survival. But, how is the drive for profits reconciled with the practice of journalism? By 1997, only fifty-eight U.S. cities had more than one daily newspaper; the newspapers in twenty-one of those cities had common ownership (e.g., Knight Ridder owns both the *Philadelphia Inquirer* and *Daily News*) and in seventeen other cities had joint operating agreements (e.g., the *Detroit News* and the *Detroit Free Press*). Thus, there are few remaining competitive daily newspaper markets in the nation.[5] In such monopoly markets, newspapers can achieve profit margins of 20 to 40 percent. Moreover, by 1997, there were 120 newspaper chains owning 1,165 daily newspapers, about 77 percent of the nation's dailies. The newspaper chains controlled about 81 percent of the nation's weekday circulation and 87 percent of the Sunday newspaper circulation.[6] The trend of increasing consolidation occurred in local radio and television news outlets as well. Former *Wichita Eagle* editor Davis Merritt notes that when newspapers are acquired by publicly traded corporations, maintaining high profit margins is paramount, and profits are often held steady or increased by cutting costs, which can impact news quality.[7]

Good journalism does cost more money. According to John McManus, passive news gathering (working from press releases, video news releases, wire services, etc.) is less expensive, but doesn't serve the public interest as well.[8] Conversely, more active discovery (attending meetings, sifting through data, investigating tips—all the kind of work typically recognized as "good" journalism) better serves public interests, but is more expensive. In his study of medium, large, and very large local television stations, McManus found pretax profits ranging from 15.8 percent to 39 percent—similar to that of the newspaper industry—and argued that stations could devote more of their resources to active news gathering and still make reasonable profits.

Philip Meyer, a journalism professor and former twenty-three-year employee of the giant Knight Ridder newspaper chain, suggests that newspapers need to adjust to profit margins lower than the 20 to 40 percent that have been possible in monopoly markets. Meyer explains that "a business whose product has high turnover and consequently huge revenues can do nicely with a low profit margin," whereas "a low turnover product needs a high margin." Thus, the high-turnover supermarket business does well with 1 to 2 percent profit margins, most retail averages 6 to 7 percent in profit margins, and low-turnover businesses such as yacht and luxury sedan sellers need much higher profit margins. Daily newspapers, Meyer says, are "more like supermarkets than yacht dealers" and need to learn to live with lower profits.[9]

But during the 1990s, the trend was not for media conglomerates to treat their news operations as the standard bearers of the free press but instead as money-making enterprises that should meet the same profit standards of every other corporate division. Thus, media corporations have squeezed news operations and news staffs and have shifted news content from government and public affairs to more ad-friendly infotainment and cross-promotional synergies, characterized by ever-thicker newspaper lifestyle sections and television newsmagazine programs chock full of celebrity profiles.[10] Meanwhile, media executives have increasingly rewarded themselves with gigantic compensation packages, regardless of how they might have damaged their company's news operations.

Antilabor Activities

The corporate news media's posture toward labor unions is evident in their own labor practices. Many of the most highly regarded news media companies in the United States have a long record of their own antilabor activities. The *Washington Post*, for example, broke its press operator union in 1975. Then-publisher Katherine Graham brought in helicopters to fly the printing plates to distant printing facilities as part of the union-busting effort. According to Martin Lee and Norman Solomon, the newspaper continues to crack down on prounion employees.[11] The *Chicago Tribune* brought in permanent replacement workers to break the unions at its new printing plant in 1985; the Tribune Company also attempted to break unions during a 1990 strike at the New York *Daily News*. The strike ended only when the Tribune Company bailed out and sold the *Daily News* to British press baron Robert Maxwell. Even the *New York Times*, in its 1994 negotiations with the Newspaper Guild of America, "proposed an end to job security, arguing that the seemingly permanent media recession requires a new discipline under which bosses may fire at will."[12]

The worst labor conflict of the 1990s at a news media corporation occurred in one of labor's traditional strongholds, when the *Detroit News* and *Detroit Free Press*, two major newspapers linked in business operations through a federally imposed joint operating agreement, colluded to break its employees' unions.[13] Six unions led nearly 2,500 workers—reporters, editors, drivers, mailers, engravers, and press operators—to walk out on the *Free Press* and *News* in July 1995 after the unions charged that management refused to bargain fairly in contract renewal talks. The newspapers immediately hired replacement workers (many of whom were readily transferred from other newspapers owned by parent corporations Gannett and Knight Ridder) to fill positions, allowing the publication of the *News* and *Free Press* to continue throughout the strike. When strikers tried to stop shipments of the lucrative *Detroit News and Free Press* Sunday edition from the Sterling Heights, Michigan, printing plant, the trucks drove full speed at picketers.[14] Later, the Detroit News Agency (DNA; the business arm for both newspapers) employed helicopters to airlift enough newspapers out of the plant to deflate the efforts of strikers. The most surprising tactic was the DNA's payment of about $480,000 to the city of Sterling Heights to subsidize police overtime for guarding the plant, which many regarded as a payoff to court the favor of the police.[15]

Management of the Detroit newspapers claimed victory for not being shut down by striking workers, but the standing of the papers in the community suffered. A boycott by readers and advertisers created huge losses during the strike, costing the Detroit newspapers more than $200 million in losses and a circulation slide of 35 percent, knocking both the *News* and *Free Press* out of their longtime perch in the Top 10 list of the country's largest newspapers.[16] Yet, from the Wall Street perspective, undermining the unions was good news. After workers ended their walkout, the *Detroit*

News proudly reported that "investors . . . didn't flinch," with Gannett stock gaining 48.85 percent and Knight Ridder shares jumping 40 percent during the nineteen-month strike.[17]

Even after striking union members agreed to unconditionally return to work in February 1997, the DNA vowed to keep its replacement workers and hire back the original workers only when positions became available. The effect was a lockout of the original employees, allowing the conflict to simmer for years longer. The National Labor Relations Board ruled in 1998 that management's unfair labor practices caused the strike, and ordered the two newspapers to reinstate workers with back pay. Both newspapers flagrantly disregarded the ruling. Moreover, the newspapers had fired more than one hundred workers for strike activity.[18]

In television news, NBC, in May 1994 contract offers with its unions, proposed to increase the amount of work done by temporary employees and to reduce the work for its 1,700 full-time employees who were union members. Under the standing contract, NBC could use daily hires— people with no health or retirement benefits—for up to 15 percent of the jobs. NBC proposed to boost the level of daily hires to 67 percent.[19] Cap Cities, ABC television's parent corporation, also has a record of anti-union strategies. When Cap Cities bought the Wilkes-Barre (Pennsylvania) *Times-Leader* in the mid-1970s, it attempted to change the union contracts that had been negotiated with the newspaper's previous owners. The confrontation resulted in a lengthy strike, violence, and permanent replacement workers at the *Times-Leader*. The workers' ultimate response was the founding of a successful competing daily newspaper, the *Citizen's Voice*, which denied Cap Cities the revenue it expected by owning the only daily in the region.[20] Disney's purchase of Cap Cities in 1995 didn't end the company's hard line toward labor. When about two thousand ABC television technical workers walked off their jobs on November 2, 1998, to protest health care issues, the company locked out the workers—preventing them from returning—and immediately replaced them with temporary workers. The locked-out employees had been working without a contract since the previous one had expired more than a year and a half earlier. Eleven weeks later, ABC ended the lockout when the union agreed to accept the original proposals, which included more temporary workers, reduced benefits, and a promise to give advanced warning on all future strikes.[21]

Even PBS, assailed throughout the 1990s as the bastion of liberal broad-casting by politicians such as Newt Gingrich and Jesse Helms, isn't espe-cially union-friendly. WNET in New York, one of the leading PBS affiliates and a production facility of PBS mainstays *The NewsHour with Jim Lehrer* (formerly *The MacNeil/Lehrer NewsHour*) and *Charlie Rose*, has reportedly outsourced several million dollars worth of postproduction video work to nonunion video services.[22] The use of outside service suppliers at WNET has the same potential effect as outsourcing in the auto industry: reduced investment in the company's own production facilities further justifies using the more up-to-date facilities of outside suppliers, and reduced use of the company's own unionized staff justifies eliminating those unionized jobs. In the end, WNET (and industries like the auto industry) may reduce its direct labor costs, as in-house union jobs are replaced with lower-paying nonunion jobs.

It would make sense, in the logic of capitalism, that news businesses wouldn't report—or would avoid reporting favorably—on issues such as labor that might damage their bottom line. Not only do the mass media work to help themselves in this manner, but they also, as Ralph Miliband argues, invariably serve as reinforcing instruments of power in the entire economic system:

> The ideological function of the media is obscured by many features of cul-tural life in these systems, for instance the absence of state dictation, the existence of debate and controversy, the fact that conservatism is not a tight body of thought and that its looseness makes possible the variations and divergencies within its framework, and much else as well. But ob-scured though it may be, the fact remains that the mass media in advanced capitalist societies are mainly intended to perform a highly "functional" role; they too are both the expression of a system of domination and a means of reinforcing it.[23]

Thus, the procapitalist function of the mass media predictably involves antiunion sentiment because organized labor necessarily infringes on the decision-making power of capital and may inhibit capital's profit margins.

The news media's ownership patterns and financial goals are a major part of explaining why the news media cover labor the way they do, but not the only part. The complete explanation needs to include not just economy but also culture—and consumerism is the link between the two.

Hailing the Consumer

The news media, of course, cannot afford to be *seen* as acting as blatant lackeys to their mogul or conglomerate owners. As James Curran notes, "the need for audience credibility and political legitimacy, the self-image and professional commitment of journalists, and the normative public support for journalistic independence are all important influences militating against the subordination of commercial media to the business and political interests of parent companies."[24] Therefore, the news media must maintain their self-described position as objective and fair reporters of events.

Edward Herman and Noam Chomsky argue that the free market configuration of the U.S. news media—with First Amendment guarantees and private ownership of the press—serves to disguise a system of media propaganda that benefits the rich and powerful and marginalizes class dissent: "It is much more difficult to see a propaganda system at work where the media are private and formal censorship is absent. This is especially true where the media actively compete, periodically attack and expose corporate and governmental malfeasance, and aggressively portray themselves as spokesmen for free speech and the general community interest."[25]

This system of propaganda, which benefits the rich and powerful, marginalizes class dissent, and simultaneously appears to be the product of a free press, is achieved by addressing the news audience as consumers rather than citizens. By addressing, or "hailing," the news audience as consumers, the news media establish a consumption-based social relationship between themselves and their audience and create an ideological frame for understanding the news story.[26] Hailing the audience as consumers, not citizens, says "you should be worried about this labor situation as a consumer, but as a citizen you need not be concerned." Through a consumer orientation, the news media serve their own economic position in relation to labor, yet also maintain a familiar, "neutral" position as they claim to be working in the interest of the audience/consumer. As noted earlier, the interests of the citizen are the fundamental questions of political power in everyday life, including policies of the environment and workplace. Graham Murdock and Peter Golding argue that as citizens, we should expect three things from our communication systems to fully exercise our citizenship:

> First, people must have access to the information, advice, and analysis that will enable them to know what their rights are in other spheres and allow them to pursue their rights effectively. Second, they must have access to the broadest possible range of information, interpretation, and debate on areas that involve political choices, and they must be able to use communication facilities in order to register criticism, mobilize opposition, and propose alternative courses of action. And third, they must be able to recognize themselves and their aspirations in the range of representations offered within the central communication sectors and be able to contribute to developing those representations.[27]

By addressing all of us as consumers, the news media diminish citizenship to mere purchasing behavior. Our "rights" as consumers concern the price, quality, and immediacy of consumable goods and services. Our democratic opposition and recourse as consumers is reduced to the hackneyed advice that we can "vote with our pocketbooks." Our contribution as consumers to the representations in the mass media is largely limited to the systematic feedback of our response (via ratings, surveys, and other audience measurement technologies) to whatever the mass media deliver to us.

The consumer orientation of the news media creates an atmosphere of "objective" coverage of industry and labor because both institutions are subject to a consumerist scrutiny of the news media. Indeed, industry's greatest fear and complaint of news coverage is the "investigative report" of businesses that have somehow betrayed the consumer.[28] The reports of Mike Wallace, CBS's *60 Minutes* newsmagazine correspondent, have attained almost legendary status in the business world. Wallace is regarded as a giant-killer of sorts, able to bring evasive business executives to their knees with his tough interviews.[29] Yet even the venerable *60 Minutes* is subject to its own corporate interests. Under pressure from the highest levels of management, the newsmagazine killed a November 1995 report on the tobacco industry. CBS feared the report—which wasn't false or libelous—would disrupt a planned sale of the network to Westinghouse. Moreover, the family that owned CBS was also involved in the tobacco business. This massive conflict of interests was dramatized in a 1999 film, *The Insider*.[30]

Although the occasional investigative report of business misdeeds suggests a lack of media favoritism toward business, it is organized labor who is the inherent loser in the media's consumer sphere. Whereas businesses are the visible creators credited with the achievements of the consumer economy, organized labor is almost always portrayed as an impediment for the consumer, either by adding costs to goods, making poor-quality products, or (via strikes or inefficiencies attributed to labor) delaying the instant gratification of consumer goods and services.

Not only do news organizations most often frame labor stories as a consumer issue, but the level of coverage of any labor story generally correlates to the level of presumed consumer relevance.[31] Because commercial news organizations envision their audience as consumers, presumed consumer impact becomes the chief criterion for newsworthiness. For example, a baseball strike idling about seven hundred unionized players is deemed much more worthy of national coverage because of inconvenienced sports consumers than a several-year lockout of more than seven hundred Midwestern industrial workers, since the lockout has scarcely disrupted the consumer market for corn byproducts. Moreover, the news media not only presume consumer interest in certain types of stories but also work to create audiences that are functional for a consumer-based, advertising-supported media system. Thus, routine news beats and topics such as business, sports, entertainment, technology, fashion, and travel fill newspaper pages and television news rundowns. Labor unions, lacking a long list of potential commercial sponsors (for both practical and ideological reasons) don't easily fit into the commercial news media's routine coverage.

That the news media address their audience as consumers isn't surprising. As James Ettema and D. Charles Whitney explain, "in an institutional conception, actual receivers are constituted—or, perhaps, reconstituted—not merely as audiences but as institutionally effective audiences that have social meaning and/or economic value within the system."[32] For advertising-supported mass media institutions, constituting the audience as consumers, and not as full citizens, provides the most economic value within the system of mass media. Thus, the news media cover labor not with an idealized *public sphere*, where it would serve as a citizen's forum for discovery and rational-critical debate but with a *consumer sphere*, where it approaches labor solely from a consumer point of view. The normalcy of the news media's consumer view on labor-management conflict has its roots in the emergence of a consumer ethos in the United States, a consumer ethos that runs hand-in-hand with the rise of the country's mass media.

The Naturalization of Consumerism in the News

Prior to the emergence of the first "penny press" commercial newspapers in the 1830s, newspapers in America were journals of opinion, supported mainly by political parties and serving mainly as political newssheets. As historian Piers Brendon notes, "Before 1830, newspapers relied on political subsidies. And, beholden to parties for information as well as lucre, journalists wrote to order, slavishly about their mentors, abusively about their opponents, viciously about each other. The press was the verbal equivalent of the pillory, the riper the billingsgate the richer the entertainment. Readers bought newspapers in order to find out who was to be vilified next."[33]

The era of the raucous precommercial press is often celebrated as a moment when a public sphere actually existed in American society. Hundreds of newspapers served as a medium for at least a limited bourgeois public sphere, where—as Jürgen Habermas describes—private people came together, "claimed the public sphere regulated from above," and engaged the public authorities "in a debate over the general rules governing relations in the basically privatized but publicly relevant sphere of commodity exchange and social labor."[34] Thus, social politics and economy became regular topics for public debate.

The precommercial press showed great democratic possibilities, but the franchise for public rational-critical debate was restricted to white, educated, bourgeois middle-class men. So, although political participation increased through the early nineteenth century, Michael Schudson's analy-

sis of that period's literacy rates, newspapers, political parties, and electoral procedures suggests that "political discourse did not become
markedly more rational and critical" at that time. Nevertheless, Schudson
argues, Habermas's ideal of a public sphere should still be "indispensable
as a model of what a good society should achieve."[35]

Ironically, as the press became more accessible in the emerging era of
Jacksonian democracy, the press moved away from the public sphere
model. Along with the Jacksonian era's innovations of universal white
manhood suffrage, public schooling, political party machinery, an egali-
tarian market democracy, and the demise of aristocracy, emerged a new
kind of newspaper: the penny press (named for the one- or two-cent selling price). Beginning with newspapers such as the *New York Sun* in 1833
and the *New York Herald* in 1835, the penny press publications quickly
gained enormous circulation by undercutting the price of the existing six-
cent journals.

The penny press marked a philosophical break with the six-penny
newspapers. In keeping with the market democracy of the times, the
penny press dispensed with political party subsidies and reader subscrip-
tions, and earned its keep through street corner sales and as an advertising forum for the growing market of manufactured goods.[36] In doing so,
the penny papers cultivated a reputation as a "free press," independent of
political manipulation. The content of the newspapers shifted from editorial debates of politics and ideology of the public sphere to a currency of
advertising and human interest "news" stories of everyday life. The new
content, distribution, and business orientation of the penny papers transformed newspapers into a consumer product for a mass audience.

By the latter decades of the nineteenth century, historian Gerald Baldasty explains, the penny press format became the dominant format for
newspapers, and news content itself had become a commodity. As Baldasty notes, business imperatives had changed the purpose of news:
"News was simply not a report of the day's events. Rather, it was a selection of reports that could be produced within a newspaper's business constraints."[37] The demand for revenues led to the blurring of news and ads.
Editors frequently dropped business-friendly "puffs"—favorable men-
tions of the newspaper's advertisers—into their news columns. Newspapers also cultivated relationships with advertisers through news profiles
of businesses or business people. For example, an 1885 *Boston Globe* article

promoted one of its top advertisers, a department store. The headline read: "Jordan, Marsh & Co. Their Colossal Sale Draws Thousands from Every Section."[38]

Newspapers also began to generate content specifically to attract a female readership, who were valued as the buyers of the stream of mass-produced goods in the late nineteenth century. By the 1880s, cooking, household hints, fashion, and society features were regular categories of news.[39] Nationally circulated popular magazines of the late nineteenth and early twentieth centuries—such as *McClure's*, *The World's Work*, the *Saturday Evening Post*, and *Ladies' Home Journal*—also used a rhetoric of consumption to orient the reading audience as active consumers.[40]

As the U.S. industrial revolution took hold, the country's population experienced a seismic shift. In 1880, about 80 percent of the nation's population lived in rural areas and small towns. A generation later, in 1920, about 80 percent of the nation lived in urban/suburban locations. This shift, and a corresponding change in work from a producer to a consumer economy, brought great challenges to American values and ideals of democracy.

By the late nineteenth and early twentieth centuries, the opposition between the managers of the still-expanding steel, mining, railroad, shipping, textile, and journalism industries and their laborers was quite clear. As David Brody notes, "corporate employers had grown too large and powerful; they were too unyielding in defense of managerial prerogatives," resulting in a rise of "rank-and-file militancy" and working-class consciousness.[41] After a series of setbacks in violent labor struggles in the 1870s and 1880s, and a depression through most of the 1890s, union membership quadrupled between 1897 and 1903. According to historian David Montgomery, "industrial growth had made possible a material abundance beyond the wildest dreams of earlier generations of humanity, without bringing prosperity, let alone contentment, to the bulk of the population. Workers' movements, national-independence movements, women's demands for social and political emancipation, and rural rebellions had the industrial world simultaneously glorying in its new splendor and trembling at the prospect of bloody barricades."[42] Thus, U.S. society at the beginning of the twentieth century stood at a dangerous juncture: Mighty industry offered mass consumerism as the reward of labor, whereas the laboring classes looked for freedom from the repressions of wage labor that made mass consumerism possible.

The newspaper industry, which in many ways epitomized the capital-labor relationships of other leading industries at that time, sat squarely in capital's corner. The press's antilabor sentiment can be traced back to the beginnings of the U.S. industrial revolution in the 1880s, when Chicago's English-language daily newspapers "cheered the execution" of the alleged Haymarket conspirators,[43] four working-class radicals who were questionably convicted of bombing a Haymarket Square rally in 1886. Labor historian Melvyn Dubovsky calls the newspaper and magazine coverage of the Haymarket bombing and trial the first national Red Scare campaign, linking all trade unionism to anarchy and murder.[44]

By the turn of the century, according to historian Jon Bekken, the commercial dailies of the heavily industrialized Chicago area "generally claimed to champion the interests of workers, but believed that the interests of labor and capital were fundamentally the same—and that both were subordinate to the 'public interest.' They strongly backed arbitration of labor disputes, opposed sympathy strikes, and called for forcible suppression of strike-related disorder."[45] The more a worker's organization leaned to the left politically, the more it could expect to be reviled in the press.

As noted earlier, Upton Sinclair, the well-known muckraking reporter of the early twentieth century, was outraged by press coverage of labor in his time. Sinclair charged that "Whenever it comes to a 'show-down' between labor and capital, the press is openly or secretly for capital—and this no matter how 'liberal' the press may pretend to be."[46] Given the shortcomings of labor coverage in the mainstream press, it is no surprise that labor activists resolved to take the matter into their own hands by publishing labor-oriented newspapers.

Bekken reports that at the beginning of the twentieth century, "the U.S. Labor movement published hundreds of newspapers in dozens of languages, ranging from local and regional dailies issued by working-class political organizations and mutual aid societies to national union weeklies and monthlies."[47] These alternative publications served an important organizing function, and many democratically invited all members to submit articles for publication. Some of these party presses with prounion messages were as popular as any commercial newspaper. According to Sam Pizzigati and Fred Solowey, "Just after the turn of the century, the largest-circulation weekly newspaper in the United States was the *Appeal to Reason*, an unofficial Socialist party paper that circulated over 760,000 copies at its peak in 1913. During the Great Depression, the newspaper of the Communist Party USA, the *Daily Worker*, saw its paid circulation climb to 100,000."[48] The high circulation of these weeklies (significant even by today's standards) was difficult to sustain, especially with the government-led antiradical campaign during World War I.[49] The U.S. government banned certain publications (such as the Industrial Workers of the World's weekly *Industrial Worker*) from the mails, while other working-class newspapers suffered libel suits, destruction of presses, or deportation of editors.[50]

Erasing Class with a Consumer Ethos

By the early twentieth century, industrialists' two greatest problems were limited markets for their mass production—the middle- and upper-class markets alone could not sustain industry's output—and chronic labor unrest, which interrupted mass production. The answer to both problems was to organize the working classes as an enormous buying public, creating mass consumption to meet the needs of mass production.[51] National advertising campaigns, social scientists, ministers, and popular writers all played important roles in redirecting American culture from a nineteenth-century production ethic of work, saving, and self-denial to a twentieth-century consumption ethic of leisure, spending, and self-realization.[52] Mass production and mass consumption were the hallmarks of this new Fordist economy.

The new consumer ethos attempted to erase visible and psychic class distinctions. Democracy that had been denied to the working classes was now promised in a modern parable, the "Democracy of Goods." According to Roland Marchand, this parable was "one of the most pervasive of all advertising tableaux of the 1920s":

> The cumulative effect of the constant reminders that "any woman can" and "every home can afford" was to publicize an image of American society in which concentrated wealth at the top of a hierarchy of social classes restricted no family's opportunity to acquire the most significant products. By implicitly defining "democracy" in terms of equal access to consumer products, and then by depicting the everyday functioning of that "democ-

racy" with regard to one product at a time, these tableaux offered Americans an inviting vision of their society as one of incontestable equality.[53]

Widespread adoption of a consumer ethos served to undermine collective class action. Stuart Ewen notes that "by the demand of workers for the right to be better consumers, the aspirations of labor would be profitably coordinated with the aspirations of capital. Such convictions implicitly attempted to divest protest of its anticapitalist content."[54] The expansion of retail credit, personal investment bankers, and public stock sales in the early twentieth century aided individual material pursuits of the Fordist regime.[55] At the same time, the new professionalized corporate public relations that emerged in the 1910s and 1920s put a consumer-friendly face on business, dissolving the image of the robber baron.[56]

The consumer ethos also determined the fate of the emerging electronic media of radio and television, as the Federal Radio Act of 1927, the Federal Communications Act of 1934, and other federal regulations defined broadcasting as a commercial pursuit. As Robert McChesney points out, corporate interests prevailed over educators, community groups, labor unions, churches, and other nonprofit groups in the debates of the late 1920s and early 1930s over the structure of the U.S. broadcasting system. Corporate interests argued that only a commercial, advertising-based system could best operate in the "public convenience, interest, or necessity" and deemed other potential guardians of the airwaves as mere propagandists. McChesney writes:

> [Commercial broadcasters] strove to attach commercial broadcasting to the ideological wagon that equated capitalism with the free and equal marketplace, the free and equal marketplace with democracy, and democracy with "Americanism." The status quo, therefore, easily became the "American Plan," where public interest was assured, as it always was, by the machinations of the marketplace. Challengers to the efficacy of the marketplace in broadcasting drew the raised eyebrows of the dominant culture as malcontent "special interests," incapable of meeting the public's needs in the marketplace.[57]

By the time of the broadcasting debates, the media was beginning to cast labor as a special interest and a strong consumer economy as America's chief concern. Even labor's greatest triumph, the National Labor Relations Act of 1935, which guaranteed the right for workers to form and join unions, was painted with the logic of consumption. The Act declared that employee-employer inequality burdened the economy "by depressing wage rates and the purchasing power of wage earners in industry and by preventing the stabilization of competitive wage rates and working conditions within and between industries."[58]

Even with its victory of a commercially based broadcasting system, business in the 1930s was challenged by the growing power of the federal government and organized labor. Corporate leaders viewed the federal New Deal programs and the prolabor laws passed in the Depression era as a threat to business's autonomy. But, after weathering the Great Depression through the 1930s and World War II of the early 1940s, in 1945 business embarked on a concerted multimillion-dollar public relations effort to ideologically place itself at the center of American society, bringing its message of free enterprise, individualism, and ever-increasing productivity and abundance to schools, churches, and the mass media. Business's public makeover included a new approach to combat unions: dropping "vocal animosity toward labor unions in general" in favor of positioning labor as "a formidable threat to the American Way."[59] The weighty resources of business, funneled through national organizations such as the Advertising Council, the U.S. Chamber of Commerce, the National Association of Manufacturers, and the Committee for Economic Development, far outstripped labor's means. Because of this, historian Elizabeth Fones-Wolf notes, "the images and ideas of business were pervasive, filling much of America's cultural space with a series of selectively distorted symbols that made it difficult, if not impossible, for Americans to discover and articulate competing visions of American polity."[60]

After the economic interruptions of the Great Depression of the 1930s and World War II, consumers were encouraged to enjoy the fruits of America's world-leader status. By the 1950s, an informal social covenant between big labor, big business, and the federal government was in place, creating the conditions for the unprecedented production and consumption of the postwar era. During this period, government primed the economy with massive federal spending, business experienced rising profit margins, and labor continued to collectively bargain for higher wages.[61]

Yet, labor's embrace of policies and rhetoric that focused on increasing wages for mass consumption wasn't imposed entirely by business, historian Lawrence Glickman argues. In fact, labor's steps toward consumerism were also enmeshed with a more progressive movement that linked production and consumption to the notion of a "living wage." In the industrial revolution, (mostly white male) U.S. workers were forced to transform themselves from independent artisans and producers to wage laborers. Working for wages was initially derided as wage slavery. But, by the late 1800s, led by the American Federation of Labor president Samuel Gompers and others, the movement toward an eight-hour day and a living wage proposed "a new, positive vision of wage labor" that provided "the ability to support families, to maintain self-respect, and to have both the means and the leisure to participate in the civic life of the nation."[62] Although this consumerist vision coincided with at least part of capital's vision of a materialist economy, it should not be discounted that labor's push for a living wage was an ideological battle fought by workers to gain economic power and respect in the new industrial economy.

As the post–World War II United States focused on consumption and upward mobility, the divisions of social class that characterized the culture of previous generations were deemphasized, particularly in the mass media. Television became the most effective purveyor of consumption and therapeutic self-indulgence. As cultural historian George Lipsitz notes, "television advertised individual products, but it also provided a relentless flow of information and persuasion that placed acts of consumption at the core of everyday life."[63] By the second half of the twentieth century, the working-class newspapers had mostly faded away, too. One of the longest-running, the Racine [Wisconsin] Labor, established in 1941, shut down in 2002—a casualty of the globalization that decimated the manufacturing industries and union population of the area.[64] It was one of the last existing independent local socialist newspapers in the United States. Aside from the more recent establishment of the Wilkes-Barre [Pennsylvania] Citizens' Voice, the remaining working class–oriented publications are generally union publications, and they have most often served as formal, undemocratic mouthpieces for union leadership.[65]

What the consumer ethos hadn't eradicated of a left-leaning working-class consciousness, the conservative postwar politics did. Communist witch hunts and antilabor legislation of the late 1940s and 1950s—well publicized by the news media at that time—effectively eliminated union

officials who had Communist Party connections.[66] Ideologically eviscer-
ated, and with the enduring anti-Communist sentiment that lasted for decades to come, unions lost the ability to create a substantial critique of the
U.S. economic system.

In the early twentieth century, labor-management conflict "was likely to
be caught, framed, and illuminated by the stark contest between organized capital and organizing labor," Dan Schiller notes.[67] In the late twentieth century, with the United States pervaded by an ethos of consumption, labor-management conflict was likely to be characterized as a
consumer issue, with no class implications. A comparison of newspaper
editorials from these two periods, describing each newspaper's own
strike situation, illustrates important differences in coverage.

A strike by *Los Angeles Times* workers in 1910 elicited this broadside
from the newspaper's editors:

> [The strikers] are mostly of the anarchic scum of Europe. They are envious,
> idle, brawling, disorderly men who hang about the deadfalls and, between
> drinks, damn as a scab every non-union industrious worker. They hate
> law, hate order, and hate the men and the conditions which compel them
> to work occasionally. Their instincts are criminal, and they are ever ready
> for arson, riot, robbery, and murder . . . They combine in labor unions
> whose honest purpose they pervert . . . to prohibit the skillful and the in-
> dustrious mechanic from accomplishing any more work in a day than the
> unskillful and lazy man.[68]

The *Chicago Tribune*, perhaps as devoted in its recent antilabor strategies as
the earlier *Los Angeles Times*, published an editorial on its workers' strike
in 1985. Exhibiting the triumph of the consumer ethos, the *Tribune* avoided
antilabor vitriol and instead made a patronizing defense of the free press
and the free flow of *Tribune* newspapers for nonstop consumption.

> [N]ewspapers are extraordinary in that their existence and the economic
> health that ensures it are critical to the free and independent flow of infor-
> mation back and forth between the government and the governed. The
> press has traditionally been the forum in which Americans debate how to
> govern themselves. And that debate does not close for the weekend, or
> shut down on holidays or take place only during normal business hours.

Neither should a newspaper, regardless of how many picket lines are put up around it or whose economic interests are affected by a strike. Publishing a struck paper is neither a comfortable or profitable exercise.

But the obligation to publish is there, constant and unceasing. And it is out of commitment to that obligation, not disrespect for the right of production unions to strike, that *The Chicago Tribune* will continue to make efforts to do so, no matter what.[69]

Of course, the *Tribune*'s seemingly neutral, objective position in the reporting of the strike masked its attempt (and eventual success) in breaking its production union with replacement workers. With its proconsumer rhetoric—who could argue with the *Tribune*'s professed dedication to be a forum for its readers?—the *Tribune* failed as a forum for debate on its own highly disrespectful antiworker strategy that included bargaining in bad faith and hiring the infamous strike-breaking Nashville law firm King & Ballow.

Playing to Consumer Fears: The Myth of Union-Caused Inflation

With a consumer ethos firmly entrenched in the United States in the postwar 1950s, a fresh news frame, adapted from economic theory, served to further thwart coverage of labor unions. This frame dropped the harsh antiunion rhetoric of earlier times and instead used the seemingly unassailable and objective authority of modern economics to blame labor unions for one of most-feared problems of postwar America: inflation. The myth of union-caused inflation began with a theory published in 1958 that became known as the Phillips Curve, after British economist A. W. Phillips. It has been one of the most enduring commonsense economic frames of the second half of the twentieth century (and is a common corollary of Dominant Frame No. 5—"collective economic action is bad"— noted in Chapter 1). Phillips based his curvilinear model on research charting unemployment and wage rates in Britain from 1861 to 1957.[70]

The Phillips Curve Frame
In its basic form, the Phillips Curve posits a consistent inverse relationship between unemployment and money wages, whereby low levels in

unemployment would result in high wages (and prices) and vice versa.[71] The Phillips Curve thus suggests a trade-off between unemployment and inflation. For policymakers, the key is determining the "natural" rate of unemployment in an economy, where unemployment is not so low that a tight employment market ignites demands for higher wages and an inflationary trend. This so-called acceptable rate of unemployment is known as the natural rate of unemployment, or NAIRU (nonaccelerating inflation rate of unemployment).[72] In the late twentieth century, the presumed natural rate of unemployment for the United States, as estimated by the Congressional Budget Office, ranged from a high of 6.3 percent in 1980 to 5.8 percent in 1996.[73] The appeal of the Phillips Curve is that it suggests that economists and government policymakers (via the U.S. Federal Reserve) can easily manipulate the economy, tightening the money supply to increase unemployment and cool inflation, or expanding access to money to heat up the economy, thus increasing inflation but lowering unemployment.

From a journalistic perspective, the Phillips Curve, although rarely identified by name in news stories, is one of the most frequently used frames for telling stories of labor's relationship to the economy. For journalists trying to cover the complex economy, the Phillips Curve offers a simple interpretive frame. In news stories using this frame, an increase in wages for workers is said to put inflationary pressure on the economy. Labor unions are most specifically implicated in such frames because collectively bargained labor contracts can increase the wages of a large number of workers at a single time. Wages are usually the largest cost of production, so, as such news stories typically presume, companies then must pass along the wage increases in the form of higher prices for consumer goods and services, which then cause inflation.

In the news, the resulting stories blare headlines such as "Organized Labor Is Seeking Big Pay Gains—Successes by Some Unions Are Leading to Worries about Wage Inflation" (from the *Wall Street Journal* in 1999)[74] and lead sentences like "Does the United Parcel Service strike signal the end of America's so-called 'Goldilocks' economy, the 'just right' combination of steady growth, low unemployment, no inflation, and rising corporate profits?"[75] (The story, from the *Los Angeles Times* in 1997, answers yes.)

President Kennedy was an early follower of the Phillips Curve's logic.

In a speech to the United Automobile Workers (UAW) in 1962, he "called for 'responsible unionism' and cautioned the union that it could set off an inflationary spiral if it used its bargaining muscle to extract wage increases that far outpaced inflation."[76] The predictions of the Phillips Curve model held up reliably in the United States through the 1960s, but several periods in the following decades revealed its shortcomings, leading to some media stories that questioned its use. For example, a *Business Week* magazine article in 1973 titled "Is the Phillips Curve Losing Its Allure?" reported on a summit of the United States' top twenty-five economists in Rochester, New York. The article noted that "inevitably, their discussions were colored by the fact that inflation has shot up to an annual rate of 6% while the unemployment rate stays stubbornly at 5%. To a growing number of economists, this confirms the suspicion that, contrary to conventional wisdom, policymakers cannot count on a predictable trade-off between the jobless rate and price movements."[77]

In 1983, when inflation and unemployment again were both high, the *New York Times* confidently spoke of "the collapse of faith in the Phillips curve—the purported trade-off between inflation and unemployment that was generally accepted in the 1960's."[78] In 1988, the high unemployment during the Reagan administration had finally subsided to 5.6 percent, renewing worries about inflation. But, the *New York Times* again reported that "most economists say the [Phillips] curve is not an accurate guide"[79] and that the theory "seems to have broken down."[80]

Yet, despite the occasional doubts and unreliability of the Phillips Curve model, it continued to be a defining frame of economic news throughout the 1990s, particularly when it came to the question of disciplining labor. For example, in August 1996, the *Boston Globe* found good news in an economic report that the number of jobs created in the previous month was lower than expected. The article reasoned that "the job news suggested the economy is good enough to keep the unemployment rate low, but not so good as to touch off a sharp rise in wages and prices."[81]

By the late 1990s, the U.S. economy continued to grow with NAIRU-defying low unemployment (below 5 percent) and inflation (below 2 percent), leading *New York Times* guest columnist J. Bradford DeLong to ask "Whatever happened to the Phillips Curve?"[82] He should have asked the other writers at the newspaper, who still seemed to be true believers in the Curve's elementary logic, especially after the Federal Reserve and its chairman Alan Greenspan increased interest rates six times between June 1999 and May 2000, just as the economy was beginning to finally realize small but long-overdue wage improvements for lower- and middle-wage workers.[83] A *New York Times* article from July 27, 2000, recited the party line on the Phillips Curve effect: "The employment cost index is known to be closely watched by Greenspan, especially since unemployment has been near historic lows. His immediate concern is that as the labor market grows tighter, employers will need to increase wages and benefits to attract and keep workers. *Business would then need to pass these costs along in the form of higher prices for its goods and services, leading to broader inflation.*"[84]

The appeal of the Phillips Curve in the late 1990s as the commonsense explanation for Greenspan's money-tightening was surprising given that the theory had been solidly debunked in professional and academic literature during the same decade. Analyses of unemployment, inflation, and wage data clearly concluded that low employment isn't inflationary and that wage inflation doesn't cause price inflation.[85] In fact, according to economists Gregory Hess and Mark Schweitzer, both of whom are affiliated with the Federal Reserve Bank of Cleveland, "it is more often that price inflation causes wage inflation."[86] That is, inflation can be caused by any number of factors (e.g., a jump in the price of electricity, oil, or natural gas), and that wage pressure occurs only after inflation has eroded the purchasing power of workers' wages.

Still, the Phillips Curve remains a resilient news frame, particularly when it serves the purpose of economic policymakers. But, as economist Bernard Corry explains, the high level of acceptance of theories like the Phillips Curve is more due to political expediency than empirical validity:

> There is obviously a strong interplay between economic ideas and political beliefs, and however much we may wish to espouse the neutrality of economic theory, the reality is far different. This interplay is a two-way process: our economics may lead us to policies that have clear political implications but—perhaps more importantly—we should be aware that our formulation of and acceptance of economic ideas may be a consequence of our prior political/philosophical beliefs.[87]

The Twisted Logic of the Phillips Curve Frame

As noted in Chapter 2, the salaries of U.S. executives rose 62.7 percent in the 1990s. Although news media reports sometimes raised an eyebrow at these salaries (e.g., noting that U.S. executive compensation far outstripped executive salaries in other countries), executive compensation escaped causal linkage to inflation.[88] A few rare news reports did discuss the matter. For example, a 1995 *New York Times* op-ed piece by Sarah Anderson and John Cavanaugh, fellows at the Institute for Policy Studies in Washington, D.C., outlined their study on the wage gap between U.S. executives and their workers. They found that in the NAFTA-aided border economy, U.S. executives were reluctant to share their largesse with a grossly underpaid Mexican workforce. The article takes aim at the trope of wage inflation:

> U.S. corporations have largely resisted pressure from Mexican unions, socially responsible investors, and other groups to provide raises to their Mexican workers that would make up for the drop in purchasing power, arguing that paying higher wages would diminish their competitive edge or contribute to higher inflation in Mexico.
>
> Such excuses are hard to swallow when you consider that the executives at these firms had no problem accepting whopping raises for themselves over the past year . . . A common argument for fat CEO salaries is that you need to pay well to attract top-notch corporate leaders. However, executives at the largest Japanese firms earn much less—a still hefty $411,200 on average last year. If the U.S. executives in our study had limited their compensation to that amount, the rest of their earnings would have been enough to give each of their Mexican workers a $1,000 raise per year. Since most of their Mexican employees are now earning the equivalent of $1,000 to $3,000 a year, this would amount to a raise of 33% to 100%.[89]

Another problem with the Phillips Curve frame in news reports is the presumption that wage increases will automatically result in price increases (e.g., the July 27, 2000, *New York Times* excerpt cited above, which says "Business would then need to pass these costs along in the form of higher prices for its goods and services, leading to broader inflation.").[90] This presumption ignores alternatives to directly passing on wage increases as price increases. For example, increases in productivity may negate the impact of wage increases. Wage increases can also be under-written with corporate profits, which—given the experience of the 1990s—may be rising much faster than employee compensation. Econo-mists Hess and Schweitzer further note that "No firm inherits the right to simply 'mark-up' the prices of its output as a constant proportion of its costs; competitive pressures strongly influence the pricing decisions of firms."[91] However, the unspoken assumption behind the Phillips Curve news frame is that when it comes to funding wage increases for workers, executive compensation and corporate profits are off-limits.

Although the wages of rank-and-file workers are summarily targeted as a cause of inflation, labor unions historically have been rebuffed in their attempts to ensure that wage increases are not inflationary to consumers. The most notable of these efforts was in late 1945, during the UAW union negotiations with General Motors over the next contract. Led by Walter Reuther, the UAW made an innovative request of the world's largest au-tomaker: Give the hourly workers a 30 percent wage increase, to make up for lost compensation during the war, and promise to not raise the prices of GM products. As Reuther declared, "we want to make progress with the community and not at the expense of the community."[92] Reuther ar-gued that GM could certainly afford to raise wages and hold prices steady because of its years of high profits, large cash reserves, new equipment furnished at public expense during the wartime effort, and a favorable economic outlook.[93]

GM balked at the request; it offered a 10 percent raise and insisted that it maintain control of its own product pricing decisions. Reuther rejected GM's offer and countered that the UAW would agree to a smaller pay in-crease if GM would open its books to scrutiny to prove its inability to pay. GM again refused, essentially arguing that it was the American way for corporations to have exclusive control over product pricing. In a full-page ad in the *Detroit News*, GM proclaimed: "America is at a crossroads! It must preserve the freedom of each unit of American business to deter-mine its own destiny. Or it must transfer to some government bureau-cracy or agency, or to a union, the responsibility of management that has been the very keystone of American business. Shall this responsibility be surrendered?"[94]

Reuther then led GM's 320,000 hourly workers on a strike that would last 113 days. President Truman intervened during the strike and established a fact-finding board to recommend a settlement. Like GM, Reuther also invoked patriotic consumer rhetoric, explaining to the board that "[The union] is defending the national policy which calls for sustaining mass purchasing power, holding the line against inflation, and restoring free collective bargaining."[95] Ultimately, though, Reuther's gambit to prevent corporations from threatening to pass along wage increases as price increases failed. The fact-finding board suggested a 19.5-cents-an-hour increase, similar to the steel industry's bargained wage increase. GM's victory ensured that management authority over questions of pricing and profits would never be seriously questioned again.

Getting Labor on the Agenda: An Uphill Battle

With the persistent power of the consumer ethos and Phillips Curve frame, getting labor's concerns into the news is an uphill battle. Given the difficulties in receiving fair news coverage, labor unions might seek advertising for themselves as an alternate way to reach the mainstream mass media audience. There have been some remarkable successes in union advertising, such as the International Ladies' Garment Workers' Union (ILGWU) radio and television campaign begun in 1975 that featured the infectious "Look for the Union Label" song that asked listeners to consider who makes their clothing. But, there have also been a number of impediments to union advertising in mainstream media. Commercial mass media have always held the power to refuse any ad as they see fit. Courts and legislatures have generally upheld this media power as a freedom of the press, although some have argued it violates freedom of public speech.[96]

For example, in one advertising campaign during the 1990s, Local 1180 of the Communication Workers of America sponsored a series of radio and television ads attacking New York City Mayor Rudolph Giuliani for ignoring tax loopholes that benefit the city's rich individuals, nonprofit institutions, landlords, and service industries. While some broadcast outlets ran the ads, others refused them because they promoted "advocacy" and were "controversial." Writer James Ledbetter remarked that the reasons for the refusals were silly: "all ads are advocacy, and WABC [a network television station that refused the ads] certainly has no record of turning away the reelection advocacy ads of officeholders."[97]

Given the regularity in which journalists use consumer-oriented frames to cover labor, it is not surprising to find that journalism textbooks actually teach this approach.[98] In one popular advanced reporting textbook, for example, journalism students are asked to consider the news value of strikes. The authors inform journalism students that "Nationwide work stoppages have a direct, often disrupting effect on the consumer. A strike in western truck gardening centers, for example, hits as close to the average family as a lockout of workers by management of a trucking industry."[99] Thus, the strike-caused inconveniences to the consumer family unit (who apparently may suffer difficulties such as quickly finding bags of garden mulch) are equated with the lost wages of a citizen worker who has been locked out of a job and whose family has lost a breadwinner.

Less obvious than textbook lessons are the commonsense styles and rituals of reporting and editing learned in the newsroom, which ultimately serve to disguise the commercial interests of the news and operate within and reify a sphere of consumer culture. The predominant style, or philosophy, of journalism is objectivity, which attempts to apply a scientific procedure to the production of news. The goal of objective news writing is to separate fact from value or emotion, reduce (or inflate) events into a story with two "sides," and use quotes as pure "data" without any reporter interpretation. As the cliché summarizing the objective reportorial stance puts it, "the facts speak for themselves."[100]

As an economic strategy, objective-style journalism is successful, and can be traced back to the restructuring of the *New York Times* by Adolph Ochs in the late nineteenth century. Robert Goldman and Arvind Rajagopal argue that "ideologies of objectivity and pluralism [are] attempts to transcend the contradictory relations of class in order to maximize market shares of the news as commodity."[101] The problems of class divisions in a democratic society still exist, of course, but discourse about class is limited by objective-style news.

While objectivity might seem to be a fair, pure method for identifying and reporting news, it has built-in biases. According to Schudson, "the bias is toward statements of fact which are observable and unambiguous; toward broad, categorical vocabulary—'say,' rather than 'shout' or 'insist'; toward impersonal narrative style and 'inverted pyramid' organization which force a presentation of facts with 'as little evocation of their real-world context' as possible; toward conflicts rather than less dramatic happenings; toward 'events' rather than processes."[102]

Another inherent bias of objective news is that it favors the status quo: official sources and viewpoints and their assumptions about the social, economic, and political order. Of course, disagreeing voices do get aired in the news media. Dissent is encouraged, for it provides the narrative conflict of many news stories. Yet, J. Herbert Altschull argues, there are limits to dissent: "[T]he counterbalancing orthodoxy is assured a voice— not only a voice but the most powerful voice, because orthodoxy is repre- sented by the powerful, whose command of financial resources and of newsworthy authority assures it of dominance in the press."[103]

Although they are indeed businesses, the news media like to avoid pre- senting themselves as institutions with the single goal of maximizing profit. As news writers and editors decide what counts as news and how to package it as a story, they can dismiss any knowledge of profit motive or bias by claiming they merely followed the accepted ways of objective news style. Thus, in the words of Gaye Tuchman, objectivity is a strategic ritual to formulate news narratives.[104] Yet, behind these strategic rituals is a simple logic for rational news departments in a commercial media sys- tem: that they compete with each other to "offer the least expensive mix of content that protects the interests of sponsors and investors while garner- ing the largest audience advertisers will pay to reach."[105]

If advertisers have a subtle influence over the news, then perhaps none would have as widespread an influence as General Motors, the nation's largest advertiser, with more than $4 billion in annual advertising expen- ditures in 1999 (nearly double the $2.6 billion of that year's next largest advertiser, Procter & Gamble).[106] The next chapter looks at how the news media covered the 1991–94 closing of a GM auto assembly plant in south- east Michigan, the second biggest labor story of the decade.

UPHOLDING CORPORATE VALUES AND DOWNSIZING GENERAL MOTORS

INTERPRETING A GM PLANT CLOSING

In 1987, General Motors (GM) unleashed one of the most memorable advertising campaigns in recent decades: Chevrolet, the "Heartbeat of America."[1] The patriotic campaign, with its pulsating heartbeat music, rapid video edits, and neon script slogan logo, was designed to create an aura of excitement for GM's largest-selling—but floundering—automobile line.

After four years, though, it was clear that the heartbeat campaign couldn't revive Chevrolet's position as the dominant automobile nameplate of middle-class America. As Chevrolet slid, so did parent corporation GM, whose share of the U.S. auto market had dropped from 46 percent in 1980 to about 35 percent in 1991.[2] Years of mismanagement and bureaucratic excess in the Chevy division and throughout the company led to jokes that GM—once the world's foremost automaker—was the heartbreak of America.

The turning point for GM came on December 18, 1991. Under pressure from Wall Street investors to respond to GM's increasingly dismal financial course, CEO Robert Stempel announced that GM would eliminate 74,000 jobs and close 21 plants by 1995. Included in the announcement was an intention to consolidate the production of Chevrolet Caprices and Buick Roadmaster station wagons by closing either the Willow Run Assembly Plant in Ypsilanti Township, Michigan, near Detroit, or the Arlington, Texas, assembly plant near Dallas. Stempel publicly denied that GM management was strategically pitting the Willow Run and Arlington union locals and communities against each other in order to see which offered the most concessions—a technique called whipsawing.[3] Nevertheless, GM's delay of more than two months in naming final plant closings ignited a competition between the local unions and between the local and state governments.

The whipsawing of the two assembly plants, and Willow Run's eventual shutdown, became emblematic of the decline of U.S. Fordist-style industrial might and the rise of a post-Fordist economy characterized by deindustrialization, capital mobility, and the decline of industrial unionism.[4] On a national level, the GM plant closings cast a long shadow on the presidential campaign of 1992. Both Bill Clinton and Ross Perot—much to George Bush's dismay—invoked the case of Willow Run in two of the three presidential debates.

The closing of Willow Run had a particular significance in the story of America's twentieth-century industrial success. In late 1940, with war in Europe, the federal government engaged the Ford Motor Company to bring its mass production expertise to build bombers. The $100 million bomber plant, constructed on farmland and old orchards near the Willow Run stream, was the largest assembly plant of the world in its time. The plant was designed to handle all aspects of production, from parts to final assembly. The production complex featured a three-quarters-of-a-mile-long assembly line, a full-size adjacent airport, and government-built temporary housing to accommodate more than 15,000 people, part of the 42,000 peak workforce at the plant. Between September 1942 and the end of production in June 1945, the Willow Run Bomber Plant produced more than 8,600 B-24 Liberator bombers.[5]

Many of the plant's workers came from the South, a pattern of labor migration that continued with the postwar auto industry. The plant's most famous worker was Rose Will Monroe, cast as "Rosie the Riveter" in a promotional film for war bonds. Monroe, a single mother of two after the death of her husband, left Kentucky for work in Michigan during the war and found it as a riveter at the Willow Run plant. The song "Rosie the Riveter" by Kay Kyser was already a hit, and J. Howard Miller's "We Can Do It" poster of a confident female industrial worker was gaining currency as the icon of women in the wartime defense industries. It was the good fortune of actor Walter Pidgeon to find a real riveter named Rose in the B-24

Bomber Plant in Willow Run, and Monroe was invited to appear in the film. Monroe, who later fulfilled her ambition to be a pilot and died in 1997 at age 77, endures as the human image of Rosie.[6]

After the war, the massive Willow Run plant was purchased by the Kaiser-Frazier Corporation, which produced a line of automobiles that by 1948 accounted for 5 percent of U.S. auto sales. But a move to market small cars contributed to the automaker's demise and led to GM's purchase of Willow Run in 1953. Between 1954 and 1992, more than seven million GM automobiles—including Chevrolet Corvairs and Novas, Pontiac Bonnevilles, Buick Roadmasters, and the final incarnation of the Chevy Caprice—rolled off the Willow Run assembly line. At the plant's automotive peak in 1973, six thousand workers built a thousand cars a day.[7]

Low demand for full-size Caprices and continued parts outsourcing by GM had slowed production by the early 1990s. Instead of introducing a new product to the Willow Run plant, as had happened so many times in the plant's history, GM shuttered the plant for good. The mothballing of the enormous Willow Run facility in Ypsilanti Township displaced 4,014 workers and devastated a southeastern Michigan community that was built around the Willow Run plant and thought it had a long-term commitment from GM. But the national news media largely applauded GM's plant shutdown as a difficult but necessary strategy for a changing world.

The News Analysis

My critical analysis of the story of the Willow Run Assembly Plant shutdown follows coverage by the evening news of the three major national television networks and two national newspapers. The time period for national coverage of the plant closing story begins with Stempel's December 1991 announcement and ends in April 1994, when GM and Ypsilanti (pronounced ip-suh-LAN-ti) Township finally settled a lawsuit over the plant's closing. During the nearly two-and-a-half-year period of the closing, ABC, CBS, and NBC generated a total of fifteen news packages to cover the story. In national newspaper coverage, the *New York Times* published thirty-one stories and *USA Today* published twenty-two stories on the shutdown. News reports on the shutdown were often linked to other traditionally valued news topics, such as the financial status of GM (the world's largest industrial corporation), the economic recession of the early 1990s, the North American Free Trade Agreement (NAFTA), and the 1992 presidential campaign. The news coverage in mainstream national news media appeared in three general chronological phases:

- Phase I: Willow Run–Arlington Competition Difficult but Necessary
- Phase II: Heartbroken and Angry Workers and Community
- Phase III: A Partisan Lawsuit Delays Success of GM's Shutdown Process

A fourth phase of the narrative (discussed later in this chapter) occurred after national coverage ended, as Texas newspapers chronicled Arlington's continuing relationship with GM. Collectively, the national and local news coverage communicated an overarching narrative that encompassed several of the dominant news frames that typify news coverage of labor: (1) the economy is driven by great business leaders and entrepreneurs, (2) the workplace is a meritocracy (despite astounding evidence to the contrary in this case), and (3) collective economic action—by labor or communities—is bad.

The moral to the Willow Run story became clear through the persistent frames in the news reports. "To frame," as Robert Entman explains, "is to select some aspects of a perceived reality and make them more salient in a communicating text, in such a way as to promote a particular problem definition, causal interpretation, moral evaluation, and/or treatment recommendation."[8] In the case of the GM plant closings of the early 1990s, the news media framing supported the dominant logic of lean and mean corporate downsizing, empathizing with displaced workers but also marginalizing collective opposition.

Although this chapter will discuss some local news coverage, the analysis focuses on national coverage because national media, unlike local media, are presumably not interested (at least initially) in favoring either of the two communities. The analysis of news framing follows the chronological news phases of the GM plant closing narrative.

Phase I: Willow Run–Arlington Competition Difficult but Necessary

When GM announced on December 19, 1991, that either the Willow Run or the Arlington plant would be closed, it denied that it was attempting to whipsaw the two local unions into a battle of wage or work rule concessions, a denial duly noted in national newspaper reports.[9] Yet, GM established a scenario that predictably created media interest. The fate of the two distant auto assembly plants set up the classic horse race frame that typifies coverage of political elections. Former *Wichita Eagle* editor Davis "Buzz" Merritt notes that it is "a popular reportorial device . . . to sort out 'winners' from 'losers.' "[10]

The story offered suspense, a looming tragedy, and a bittersweet victory. None of the sixty-eight national television and newspaper reports asked why GM needed to create such a competitive atmosphere between Willow Run and Arlington, the only two plants in GM's round of closings to be squared off directly against each other. Instead, reports quickly accepted the competition as a difficult but necessary part of GM's recovery. With journalism's rituals of objectivity, GM's denials of whipsawing were recorded and treated as fact, even as the same reports oftentimes charted the increasing competition between Willow Run and Arlington. In essence, journalism became the agent for whipsawing.

A December 20, 1991, *USA Today* article illustrates the consequences of objective-style reporting. The entirety of the article's discussion on whipsawing consisted of two sentences representing opposing points of view: "Some autoworkers claim GM is forcing Arlington and Willow Run to compete in offering concessions. GM denies the charge."[11] Under the ritualistic style of objectivity, offering two competing points of view makes the article balanced, fair, and objective.[12] The objective approach gives each quote equal weight regardless of what might be evident to the journalist.

Without any sense of irony, though, the same *USA Today* report later publicized and promoted the whipsawing that GM denied. The story concluded with a summary of pros and cons about the Willow Run plant: "Advantage over Arlington: Is closer to suppliers, assembly cost per car is lower[.] Disadvantage: Plant is older, unions may not agree to concessions[.]" Only by adhering to the practice of objective-style journalism could journalists both report GM's denial of whipsawing without criticism and sportingly handicap the competition of the two plants. By treating whipsawing as a necessary and expected situation, the news media sanctioned competition between workers and communities, and alleviated GM of responsibility for the nasty civic battle that would ensue. This objective-style account consequently positioned any potential labor union opposition to the GM plan as a bad thing.

A report by ABC's Chris Bury on January 24, 1992, in the midst of the more than two-month whipsawing period, again closed off rational-critical debate about the Willow Run–Arlington competition. The report began by documenting the anxious struggle of the Ypsilanti and Arlington communities to save their plants, a struggle that had come to include promises of millions of dollars worth of new tax breaks and state contracts from Texas Gov. Ann Richards and a pledge by Michigan Gov. John Engler to match the Texas concessions. In the middle of the report, Bury briefly addressed the ethical issues of the political rivalries created by the plant closing delay.

BURY (voice-over): Ypsilanti's city manager accuses GM of playing the two regions like a whipsaw.

HERBERT GILSDORF, CITY MANAGER: It looks to me like they're trying to wring every possible concession, every possible buck they can out of the local communities and the state government. I don't think that's really the right thing to do.

BURY (in front of the GM building in Detroit): Executives here at General Motors declined to be interviewed but denied playing Michigan against Texas for the best deal. According to GM, the decision will hinge on which plant can produce the best cars at the lowest cost.

Bury's objective stance leaves him in the role of GM public relations officer, as he announces the GM position without any evaluation. Such rituals of objectivity, Michael Schudson notes, make journalists "mere stenographers"—or in the case of broadcast reporters—mere spokespeople.[13] Interestingly, the rituals of objectivity are practices designed to protect the reporter and his or her editors from accusations of bias. Journalists can respond that they are only doing their job the way it's always done; they are just reporting the facts. Ultimately, though, this strategy precludes journalistic responsibility (see Chapter 3 for a discussion of objectivity and its built-in biases).[14]

What Bury might have said is that GM's decision would most likely hinge on the plant that can produce cars at the lowest net cost, after all possible incentives are included in the accounting. Of course, objectivity does not mean that journalists report stories value-free. Quite the opposite: All news stories implicitly suggest certain values, and it is the unquestioned, commonsense values that are the so-called neutral social values on which most news stories are based. Herbert Gans explains that "the values in news are rarely explicit and must be found between the lines—in what actors and activities are reported or ignored, and in how they are described."[15]

News media reports in this case embraced the post-Fordist logic of flexibility. In other words, the news endorsed worker concessions, layoffs, mass firings, human-replacing technology, and capital mobility as the key to sustaining corporate profitability and economic health. By doing so, the news media failed to acknowledge that corporate strategies are choices, not inevitabilities. Corporations make a choice when they favor short-term profits over long-term gains; they make a choice when they hold stockholder interests far above community interests; they make a choice when they treat workers as flexible expenses instead of investments.

Despite the possibilities, objective journalism, as Robert McChesney notes, "effectively internalize[s] corporate capitalism as the natural order for a democracy."[16] As a result, the news portrays decisions of corporate capitalism as the only possible alternative, casting choices such as downsizing as the inevitable reality with which we all must live. Economist David Gordon tracks the corporate squeeze of working Americans back to the late 1960s and early 1970s, when the postwar Fordist economy began to decline in an economic stagflation of slow growth and high inflation. According to Gordon, "U.S. corporations could have tried to revive profitability by taking either the high road or the low road. Moving on the high road would have required providing workers the carrot of improving real wages and renewed job security as well as addressing the productivity slowdown directly by involving workers more fully and cooperatively in production." Instead, Gordon explains, most U.S. corporations took the low road and the "stick" approach, "squeezing and scolding our workers, cheapening labor costs, and trying to compete economically through intimidation and conflict."[17]

This approach had the desired effect on U.S. workers' psyches: A *New York Times* poll in early 1994 found that two-fifths (39 percent) of American workers "expressed 'worry,' either a lot or some, that during the next two years they might be laid off, required to work reduced hours, or forced to take pay cuts."[18] The problem, according to Robert Reich, is that this so-called lean and mean approach to greater profitability works only in the short run. In the short term, management compensation skyrockets, the corporate balance sheet looks more profitable, and retail consumers may indirectly benefit through lower prices. In the long run, such strategies produce "suspicion, insecurity, and opportunism" in the business and community because "employees know that they can be sacked at any time."[19] Plant closings in particular can lead to a breakdown in community cohesion and values and can foster an "anti-union animus," with the blame for the shutdown directed at the union, according to economists Bluestone and Harrison.[20]

With declining real wages and benefits, even in times of rising corporate profits and Wall Street records, corporations created worker incentive via job insecurity and a heavier managerial and supervisory apparatus—bureaucrats who Gordon calls the "Stickwielders." Contrary to the myth that U.S. businesses in the 1980s and 1990s have become lean and mean, the majority of U.S. corporate organizations have grown "fat and mean" in Gordon's words. Production workforces may have been downsized in recent decades, but "the weight of the bureaucratic burden has actually been growing, not contracting, through the mid-1990s."[21] The resulting economy thus featured huge monetary rewards for the corporate elite,[22] a flourishing managerial class, and an increasingly disciplined production workforce.

Nevertheless, journalism's acceptance of the lean and mean mythology ensured that GM's whipsawing would not be framed as an attack on workers but instead as a logical business move toward greater efficiency. At the same time, though, reports portrayed United Automobile Workers (UAW) criticism of whipsawing as an attack on GM. A *New York Times* story about UAW vice president Stephen Yokich's response to GM's actions was headlined "Playing Rough with GM."[23] This example corresponds with Hayg Oshagan and my analysis of Willow Run coverage in four newspapers.[24] That study noted that while the UAW is often cast with negative frames as a stubborn, inflexible menace to GM, it is also portrayed with positive frames but only insofar as it accedes to GM's shutdown plans with flexibility, reasonability, and efficiency. Yokich and the UAW were thus framed as headstrong obstructionists when they disagreed with GM's cost-cutting plans.

In national news coverage of the GM assembly plant whipsawing, journalists framed the Willow Run–Arlington competition as necessary, even after GM's Stempel presumably undercut the need for suspense. The lead paragraphs of a *USA Today* story on January 13, 1992, laid bare the cynicism of GM's whipsawing strategy:

> General Motors Corp. is telling mayors, governors and business leaders it won't accept special deals intended to keep their communities' GM plants open.
>
> Chairman Robert Stempel said Sunday that GM already has the information it needs to decide which U.S. and Canadian assembly and parts plants to close.
>
> Stempel says he's telling local leaders, "Thank you very much . . . but don't do anything for General Motors. We haven't asked anybody for anything, and we don't expect to."[25]

Stempel didn't have to ask for concessions because the news media's framing of the decision encouraged what has become a standard political practice. Moreover, neither *USA Today* (the only news organization of this study to carry Stempel's denial) nor ABC, CBS, NBC, and the *New York Times* asked the obvious question that might have weakened Stempel's executive authority: If GM already has the information necessary for a decision, then why doesn't it announce its decision and end the whipsawing competition now? Journalists also might well have asked Stempel why GM didn't have the appropriate information about its own plants to make a decision when it first announced shutdown plans a month earlier.

Phase II: Heartbroken and Angry Workers and Community

The UAW Local 1776 at Willow Run, confident of their record of producing high-quality cars for $300 to $400 less per unit than the Arlington plant,[26] took Stempel's word that special deals and concessions would have no impact on the decision. If the decision would go to the plant producing "the best cars at the lowest cost," Willow Run was the clear choice. So, while the union local at Arlington unilaterally voted to permit a third eight-hour shift at their plant, undercutting the national UAW contract with GM, the Willow Run local made no special concessions. And, while Arlington and Texas ultimately put together a package of concessions to GM worth $23 million, township and state officials in Michigan decided to add no other incentives to the tax abatements that GM already enjoyed at its Willow Run site.

When GM announced on February 24, 1992, that the Willow Run plant had been selected for closure, journalists framed the story as evidence that workers must adapt to a post-Fordist logic of flexibility. GM's own standards of "the best cars at the lowest cost" and no "special deals" were conveniently forgotten as the news retold the fable that lean and mean was the only route to economic success. The fact that GM strategically combined the plant closing announcement with the release of its loss statement for 1991 ($4.45 billion in losses, including a one-time $2.8 billion loss to cover plant closing expenses) further rationalized the need for closings, layoffs, and worker concessions.

Two consecutive reports by NBC's Jim Cummins demonstrate how the same video footage can be framed first to suggest worker uncertainty and later to pinpoint workers' response to concessions as the definite cause for plant failure and success. On February 23, 1992, Cummins reported that the tension in the two communities was about to end:

CUMMINS: In the two months since GM announced one of the plants would have to close, the workers and their families have had to struggle with the uncertainty.

[VIDEO: Some Willow Run workers at a meeting, clapping hands and singing "Solidarity Forever."]

CUMMINS: In Michigan, they reaffirmed their union solidarity, while in Texas they voted to make concessions, if that's what it takes to save their jobs.

[VIDEO: Willow Run worker footage dissolves to Arlington worker walking through hallway of union offices to doors with a sign that reads "Polls open 7:00 A.M. Vote Today."]

On the following day, Cummins' story on the Willow Run closing announcement used the same video clips, but created a modern-day fable about the value of union concessions:

CUMMINS: When GM announced in December that one of the plants would have to close . . .

[VIDEO: Cummins' narration pauses this time, allowing the video soundtrack of Willow Run workers singing "Solidarity Forever" to swell for emphasis.]

February 24, 1992, *NBC Nightly News*. Reporter Jim Cummins: "When GM announced in December that one of the plants would have to close, the UAW workers in Michigan reaffirmed their union solidarity . . ."

". . . while union workers in Texas were going to the polls and voting to make local contract concessions to the company, to save their jobs."

CUMMINS: . . . the UAW workers in Michigan reaffirmed their union solidarity, while union workers in Texas were going to the polls and voting to
make local contract concessions to the company, to save their jobs.
[VIDEO: Dissolves to same video clip of Arlington worker walking toward
union voting room.]

So that the moral of the fable was not lost on the audience, Cummins
concluded by remarking "the workers in Texas made concessions, and
now they're celebrating." The fable of worker concessions framed stories
at the *New York Times* as well. A March 1, 1992, article by Thomas C. Hayes
argued that concessions were the chief reason for Arlington's success,
while also reporting (in objective style) GM's contention that concessions
did not figure into its decision:

> A key agreement was to offer a round-the-clock production schedule,
> using three crews and three work shifts. American auto makers have not
> run three-shift schedules for 20 years. Mr. [Arthur C.] Hester [manager of
> the Arlington plant] said the change addressed GM's desperate need to
> pare manufacturing costs per car.
>
> Union members here were voting to approve the schedule changes on
> the same day in December that Robert C. Stempel, GM's chairman, an-
> nounced the possible plant closing. Union leaders at Willow Run did not
> counter with offers to change work rules or schedules.
>
> . . . City and state officials here [in Arlington, Texas] also offered a vari-
> ety of tax breaks and other incentives potentially worth as much as $23
> million over several years. But, GM said it based its choice on "internal
> business factors" and not on such incentive packages.[27]

The convergence of a narrative frame that argued concessions were the
key to success with the apparent acceptance of GM's statements that concessions did not matter created stories with high levels of contradiction.
The same article also paraphrased the plant manager, who attributed the
decision favoring Arlington to "labor peace." The unproblematic acceptance of the manager's statement suggests that doing nothing (what Willow Run workers did) is somehow a hostile (bad) posture, whereas voting
to accept concessions (what Arlington workers did) is a peaceful (good)
stance.

Ironically, the hands-off approach of objective reporting that allows such contradiction is also argued to be the source of reporters' credibility. Such objective-style reporting created other indefensible juxtapositions. The *New York Times* front-page story covering GM's February 24 announcement of plant closings contained a subheading called "Spreading the Pain:"

> GM is taking some important symbolic steps to show that it is trying to spread the pain to executives. For example, the auto maker confirmed today that it had trimmed a special executive pension that pays Roger B. Smith, its former chairman, more than $1.1 million a year.
>
> The revised pension plan, which also affects 100 GM executives who have retired since 1990, would mean an annual payment to Mr. Smith of slightly less than $1 million. GM said it would save $14 million annually from the revisions.[28]

The *New York Times'* attempt to impose journalistic balance on an inherently unbalanced situation thus created the outrageous comparison of sacrifice between the more than four thousand workers who had just lost their jobs and an elite group of retired GM executives who, incidentally, presided over GM's decline. *New York Times* reports notwithstanding, most of the economic pain of the shutdown was spread around Ypsilanti Township, the surrounding communities, and the households of its 4,014 workers. Economists at Eastern Michigan University in Ypsilanti predicted that up to 18,000 jobs could be lost from the area as the plant closing rippled through the local economy, affecting parts suppliers and other related industries.[29]

The community's tax base would also be affected. Even with several million dollars in tax abatements for the Willow Run plant, GM still paid $3.6 million in local taxes a year, 8 percent of the township's total tax revenue. As Bluestone and Harrison have documented with other plant closings, the shutdown created a state of "community anomie" and anxiety.[30] The workers showed signs of stress: in less than two months, in the period between late April and early June 1992, five workers—all in their late thirties or forties—died. Four had heart attacks, and one an aneurysm. The normal death rate among Willow Run workers was about one death in three months.[31]

After the closing, news coverage shifted to a theme of heartbroken and angry workers and community. News relating to the Willow Run plant in 1992 after the February closing announcement focused on the implications of angry Willow Run workers on the presidential election. In Michigan, the relevant campaign period ran from a few weeks before the March 17 state primary and again before the national election in November. The *New York Times*, which devotes many pages to presidential election strategies, accounted for most of the Willow Run coverage during this period. Although the stories of hurt and anger did give disillusioned Willow Run workers a voice, the coverage also demonstrated the limited public sphere in which workers' voices are considered legitimate. Thus, it is likely that the several *New York Times* stories about Willow Run workers clustered prior to the spring primary election and the fall presidential election would not have been written had it not been an election year and had not Michigan been a traditionally important state in presidential elections.

A March 13, 1992, *New York Times* story by Jeffrey Schmalz featured a sociological sketch of Willow Run workers in the week before the Michigan primary: "In two days of chats and interviews at bowling alleys and shopping malls, outside automobile plants and inside union halls, people in this city 30 miles west of Detroit spit out venom and hurt and cynicism unlike anything in similar interviews in Maryland and Florida: Government is corrupt to its core, the tool of the wealthy. Ignore what most politicians pledge. They either lie or are helpless to make real changes."[32]

Unfortunately, the only public action credited in the article as an outlet for cynical and economically dislocated people was voting—the very activity that generated such cynicism. Instead of discussing the possibility of other democratic options for these beleaguered citizens (e.g., movements to strengthen national labor policy, to expand the social welfare safety net, to promote corporate responsibility), the story spent the remainder of its space discussing if presidential candidate Jerry Brown was the only chance of salvation for workers after Senator Tom Harkin withdrew from the race. It is no wonder that citizens, "aware of the dilemmas and powerlessness that the structure of the political market imposes on them . . . have responded by manifesting the symptoms (e.g., non-voting) of what social scientists have termed 'political alienation.'"[33]

Perhaps the best reporting during the entire Willow Run shutdown was Sara Rimer's five-part series titled "Closing Willow Run" in September and October 1992, along with two additional stories she filed from the

Ypsilanti area for the *New York Times*. Rimer's lengthy stories chronicled the history of the Willow Run plant from its beginnings as a World War II bomber plant. She told the story of Willow Run workers—many of them came from the U.S. Appalachian region and nearly 20 percent were women. Another article offered a rare account of GM management's responsibility for designing the poor-selling Chevy Caprice, the Willow Run–produced car that "illustrates one of GM's biggest problems: It's stubborn—some say arrogant—insistence on doing things its own way long after the market has passed it by."[34] Rimer's story on September 7, 1992, even exonerated (somewhat belatedly) the Willow Run workers from blame:

> "The auto industry has gone through a ruthless shakeout," said Harley Shaiken, an auto analyst at the University of California at San Diego. "These people are paying the price. . . .
>
> "Willow Run was a very cooperative plant," he said. "What makes this such a bitter experience for those workers is that they played by the rules, and the rules got switched. And nobody told them."[35]

Like the several *New York Times* articles that ran before the primary election in early March 1992, the "Closing Willow Run" series ultimately served as a long feature on the political atmosphere among autoworkers in southeast Michigan. The series' third article, subtitled "Taking the Anger to the Polls," captured the implicit aim of the series, which ran two months before the presidential election. Although the third article marveled at the union workers' renewed political interest, their motivation remained cynical. Their main reason for supporting Clinton (their backup candidate after both Harkin and Brown dropped out) was that he was "not Bush."[36]

A CBS report during the same election campaign period portrayed the Willow Run workers in a similar manner: an important block of voters who represent the American Dream gone awry, and whose skepticism made them a difficult obstacle to political victory in Middle America. Richard Threlkeld's October 7, 1992, CBS report consisted of discussions with Willow Run workers about presidential candidates and the NAFTA, which both Bush and Clinton embraced as a cure to U.S. economic ills. Threlkeld concluded that "it may well be that in the long run, the free trade agreement will be good for Americans. But the autoworkers of Michigan are understandably worried about the here and now."

The CBS package wasn't about how to remedy problems in the free trade agreement (Threlkeld made approval of NAFTA sound favorable and inevitable) but instead to suggest that the idea of NAFTA had not yet been sold to voting Michigan autoworkers, an important political constituency. The story fell far short of any attempt to reduce cynicism in public life. In order to alleviate such social pessimism, many journalism professionals and academics argue, journalism must do more than just telling the news and reporting the decline of a community. According to civic journalism advocate Davis Merritt, journalists need to envision public life beyond electoral politics: "Public life is the means by which democracy is expressed and experienced. It is not politics alone. Politics is the mechanism by which our constitutional government functions. Public life involves more than just that, and includes any activity where people try to achieve common goals or address common problems."[37]

In Phase II of the plant closing narrative, the news media came closest to creating a public sphere (recall from Chapter 1 that Jürgen Habermas used this term for a democratic forum where the public can engage in discovery and rational-critical debate).[38] Yet, the public sphere in this stage is illusory; in hegemonic fashion, the news feels the pain of displaced workers but does little to encourage alternative frames of discourse on downsizing.[39] In the fall of 1992, the news media could have begun to reinvigorate public life by creating an open dialogue on policies such as NAFTA and corporate downsizing. Instead, the news publicized NAFTA and downsizing as the inevitable and only possible solutions to guarantee the health of U.S. business. Phase III of the Willow Run news coverage completes the hegemonic narrative by marginalizing democratic—and oppositional—action by the Willow Run community, and again minimizing chances for a public sphere where people try to address common problems.

Phase III: A Partisan Lawsuit Delays Success of GM's Shutdown Process

In the months following the announcement to close the Willow Run plant, the Township of Ypsilanti filed a lawsuit against GM for breach of contract. The lawsuit created a unique opportunity for the news media to facilitate a rational-critical debate on public life and what should be the

common goals of business, government, and citizens. The lawsuit constituted a real (and rare) public action of a small community against America's largest industrial corporation.

Ypsilanti Township claimed that GM had violated its promise to maintain jobs at the Willow Run facility in return for twelve-year tax abatements granted in 1984 and 1988 worth $13.5 million. Tax abatements, de-
signed as a last resort to retain foundering industries, had become a
benefit routinely expected by GM. From 1975 through 1990, GM requested
and received more than $1.3 billion in tax abatements from Ypsilanti
Township on investments and additions at Willow Run and another
nearby plant. In the state of Michigan, GM has been one of the most frequent benefactors of industrial tax breaks, receiving more than 120 municipal property tax abatements.[40] According to Reich, there is a sad irony in
such tax breaks: "The executives of General Motors, for example, who
have been among the loudest to proclaim the need for better schools, have
also been among the most relentless pursuers of local tax abatements."[41]

Unfortunately, journalists neglected the opportunity to facilitate a public debate about the relationship among industry, government, and citizens. Instead, the news media uniformly framed the lawsuit as a futile action and a pesky irritation hampering GM's path to progress and recovery.
On the first day of the trial, January 11, 1993, NBC's Fred Briggs already
discounted the lawsuit's chances for success: "The township wants the
plant kept open. That's not likely. What *is* [likely] is some type of financial
settlement."

When Washtenaw County Circuit Court Judge Donald E. Shelton ruled
on February 9, 1993, that GM had indeed violated the contract implicit in
the tax abatements it had received from the township, journalists framed
the lawsuit's success as a fluke and portrayed the decision as GM's loss,
not the citizens' gain. The *New York Times* headline read "GM Blocked
from Closing Auto Plant," while the story called the decision merely a "re-
prieve."[42] *USA Today*'s headline stated "Judge: GM Can't Close Plant,"
with the story giving the ruling "little chance of surviving GM's promised
appeal."[43] Like the print stories, a February 9 CBS package by Jacqueline
Adams suggested the ruling offered "at least a ray of hope" to towns and
workers, but argued that the decision "may well be overturned."

NBC's story on February 9, 1993, dismissed the decision as an unfair and costly annoyance to GM and perpetuated the myth about the value of concessions. The package was reported by Mike Boettcher:

> BOETTCHER: GM's attorney said it would cost the automaker $300 million a year to keep the plant open.
>
> LEE SCHUTZMAN, GENERAL MOTORS ATTORNEY: I think it's very difficult for a judge in a community in which this is occurring to rule against the local government.
>
> BOETTCHER: Ypsilanti, a city that lives or dies with the auto industry, breathed a little easier after the ruling. GM had hoped to close the Ypsilanti plant this fall as part of a major cost-cutting plan, and consolidate operations in Arlington, Texas. Workers at Arlington's GM plant had agreed to labor concessions, and their factory was chosen to stay open over Ypsilanti's.

Boettcher's suggestion that labor concessions made Arlington the more attractive choice for GM's cost-cutting overlooked a confidential GM document that was publicly released against GM's wishes by Judge Shelton in a pretrial hearing on December 16, 1992. The document, ignored by all three networks, *USA Today*, and reported by the *New York Times* only in a short Associated Press story, revealed that GM "had estimated it would save more than $74 million a year by using the Willow Run plant," confirming what Willow Run workers had long claimed.[44] Moving to Arlington would only result in short-term savings, the GM document stated. This information had the power to disrupt the dominant news frame of the plant closing decision. Nevertheless, the labor concessions fable remained the news frame of choice for mainstream journalism.

Mainstream journalism also framed the Ypsilanti Township suit as a fight and victory for the UAW, not the entire township community. All four of the reports on the Circuit Court decision noted that autoworkers cheered the ruling. The televised reports on NBC and CBS both used the same video footage that zoomed in on a group of Willow Run workers (recognizable in their UAW jackets) in the courtroom for a reaction shot when Judge Shelton announced the court order. Other courtroom spectators were invisible to the news camera. It is worth noting that the case's plaintiffs were Ypsilanti Township, the County of Washtenaw, and the State of Michigan. The UAW (along with the Michigan Education Association) participated only as amicus curiae (friend of the court), voluntarily providing information to the court. Although the news framed the lawsuit as a delay tactic that would benefit only union workers, Judge Shelton's opinion linked the Willow Run case to much broader issues of public life:

> Contrary to the approach of the defendant in this case that "what is good for General Motors is good for the country," the truth is, as this case demonstrates, that what is good for General Motors may only coincidentally help, and often hurts, many of our people. Industry is the source of many of the jobs in our nation and it may well be that our nation needs a new relationship of trust and cooperation between government and industry in order to compete with heavily subsidized industries from other, perhaps less democratically and socially sophisticated, countries. But such an effort must be national in scope and must be a real partnership with industry, not one in which industry simply view government as a part of its "business climate" and another opportunity to increase profits.
>
> . . . The local governments of this State are placed in a position where they feel that they have no choice but to give taxpayers' resources away under a statute which does not mandate that they receive anything in return for those foregone taxes.[45]

Unfortunately, the mainstream news media chose to ignore this portion of Judge Shelton's opinion, leaving a well-laid map for public debate to be filed away in courthouse cabinets.

GM attorney Lee Schutzman had publicly inferred that Judge Shelton's decision was politically motivated. The same thing, of course, could be said for the subsequent State Court of Appeals decision on August 3, 1993. Whereas Schutzman suggested that it is "very difficult" for a county judge to rule against a local government, it could also be suggested that it might be just as difficult for a state judge to rule against the state's largest and most powerful corporation. In fact, the State of Michigan was a reluctant partner in Ypsilanti Township's lawsuit against GM. The state tried to rush the suit directly to the appeals court, and was involuntarily listed as a plaintiff on the circuit court case only after Shelton applied the law requiring the state to be added as a plaintiff.[46]

Any news media discussions of fairness or allegations of political motivation had ended by the time of the Court of Appeals decision. Only CBS and the *New York Times* even bothered to present stories on the appeals court reversal, which permitted GM to close Willow Run. Both stories failed to include the philosophical underpinnings of the decision, which offered an amazingly industry-friendly alternative to Judge Shelton's more expansive vision of public life. The appellate court decision argued, in part, that "the fact that a manufacturer uses hyperbole and puffery in seeking an advantage or concession does not necessarily create a promise."[47] The *New York Times* story on the appellate court decision noted that "the legal proceedings have come to resemble a condemned prisoner's efforts to fend off execution," a metaphor that both communicated the frustration of the Willow Run community and suggested who—in the eyes of the news media—the lawful and unlawful parties were.[48]

On September 3, 1993, the Michigan Supreme Court, Ypsilanti Township's last legal hope, denied an appeal, letting the Court of Appeals ruling stand. The Willow Run Assembly Plant was then permanently closed. A few stories along the way suggested GM might want to bring a new product, such as the popular Saturn models, to the Willow Run plant.[49] These stories conveyed the theme that things were improving for workers and community, a hopeful news frame common to coverage of unemployment.[50] Nevertheless, by 2003, the plant had still not returned to production.

End of the National News Coverage

The national news coverage of the Willow Run shutdown had fizzled out along with the plant's future, but it ended with two upbeat newspaper stories that provided a rather ironic coda. On April 24, 1994, the *New York Times* reported that GM and Ypsilanti Township had resolved the issue of GM reimbursing the township for tax abatements. The settlement called for GM to invest more than $80 million to expand production at its existing Hydra-Matic transmission plant, located next to the closed Willow Run assembly plant. A GM spokesperson said that the investment would not create any new jobs. The article also noted that the "town and county will provide 12 year abatements worth 50 percent of the property taxes on the new investment"[51]—the same kind of twelve-year, 50 percent tax abatements that were the subject of the Willow Run lawsuit. Thus, the suit ended with GM spending money to upgrade its own facility and getting its usual tax subsidies.

Two weeks later, on April 29, 1994, the front page of USA Today's "Money" section proclaimed, "Good Times Roll; Perseverance Pays Off for Autoworkers."[52] The article suggested a sense of resolution—through financial reward—for autoworkers (at GM and elsewhere) who had put up with the industry's instrumental approach and lean and mean directives. Now, production was increasing, and workers were flush with cash from lots of overtime hours. The story comes full circle on how the news media frame forsaken autoworkers. The happy story of the auto industry's resurgence, as the USA Today article tells it, is that Chrysler engine-plant worker Joe Holland had a bonus large enough to take his family to Disney World, just "what Super Bowl champions do." Thus, success for the autoworker is not defined in improved relations with management, better working conditions, or more job security but instead in the ability to be a good consumer. Consumerism represents back to normal in the narrative scheme of mainstream journalism.

Although the April 29, 1994, USA Today story proclaimed the good times were back for Michigan autoworkers, it also hinted at lingering worker discontent. The article reported that employment levels were still low and that the pleasure of occasional overtime work had become a constant burden. The reporters returned to engine-plant worker Joe Holland: "Huge bonuses—some as big as $8,000 were common at the Trenton Engine Plant because workers have been averaging 6 or 7 hours of overtime a week. The work is tiring and stressful, Holland says, 'but when you have a little more money in your pocket, it sort of eases the stress.' "[53]Holland's feeling that the extra money "sort of" eases the stress of constant weeks of more than forty hours of labor foreshadowed the problems the auto industry would encounter later that year. High demand for automobiles greatly outstripped supply at Chrysler, Ford, and especially GM, sometimes creating several-month delays for the delivery of new cars.[54]

GM's lean and mean strategy to please Wall Street in 1992 had left the auto giant unable to cope with consumer demand by 1994. The Detroit News reported that GM needed at least 300,000 more trucks to keep up with demand, yet the closed Willow Run plant wouldn't be a candidate for resurrection.[55] Workers at the GM facility in Flint, Michigan's Buick City complex who were making the highly coveted GM trucks were exhausted from work speedups and required overtime, and they experienced a significant rise in repetitive motion injuries and stress-related ailments. The 11,500 overworked Buick City workers went on strike on September 17, 1994, to get some relief. Five days later, a reluctant GM agreed to new safety provisions and the hiring of 779 workers—the first new GM production workers in eight years.[56]

Out of the National Eye: GM's Destabilizing Effect on Arlington

For nearly two-and-a-half years, the national news media spun a narrative of economic hope and tragedy in covering GM's downsizing. The stream of stories ended in 1994 on a happy note: the recession was over, the economy was booming, worker perseverance in Arlington paid off, people were getting on with their lives.

Meanwhile, in Arlington, Texas—as the national news media turned their eyes away—the prize of being the most flexible workforce slowly lost its luster. During the whipsawing battles of 1992, Texas newspapers such as the *Dallas Morning News* and *Houston Chronicle*, along with national media reports, had congratulated Arlington workers on their flexibility, which would reportedly save the plant's 3,327 jobs and create a thousand more. On February 25, 1992, the day after GM announced Arlington would stay open, a celebratory *Dallas Morning News* front-page spread identified worker flexibility and community concessions as the central elements for retaining jobs: "The strategy was simple and straightforward: tireless lobbying and gentle arm-twisting, sweetened by an eye-popping package of labor and economic incentives."[57] An editorial in the same issue of the *Morning News* stated that "teamwork" saved the Arlington plant and extolled the inspirational "willingness on the part of workers to make some personal sacrifices." Downstate, a *Houston Chronicle* editorial on the same day concurred in the praise of good laborers:

> Surely much of the credit must go to the quality and cooperative spirit of the Texas work force . . . The Texas workers already enjoyed the reputation of being more flexible than employees at the Willow Run plant near Ypsilanti, Mich. The word is that the Texans were more willing to make changes and accept new and more efficient ways of operating the plant.

. . . In today's increasingly competitive world, a work force which can
accept new ideas for more efficient production is vital for a company's survival. Texas workers apparently had the edge.[58]

The editorials seem to be inspired by managerial textbooks. The phras-
ings are subtle, but illustrate that "teamwork," "cooperative spirit," and
"flexibility," are often euphemisms for a "team" or "quality" organizational strategy in which a disciplined workforce ultimately accepts top-
down managerial policies and unilateral sacrifices instead of truly partici-
pating in joint decision making.[59]

As it turned out for the Arlington workers, the idea of being a flexible
and concessionary workforce was more important than the actual concessions. The Arlington union local's vote to add a third shift was cited as the
primary concession that won GM's favor. Yet, round-the-clock production
was unnecessary for manufacturing GM's increasingly unpopular large
sedans. By 1996, production of the Chevy Caprice, Buick Roadmaster, and
Cadillac Fleetwood sedans had slipped from two shifts to one. The sedan
production at Arlington was phased out completely at the end of that year.

Keeping the Arlington plant open required winning a new GM product
to build, and again it was the workers and community who were expected
to make concessions. GM proposed to convert the plant to truck production, investing $264 million to create what the automaker refers to as a
"flex-build" plant. The plans called for reducing the union workforce
from 1,900 to 1,350 and outsourcing many jobs to Lear Seating Corp. and
Mackie Automotive Systems, two nonunion suppliers who would locate
plants in Arlington. GM also proposed that it get city property tax abatements worth at least $11.7 million over ten years for its plant improve-
ments (which it later received). Finally, GM said that it would commit to
maintaining production at the Arlington plant for two years—until mid-
1999—when Arlington would again be considered for shutdown.

At some point in 1996, the workers at Arlington had tired of being the
only flexible members of the GM–union team. The top two union officials
who negotiated the proposal to bring truck production to Arlington were
voted out of office in local UAW elections by workers concerned about
agreements for more outsourcing, the continual erosion of union jobs, and
GM's short-term commitment to the plant. Nonetheless, a front-page *Dallas Morning News* story praised the two deposed union officials as "the un-

sung heroes of Texas truck production."[60] The article also attempted to pin union disagreement not on the admirable, "cooperative," longtime Arlington employees, but on the uncooperative, "political" Arlington workers who had recently arrived from Willow Run and other closed plants.

The *Dallas Morning News* continued to sell GM's hard bargain as a great deal for the community and local UAW members. In a December 13, 1996, editorial, the newspaper—with no apparent sense of irony—hailed GM as a stabilizing force in the community: "Under the current plans, the local GM plant will have trucks to build until mid-1999. While this may seem a flimsy agreement at best, the automobile manufacturer's commitment to Arlington is much greater. Adapting the Arlington plant to build trucks and sport utility vehicles, regardless of how non-committal GM officials are, speaks volumes to the business, the workers and their families in stabilizing a huge economic force in this area."[61]

In another editorial, on February 28, 1997, the *Morning News* urged workers to again be cooperative and approve the pending contract with GM. The newspaper said GM was giving a "big concession" to workers by allowing them to compete for the outsourcing jobs at Lear and Mackie. Rather cynically, the editorial stated, "Whether the union can effectively compete for those jobs remains to be seen; however, GM management is at least recognizing that the union should have the opportunity to bid on such work."[62] The editorial also signaled that the *Dallas Morning News*'s characterizations of Arlington autoworkers as efficient, quality-minded, and flexible could easily shift to old stereotypes of union workers as inefficient, unproductive, and overpaid.

The Arlington union members were not impressed by GM's miserly concessions and resisted the pressure of the February 28 *Morning News* editorial headline, which read: "Sign on the Dotted Line; Union Members Should OK GM Contract." In March 1997, the Arlington autoworkers voted down, for the first time ever, a local contract with GM, shocking those who expected the Texas workers to be forever docile. But, the standoff did not last long. In June 1997, full-size Chevy and GM trucks and sport utility vehicles began to roll off the Arlington assembly line, and in the following month the UAW Local 276 approved a new contract with GM that offered more lucrative overtime hours to skilled tradeworkers and protected a few dozen jobs from outsourcing.

Although GM gained temporary peace with its assembly plant workers, its long-term practice of demanding tax abatements from the schools and city government was affecting the community at large. After years of tax concessions to GM—the world's largest industrial corporation—the Arlington school district was left in such poor condition that it could not afford to give up the tax revenue by handing out more abatements.[63] On the city level, GM still enjoyed significant tax breaks, paying $872,012 in city taxes and having $289,712 in taxes abated in 1996.[64] The abatements also cut into municipal services. For example, the neighborhood of East Arlington, built more than forty years ago to house workers of the then-new GM plant, was falling into disrepair. The city needed more housing code enforcement inspectors, but was unlikely to come up with the money. The cost of more inspectors—approximately $250,000—was less than a year of city tax abatements for GM.[65]

The biggest GM–induced upheavals for Arlington, however, were in the implicit elements of the approved labor contract. The final contract allowed GM to eliminate more than 200 jobs to pare the plant's unionized workforce to about 1,500, a steep (over 60 percent) drop from the 3,800 workforce five years earlier. The remaining Arlington assembly workers of UAW Local 276 did well under the contract. According to Local 276 president Lonnie Morgan, when the plant went down to one shift, 546 workers went on preretirement leave and others were offered a "superenhanced" transfer package. "No one was laid off to the street," Morgan said.[66]

But the story of "winning" a new product line for GM included selling out a new generation of workers at Mackie Automotive Systems and Lear Seating Corp., who assembled the same parts once done inside the Arlington plant but for less than half the wages. For example, at the Mackie plant built adjacent to GM's Arlington assembly plant, three hundred workers preassembled and sequenced 90 percent of the auto parts used next door at the GM plant. On November 18, 1997, these three hundred Mackie workers (represented by UAW Local 129, a different local than the one representing the GM Arlington workers), frustrated by work conditions, medical and pension benefits, and a $6.50 starting wage, went on strike. The strike set up the uncomfortable daily situation of the well-paid Arlington GM workers driving by the pickets of their Mackie UAW brothers and sisters, whose low-paying jobs they had essentially agreed to in their contract with GM. (A similar situation occurred in Oklahoma City, where Mackie workers also walked out.)

The strike initially shut down GM's Arlington plant and the Lear plant (where workers started at $9.00 an hour). Mackie then hired temporary workers to keep parts flowing into the neighboring GM assembly plant. UAW workers at the GM plant said they had no choice but to accept the scab-assembled parts, since they could be replaced if they stopped working. However, some GM-Arlington workers represented by Local 276 were angered by their union's weak support of the Mackie workers. One anonymous letter of protest, dated December 1997 and claiming to be "sent to all UAW locals in our area and to the international union" assailed Local 276 leaders and urged support for striking Local 129 workers at Mackie. The letter said, in part,

> Look what our own leadership is doing to our brothers and sisters at Mackie. Our leadership tells us they do not want us to get involved because it may keep us from drawing unemployment if we were to have to cancel production due to Mackie's situation . . . I say to hell with our leadership and let's help our brothers and sisters instead of almost running over them to get into G.M. gates and crossing their picket lines. REMEMBER IT WAS THIS LEADERSHIP THAT GAVE AWAY ALL THOSE JOBS TO MACKIE. We owe it to them.[67]

The Mackie strikers hit a raw nerve in a community that had unfailingly embraced business. On January 24, 1998, a report in the *Fort Worth Star-Telegram* (a newspaper that frequently granted a guest column to Arlington Chamber of Commerce president David Sampson for his antiunion rants) noted that "[The Mackie strike has] been a blow to [Mackie's] image. Last month, some City Council members even discussed amending tax abatement policy to reduce abatements companies can get if they pay their workers below a certain wage. Mackie received a tax abatement early last year."[68]

Meanwhile, North Texas Jobs with Justice activists led an effort to stop a local mission from bringing homeless people from the Arlington Night Shelter to the Mackie plant to work as scabs. Mission Arlington had a $40,000 grant from the city to transport homeless individuals to job sites and children to day care. Jobs with Justice had to explain that sending unemployed homeless individuals to work as scabs undermines striking workers and ultimately doesn't help the poor.[69]

The strike at Mackie ended in January 1999. The union (Local 129) finally won its proposals for a $9.00-an-hour starting wage and better benefits. But, with the long duration of the strike, most striking Mackie workers—lacking sufficient financial resources to weather a fourteen-month strike—had already drifted off to other jobs.[70] Meanwhile, workers at the Arlington GM plant dodged the threat of closure again in 1999, as GM awarded them the production of a new line of trucks beginning in the second half of 2000.[71] Mackie responded with announcements for a new supplier plant on Arlington's north side and up to one hundred additional jobs.

Choosing Which Stories to Tell

All too often when we talk about the economy, we fail to acknowledge that corporate strategies are *choices*, not inevitabilities. Corporations choose to favor short-term profits over long-term gains, to value stockholder interests above community interests, and to treat workers as flexible expenses instead of investments.

While they would rarely acknowledge it, news workers make conscious choices, too. The news hides behind a veil of objectivity, but tells stories that generally serve the core dominant values of U.S. capitalist society—including those of their own profit-maximizing corporate owners. The heavy business control of mainstream mass media ultimately limits the scope of ideas presented and range of debate in the news media, blocking the potential for wide-ranging democratic discourse. The national news media story of Arlington and Willow Run illustrates how news media can run with one dominant interpretation of events, going so far as to ignore information that doesn't fit into the dominant frames (e.g., GM's admission that Willow Run was the less expensive plant per unit and Judge Shelton's opinion that linked the Willow Run case to broader issues of public life) and ending a story with a positive, capitalism-affirming sense of closure.

However, while commercial media seek to frame media content for dominant class interests, they must ultimately address alternative class experiences in some manner, lest they lose their popular credibility. Because hegemony is a process whereby consent must be constantly won, mass media occasionally include content that critiques capitalist logic and may attempt to broaden discussion on economic and class issues. This small window provides the only opportunity for labor to get its story told in mainstream news media. And the kind of story that gets told is partly labor's choice, too. A compliant, concessionary union that practices business unionism fits perfectly into the lean and mean mythology of the necessity of sacrifice. But, when labor uses principled civil disobedience and other creative means to highlight inequities—such as the refusal of Mackie workers to work for less than a living wage in unsafe conditions—news media can be compelled to depart from traditional story frames.

Before the Reagan era of downsizing had begun, sociologist Herbert Gans noted that U.S. news "has an optimistic faith that in the good society, businessmen and women will compete with each other in order to create prosperity for all, but that they will refrain from unreasonable profits and gross exploitation of workers or customers."[72] News media's optimistic faith in business is hard to counter. But if labor can offer dramatic stories that point out the folly and contradiction of the euphemistic "downsizing," they can ultimately create the opportunity to discuss socioeconomic alternatives.

Unfortunately, the national news checked out of the Arlington story after 1994. But what happened in Arlington is a story of national and international importance. Mackie Automotive Systems isn't a struggling small local business but a large multinational corporation headquartered in Oshawa, Ontario, and by 1999 employing 2,400 in Canada, Mexico, the United States, England, Germany, and Poland. As a supplier, Mackie is the remora to GM's shark, regularly feeding off GM assembly plant locations as a cheap outsourcer of work previously done by GM in-house. By 1999, fourteen of Mackie's sixteen plants served GM operations.[73]

Moreover, since the national news media checked out of the story, it has become evident that GM's heralded cutbacks of 1992 have been far from equitable. As GM sought to increase outsourcing, spurring the debilitating summer 1998 GM strikes, *Business Week* reported that "GM's senior management ranks have ballooned 47% since its 1992 reorganization."[74]

Of course, local action only goes so far in dealing with corporations that have national and global means and leverage. For U.S. news media to put the situation of downsizing and outsourcing at GM on the national radar again—and for labor to get the right kind of coverage—requires a sus-

tained effort and creative civil action by the UAW and its international affiliates. The UAW should have plenty of solidarity-building opportunities.
As the Arlington case illustrates, GM's continuing strategy is to gain concessions by committing product lines to assembly plants only for a few
years, putting workers' jobs in a regularly threatened status. GM also
threatens to export more jobs to domestic and foreign outsourcers. In fact,
in 1998 GM formally announced plans to spin off its Delphi parts subsidiary into a separate company and to use modular construction meth-
ods (i.e., outsourcers build the major components, and GM only assem-
bles the final modules). Carrying this style of production to its extreme,
GM and other automobile companies of the future may become completely white-collar corporations, marketers of automobiles that they design but don't produce.[75] Symbolic of this strategy is the fact that with the
completion of its spin-off of its $6.2 billion Dephi division in 1999, GM—
who had been the world's largest industrial corporation since the 1930s—
slipped behind Ford in the rankings.[76]

If the UAW intends to garner and sustain public support and favorably
frame news coverage in this new economy, it needs to shed its conservative, insular approach and take a principled stand for workers experienc-
ing poor pay and working conditions at places such as Mackie and Lear—
about 90 percent of auto parts suppliers are unorganized[77]—and at GM
suppliers across the U.S. border. As the anonymous letter writer of UAW
Local 276 wrote, "We owe it to them."

5

THE EAGLE IS STRANDED

THE AMERICAN AIRLINES FLIGHT ATTENDANT STRIKE

The case of General Motors' shutdown of the Willow Run, Michigan, assembly plant has the narrative elements of the traditional image of labor: mostly male blue-collar workers earning a union-bargained living wage, a large industrial union (the UAW), and a large industrial corporation exporting northern Rust Belt jobs to the South in the name of cost savings and greater efficiency.

The case of the 1993 flight attendant strike of American Airlines does not fit the traditional image of labor. Yes, the company is large—by the early 1990s, American was the nation's biggest airline. But the union's more than 21,000 flight attendants were mostly female (85 percent), in many cases earning inadequate wages (starting at less than $15,000 per year). The union—the Association of Professional Flight Attendants—was mostly unknown, with no history of political power, and led by a woman. The targeted business was a service industry that could not export jobs but could replace workers. Perhaps the most unique feature of this strike is how the typical image of the flight attendant is so far removed from the media's image of a union worker. Whereas union workers are stereotypically portrayed as "fat, lazy and insubordinate,"[1] those three adjectives are not conjured up by the image of flight attendants, whose very jobs depend on them being thin, active, and agreeable.

Flight attendants have long been subjected to sex, age, and race discrimination. In fact, one of the most compelling reasons to hire women for the job beginning in the 1930s was that airline executives thought "it would be difficult for potential travelers [mostly men] to admit fears of flying when young women routinely took to the air as part of in-flight crews."[2] In the following decades, "only good-looking, slender, unmarried, nonpregnant women could be employed or remain employed on the airlines." Age discrimination eliminated flight attendants who reached their early thirties, and racial discrimination kept flight attendant crews almost all white into the 1960s. Several airline marketing campaigns (e.g., National Airlines' "Fly me," and Continental's "We really move our tail for you")[3] continued to foster the idea that flight attendants—"stewardesses" at that time—were little more than sexy waitresses of the sky. By the 1970s, things began to change: four independent flight attendant unions had emerged, men slowly reentered the position, and flight attendants began to demand greater respect as workers.

The airline industry, which had long treated flight attendants with an attitude of patriarchal condescension, was apparently still not willing to treat them as professionals in the 1980s. For example, in contract negotiations with TWA in 1986, the airline demanded the flight attendants take larger pay cuts than the machinists or the pilots. According to the union leader for the TWA flight attendants, TWA owner Carl Icahn "told us that we were secondary incomes, that we were not the main wage-earners in our families, and that we should accept bigger cuts than the pilots or mechanics."[4] Although Icahn denied the statement, he persisted in his demand for greater cuts for the flight attendants' wages. The TWA flight attendants walked out over the dispute. Icahn then hired young replacements, rushed them through training, and paid them a much lower annual salary of about $10,000. Later when the strike ended, the former flight attendants were hired back only as positions became available, and only at the new lower pay scale.

Icahn's success with breaking TWA's flight attendants union, hiring replacement workers, and extracting millions of dollars in salary savings must have been reassuring for American Airline's chairman/CEO Robert Crandall when the company's flight attendants moved toward striking in November 1993. Crandall had avoided such tough measures a decade earlier when he was able to get all of American's unions to agree to a dual wage scale. Beginning in 1983, new flight attendants, machinists, baggage handlers, pilots, and ticket agents were hired at a lower "b-scale" wage.

The key to getting American's unions to agree to the two-tier system, according to author Thomas Petzinger Jr. was the guarantee that the existing employees would maintain their high wages and would be able to benefit from the advancement opportunities of American's planned expansion. The additional "stick" that American wielded was "a massive war chest, the means to win a war of attrition should the unions refuse to approve the two-tier wage scheme."[5] For flight attendants, the new system meant that flight attendants making $30,000 would be working side-by-side with new hires making less than $15,000 a year.

Subsidized by a workforce increasingly consisting of b-scale workers, American embarked on an unprecedented growth plan in the 1980s, moving its headquarters from New York to Dallas and establishing major hubs in Dallas–Fort Worth, Chicago, Nashville, and Raleigh-Durham, buying Eastern Airline's Miami hub and Latin American routes, expanding into Europe, and instituting the industry's first frequent-flier plan. Crandall's evidently brilliant management move had a flaw, though:

> The one nagging problem with an expansion fueled by b-scalers, of course, was that the low-paid newcomers quickly came to realize that they were receiving distinctly unequal pay for equal work. This presented Crandall with a labor relations problem in the short term and in the years ahead with a significant strategic challenge: maintaining b-scales past the point at which the b-scalers themselves attained the majorities of the unions that represented them.[6]

By 1990, American (with its distinctive eagle wings logo and patriotic red, white, and blue colors) had surpassed United as the nation's leading air carrier. The airline had also reached another, more portentous milestone: b-scale workers now made up more than half of the company's workforce.[7]

Mainstream News Media Cover the Strike

If we recall James Carey's statement that "news is not information but drama," then we can remind ourselves that national news stories of a strike will not necessarily provide a comprehensive account of the events.

Instead, the news delivers just enough information to frame a compelling drama—one that both stirs the audience with familiar narratives and fits within the journalistic value of objectivity. Most typically, the news dramatizes a strike by pitting labor against management, with the economy's mighty consumer as the jilted third party.

The story of the 1993 flight attendant strike against American Airlines is a perfect example of such a strategically framed drama. As noted in Chapter 1, the news media largely framed this strike as a story of consumer inconvenience and expense, precluding rational-critical debate of class and compensation issues in the airline industry or of the ways in which the airline industry had been managed since its deregulation in 1978. With "impact on the airline passenger" as the central organizing theme, the news media left out of the story a number of important details that could have helped their readers/viewers make an informed judgment about the strike. Instead, the national news media whipped up a story of an intractable airline conflict that left consumers waiting in the wings.

The Travelers' Advocate

The timing of the strike by the American Airlines flight attendants—just before Thanksgiving—fit the news media's consumer-based view of labor-management conflict. About 95 percent of the 21,000 flight attendants walked out on Thursday, November 18, 1993, exactly a week before the Thanksgiving holiday, and one of the busiest air travel seasons of the year. The Association of Professional Flight Attendants planned the strike to last no longer than eleven days, with the knowledge that should American try to employ replacement workers, minimum Federal Aviation Administration standards required at least a ten-day safety training program for them.

With the travel plans of American's usual 200,000 passengers a day disrupted, finding an upset passenger was not difficult for the news media. ABC, CBS, and NBC broadcast a total of eighteen news packages during their evening newscasts, but limited coverage to the immediate strike period of November 18 (when the flight attendants walked out) to 23 (when they returned to work). The two mainstream national newspapers offered more extensive coverage over a longer period of time, with *USA Today* filing a total of thirty-three stories between October 21 and December 2, and the *New York Times* publishing thirty stories between October 14 and December 12.

For the three major news networks, the difficulties between the nation's top airline and its flight attendants didn't even merit a package report until November 18, when the threatened walkout began and peeved consumers were in great supply. For the television networks, stories of traveler woe were more important than trying to explain the factors behind the strike, as illustrated in a report by ABC's Bob Jamieson on November 19:

> JAMIESON [over VIDEO of flight attendants on a picket line]: While American and its striking flight attendants argued over who was winning the labor dispute, [cut to VIDEO of long lines in an airline terminal] angry passengers declared both losers.

> JAMIESON [over VIDEO of customer in terminal with American Airlines representative]: Many blamed American for stranding thousands at airports like Chicago's O'Hare by promising flights would operate when they did not.

> FEMALE CUSTOMER #1: I've been on the phone for two days, rescheduling. They tell me one thing, then they lie to us.

> FEMALE CUSTOMER #2: For people that have international flights booked months in advance, trips that come once in a lifetime, it's pathetic.

> JAMIESON [over VIDEO of picket lines with flight attendants chanting "American's lying, we're not flying"]: Others lashed out at the attendants for striking in the days before Thanksgiving.

> MALE CUSTOMER #1: I blame it on the people who are striking. I don't think they are hurting the airlines as much as the passengers.

> MALE CUSTOMER #2: I hope they replace all their flight attendants.

On November 20, NBC's Gary Matsumoto trumped Jamieson's story of anonymous traveler misfortune with a dramatic package focusing on the odyssey of the Seffren family of Illinois as they tried to meet their Princess Cruise in San Juan, Puerto Rico before it left port for a Caribbean tour. In his on-camera stand-up in O'Hare, Matsumoto explains "This one family of 26 holiday travelers has lugged hundreds of pounds of suitcases through three different airports, several different terminals, and has spent nearly a hundred extra dollars in skycap fees." Matsumoto later noted that the cruise line, not American, finally made the arrangements for the

November 19, 1993, *ABC World News Tonight.* For the television networks, stories of traveler woe were more important than trying to explain the issues behind the strike.

Seffrens to fly to San Juan via several connecting flights and still meet their cruise ship on time. Still, he said, it wasn't clear how the extended family would return from the Caribbean once the cruise ended seven days later.

USA Today and the *New York Times* also joined the abandoned traveler narrative. A November 22 story by *USA Today* began: "Misery reigned over U.S. airports Sunday as a strike by American Airlines flight attendants hobbled the carrier, leaving passengers stranded and tempers frayed." The report then cited reactions from immobile passengers at six airports across the country:

> Miami International Airport: Newlywed Joanie Smith of Newtown Square, Pa., sat in a chair while her husband, David, slept at her feet. The Smiths planned to spend their honeymoon in the Caribbean.
>
> When the strike canceled their flight from Philadelphia, they managed to book a USAir flight to Miami. There, they learned the American flight to Aruba had been canceled three days straight.
>
> "I feel so angry, I feel like . . . yelling at (the strikers)," Smith said. It's my honeymoon. I've had no sleep, no rest."[8]

The *New York Times* used a similar narrative approach in a November 20 report:

> Like a coast-to-coast blizzard, the strike by flight attendants has hamstrung travel throughout the nation, upending plans for business meetings, family reunions, vacations, even weddings.
>
> "We've been planning this vacation forever," said Sue Karnes, whose flight to San Juan, P.R., had been delayed for five hours and counting, as fellow would-be passengers slept in chairs. "We're supposed to be on a cruise that leaves tomorrow. We paid $2,600, and it's nonrefundable."[9]

The *New York Times'* simile of "a coast-to-coast" blizzard to describe the consequences of the strike on customers is not surprising. The sound bites and quotes from the frustrated, angry passengers could almost be lifted from the stories the news media routinely do when bad weather shuts down airports. Although the resulting canceled flights and missed connections are similar outcomes, the causes of bad weather and strikes are different: One is an act of Mother Nature; the other is an act of people. Yet, coverage of airline industry labor conflict puts consumers in the same state of powerlessness that bad weather does. Like the case of a bad winter blizzard or summer thunderstorms, the news reports seem to be communicating that there's no use in trying to make sense of a strike—we're all helpless in its wake. Thus, the passenger sound bites and quotes are rarely about what those people understand about the strike, but only how they feel about their immediate situation.

Even after the strike had ended, *NBC Nightly News* apparently felt that the story of the worried and angry traveler merited top billing in its newscast. On November 23, the day after the strike ended, anchor Tom Brokaw led off the newscast this way:

> BROKAW: Good evening. Thanksgiving travel is underway tonight—the busiest travel time of the year in this country. And it is a little chaotic at this time, but it would have been much worse if American Airlines were [*sic*] still on strike. NBC's David Bloom now takes us through the travel prospects for the next few days.

Bloom's report was a compendium of bad things that could happen to holiday travelers—such as the already-ended American Airlines flight attendant strike, a possible work slowdown at United Airlines, crowded air terminals, cranky children, and bad weather. His voice-over narration began "American's planes are flying but many of the passengers are still grumbling." Later he alerted the viewer that "travel experts predict Thanksgiving weekend blues." A source from a travel magazine warned in a sound bite to "expect crowds . . . a lot of angry and frustrated people, and lots of crying babies." Next, Bloom noted that a potential work slowdown by United Airlines machinist and pilots union members could result in delays. Bloom concluded (over video of a weather satellite image, a man shoveling snow, and an icy freeway pileup) with "the last bit of bad news, the weather—a storm heading east across the Plains."

Thus, strikes and work slowdowns are equated with nasty winter weather, angry strangers with suitcases, and someone else's incessantly crying baby—all bad things that give us the blues. These are unpredictable events, NBC seems to say, that weigh against our holiday happiness and render us powerless. We cannot understand or prevent such situations, we must only try to avoid them and hope they don't happen to us.

So, what the mainstream news media gave their audience in this time of crisis was mobilizing information of a consumer sort. For example, *USA*

Today (which is heavily dependent on the travel industry, with about 20 percent of its circulation supported by bulk sales to hotels and airlines)[10] provided three stories in a five-day period that directly addressed airline fliers with advice. A November 19 report, entitled "What to Do If You're Flying During the Strike" provided a question-and-answer list and was followed by "Advice, Refunds, Options," on November 22 and by "Playing It Smart with Your Ticket" after the strike on November 23. Even the *New York Times* took the consumer hotline approach with its own November 19 question-and-answer report on tickets and flight availability, aptly titled "Advice for Travelers During the Strike."[11]

The Traveler's Advocate, Ergo the Business Advocate

It is an attractive and enduring myth that the news media in the United States operate in a free market, presenting all possible views, thus allowing truth to prevail with an informed citizenry in the marketplace of ideas.[12] As Michael Schudson has noted, the utopian model of the active, informed citizen operating in a free marketplace of ideas has given way to the contemporary reality of what Schudson calls the *monitorial citizen*—the citizen who keeps an eye on the sociopolitical scene, but only acts when necessary. For the monitorial citizens of today, more private but always scanning the informational environment and "poised for action" when needed, the news media seem to be crucial. Schudson writes: "All that is required to criticize the present state of affairs is to know that some serious injustices persist, that some remediable conditions that limit human possibility lie before us, and that resources for reconstituting ourselves can be found."[13]

Schudson's concept of the monitorial citizen is useful in explaining the state of civic activity in the United States. I would agree that most Americans are still willing to act on serious injustices, given adequate explanatory and mobilizing information. Yet, to use the example of labor in the United States, I would suggest that the monitorial citizen who informally scans the mainstream news media on a regular basis comes up woefully short on sufficient information to know the injustices that persist in U.S. labor relations and to discover the resources to remedy the situation.

In the case of the flight attendants' strike against American Airlines, the news media gave the anxious airline passenger mobilizing information on how to get from point A to point B, but treated the monitorial citizen to a superficial tit-for-tat that presented some of the competing claims of the union and company but never investigated the truth of the claims. The final product is a journalism of stenography, not of inquiry or analysis. Even the *New York Times*, generally lauded for the insight and analysis it provides for readers, threw its hands up at trying to sort out the information. An October 24, 1993, story by Barbara Presley Noble had one of the most indeterminate leads ever to begin a story in the "newspaper of record":

> Objective reality is the uninvited guest to virtually any labor-management negotiation, but rarely more so than in the current lengthy dispute between American Airlines and one of its unions, the 21,000-member Association of Professional Flight Attendants. Perhaps Srinivasa Ramanujan, the late Indian mathematical genius, could untangle the airline industry's wizardly compensation formulas and arrive at a kernel of pure truth.
>
> Mere mortals wait in vain for any fact, factoid, or fact-ette to stand up and bark. Are flight attendants still getting the shaft a decade after they made concessions, including allowing the company to impose its two-tier wage system, to save jobs and, supposedly, the airline? Or is American a benevolent employer, simply seeking flexibility to allow it to compete in what every American man, woman, child and kitty cat by now agrees is a killer industry?

Unfortunately, the mere mortals reading the story would also wait in vain for any kind of journalism investigating and weighing the competing claims. The article's lead paragraphs quickly define the situation as a story of competing compensation claims and declare any further understanding of the situation to be impossible.[14] Thus, the mere mortal reader is quickly discouraged from ever knowing the inequities between labor and management in this case. If the *New York Times* can't evaluate the principles of each side's stance, a reader might conclude, how can anyone else?

Given the limited mainstream news coverage of the strike's issues and the lack of assistance in sorting through the ethical merits of the airline's and union's claims, the news audience is left to evaluate the strike from a consumer perspective. The consumer is therefore directed only to ask which side is most concerned about keeping the planes flying and keeping ticket prices low. The easy answer from this perspective is American Airlines.

The *New York Times'* nonevaluative framing of the strike was generally consistent with the approaches taken by ABC, CBS, NBC, and *USA Today*. The conflict, these news outlets seem to agree, was between an airline that wants to cut costs via reduced staffing, changes in work rules, and increased flight attendant health care contributions and flight attendants who feel squeezed after years of concessions and comparatively low wages. As with the story of General Motors' Willow Run Assembly Plant shutdown, the news media reports approved of the post-Fordist logic of flexibility. Thus, the news characterized American Airlines' "hard-nosed" dealings with its flight attendants as the only possible path for American and the rest of the airline industry. For American to survive in the contemporary economy, the reports generally concluded, workers needed to flexibly accommodate management's strategies to control labor costs.

A November 22 *USA Today* article even explicitly linked the cost-cutting and consumer ticket prices issues:

> The strike may even be an image winner for American if it succeeds in cutting costs and lowering fares, says James O'Donnell, a consultant and former Continental Airlines marketing executive.
>
> "American's frequent fliers are business people who know how to add and subtract," O'Donnell says.[15]

Thus, from a journalistic standpoint, advocating a cost-cutting strategy that undermines labor is not necessarily a probusiness bias (although it is) but an acceptable objective, neutral, proconsumer position. In other words, the consumer-oriented ends justify the antilabor means.

The Myth of Labor Costs

The airline industry was losing money in the early 1990s. By most accounts, industrywide losses from 1990 to 1992 totaled $10 billion.[16] American, which had become the leading airline in the nation, represented a sizable chunk of the industry losses (see Table 5.1).

Table 5.1 American Airlines: Net earnings (loss) in millions, 1986–1998*

1986	1987	1988	1989	1990	1991	1992	1993	1994	1995	1996	1997	1998
279	198	477	455	(40)	(240)	(935)	(110)	228	162	1,016	985	1,314

*Data from 1996 and 1998 AMR Corporation Annual Reports.

American chairman/CEO Robert Crandall developed a simple solution to increase profitability: "controlling" labor costs. The flight attendant contract that came up for negotiation in 1993 was the first major labor contract negotiation with American in the 1990s. Most flight attendants were working under the low-wage b-scale system initiated in 1983 and were looking for compensation for enduring a decade of concessionary wages as a union. As the economy lifted, American was also expecting to show its first profit since 1989, with third-quarter 1993 earnings of $118 million. As contract talks began, American had decided to maintain its b-scale wage system, even if it meant pushing the flight attendants to a strike and having to intimidate them with the threat of replacements. The mainstream news stories adopted the logic of American's cost-cutting strategy without question.

Were there other reasons for the airlines' huge losses and other options for increasing profitability? According to the *New York Times* on November 20, "Airline labor leaders are making the point in many public forums that the airlines managers, not the workers, are to blame for the $10 billion in losses industry-wide from 1990 to 1992."[17] The *Times* never elaborated on the management inefficiencies, though, so the airline labor leader's point reads like baseless allegations. The same article also suggested that Crandall had no other alternative than to squeeze unionized workers: "Mr. Crandall is now looking to labor as, in effect, the banker of last resort."

CBS News correspondent Monica Gayle was more unequivocal in her analysis of the labor dispute in a November 20 report: "At issue were wages, staffing, and work rules. In an increasingly volatile market, American Airlines is trying to cut back on its only variable cost, which is labor, in order to [VIDEO of a Southwest Airline jet taxiing] remain competitive with smaller, leaner airlines."

Like CBS, a November 19 *USA Today* story characterized the need to pressure labor as a simple fact, not as a management choice or opinion. "Labor is one-third of an airlines' operating costs, twice the expense of fuel. Airlines have no control over most costs, so they're going after their workers."[18] The lack of attribution in the CBS and *USA Today* reports is important. Journalists generally attribute statements of opinion; for example, "Airline labor leaders are making the point . . . that the airlines managers, not the workers, are to blame." Statements that are commonly verifiable and agreed on, such as "the airlines lost $10 billion between 1990 and 1992," are generally not attributed. By stating that "airlines have no control over most costs" and that "American Airlines is trying to cut back on its only variable cost, which is labor," the news audience is led to believe that pressuring the flight attendants is the only way for American to remain a viable company. Yet, nearly every expense (the *USA Today* story later lists, in order, the major costs of airlines: labor, fuel, travel agent commissions, maintenance, aircraft leases, food, interest, landing fees, advertising) is variable, depending on how an airline is structured and managed and which resources are conserved or not.

Later in the same November 19 *USA Today* article, the reader did get some alternative reasons for American's financial problems, but in an attributed form: "There is plenty of blame to go around, and labor unions say management needs a scapegoat. Airlines can't seem to resist jumping into fare wars. And they're married to hub-and-spoke systems that force pilots, flight attendants and expensive jets to wait hours in airports before feeder flights arrive."[19] In this case, the critique comes from labor, which might be dismissed by the reader as a biased source. The newspaper, however, did little to investigate the merits of labor's claims of airline mismanagement. *USA Today* could have gone back to its own files from the previous year and found evidence of American's disastrous decision to initiate a new fare scheme in the spring of 1992, which precipitated an industrywide price-cutting fare war. In an April 17, 1992, article, *USA Today* announced:

> American Airlines' new fares—a hit on Main Street—are playing to mixed reviews on Wall Street.
>
> The cheaper, simpler fare structure that American announced last week—largely matched by the industry since then—has sent airline analysts scrambling to reduce their earnings estimates.
>
> . . . American says it will lose $100 million in revenue this quarter . . .
>
> Long term, American says its new fares eventually will generate $300 mil-

lion to $350 million in additional annual revenue and will restore profits to an industry that has lost $6 billion in two years.[20]

But American grossly overestimated its profits. The price war lasted through June 1992, attracting plenty of new fliers but at disastrously low prices. An editorial in the *St. Louis Post-Dispatch* noted that "the tremendous number of tickets sold has generally been at prices roughly a third or less than the cost per seat-mile of actually flying passengers to their destinations. No one can yet calculate the financial effect on the industry, but it could wipe out any chance for airline profits in 1992."[21] For American, that year's loss was $935 million, its worst year ever.

Other ongoing managerial problems included the huge expansion and establishment of American transportation hubs in the 1980s that Crandall argued would save American. By the early 1990s, there were just too many airline seats in the industry for the number of flying customers (hence the ultimately damaging fare wars to drum up business). By the 1990s, competitor Southwest Airlines had become the model airline of the industry. Crandall admitting to wanting to emulate Southwest's more efficient work rules, which kept pilots and flight attendants in the air more hours each week. Yet, the hub-and-spoke system of American and other major airlines required crews to wait in terminals for hours until passengers on connecting flights arrived. Conversely, Southwest's business was built on shorter point-to-point routes, allowing flight crews to fly back and forth without long waits.

Finally, one of the chief reasons why the airline industry was suffering in the early 1990s was that the United States was suffering from a recession. Even American Airlines' own official statements on the reasons for the financial problems of the early 1990s cited managerial problems, not labor costs. The 1996 Annual Report for AMR Corporation (American's parent company) explains:

Unfortunately, in the late 1980s and early 1990s, the efforts of many carriers to build large networks created excess capacity. In the weak economy of the early 1990s, excess capacity meant empty seats, which forced carriers to cut fares in an effort to stimulate demand. In recent years, the industry has slowed its rate of growth, and as the U.S. economy recovered, demand increased. Thus, the airlines have recently been flying fewer empty seats while keeping fares at more compensatory levels.[22]

In retrospect, then, hounding already low-paid, hard-working flight attendants for more concessions was not the only possible response to American's profitability problems, but may have been the easiest knee-jerk response to the bottom line, particularly when the news media were willing to demonize the flight attendants on behalf of the almighty consumer.

Daring to Strike and Scaring the Strikers

On the first day of the strike (November 18, 1993), NBC's Jim Cummins concluded his report with a brief attempt at historical context. Narrating over file footage of striking Eastern Airlines machinists and an Eastern jet taxiing on a runway, Cummins stated: "This is the largest airline walkout since the machinists struck Eastern Airlines in 1989. That strike was the beginning of the end for Eastern, which is not in business anymore." Although Cummins' comparison is sketchy at best, his conclusion—that the striking flight attendants could selfishly pull the entire airline under—is quite clear.

The causality that Cummins implies about the machinists walkout and Eastern's demise does not fit with the facts of Eastern's collapse, however. Frank Lorenzo, the chairman of Texas Air (which had purchased Continental Airlines in a debt-heavy transaction in 1981 and run the airline into bankruptcy two years later) bought Eastern in 1986 and pushed for concessions from Eastern's machinists unions. Yet, the rationale for further labor cost-cutting was missing—Eastern's labor payroll was hardly inflated after a decade of worker givebacks. According to transportation researchers Paul Dempsey and Andrew Goetz, "Eastern's employees surrendered $1.14 billion in concessions between 1979 and 1988. Eastern enjoyed the lowest labor costs in the industry, with only nonunion Continental having lower wages."[23]

In fact, the problems of Eastern were managerial. Under Texas Air's ownership, Eastern was led by the same management team that pushed Continental into bankruptcy, which allowed it to dispose of its labor contracts. The Texas Air management team also exhibited little care for Eastern. According to Eastern's bankruptcy examiner, Lorenzo and his Texas Air team stripped between $284.5 and $403.1 million in assets from Eastern and redirected them to Continental Airlines, Texas Air's other subsidiary. For this kind of management, Lorenzo was paid handsomely, reportedly more than $1.25 million in 1988.[24] With this history in mind, one might credit the "beginning of the end for Eastern" to the tenure of Lorenzo or even to the questionable tenure of Eastern's previous head, Frank Borman, the Apollo astronaut. (Just before Eastern was handed over to Lorenzo in 1986, Borman and the rest of Eastern's top managers softened their exit from the company by giving themselves $7.3 million in golden parachutes—a disturbing action by a management team that had demanded cuts from workers throughout the early 1980s.)[25]

Amazingly, one news report in *USA Today* on November 24, 1993, titled "Lorenzo Knows the Woes of Crandall," rationalized the short-term economic schemes and antilabor strategies of the two airline bosses who had goaded their unions to strike and attempted to generate sympathy for Crandall and the resurrected Lorenzo as misunderstood visionaries. The story read, in part:

> The chairman of the last big airline to go through a crippling strike— Frank Lorenzo—has some sympathy for American Airlines chairman Robert L. Crandall.
>
> "You just hate, hate, hate a strike," said Lorenzo, who was running Eastern Airlines when workers led a March 1989 strike that contributed to the company's bankruptcy.
>
> . . . Lorenzo was portrayed by the unions as money-grabbing villain who destroys the airlines. Years before he acquired Eastern, he took Continental Airlines into bankruptcy court where he was able to void union contracts.
>
> Lorenzo, however, says he was responding to the same pressures as Crandall—to bring down the costs of big airlines to compete with fledgling carriers.
>
> "Crandall is doing what he must to look out for the long-term," Lorenzo said. "The long-term economics of these carriers is in a squeeze. Bob's doing what he can."[26]

The story thus reiterates labor wage-cutting as the only route to airline success.

The news media also functioned to publicize American's threats of replacement workers. The specter of replacement workers was, of course, known to striking flight attendants. Because of this possibility, the flight attendants strategically limited their strike to eleven days, knowing that replacements required a minimum of ten days of safety training. For American to replace all of the strikers, hiring and training of potentially 21,000 replacements would have had to begin the day the strike commenced. The flight attendants also knew, as did American, that airline workers are covered under the Railway Labor Act and protected by law from being *fired* for being on strike. So, although a company may hire permanent replacement workers during a strike, the company is obligated to take back any workers involved in a walkout, as positions become available.

The *New York Times* and *USA Today* both mentioned the prohibition against firing striking workers in their coverage and acknowledged the union's eleven-day-strike strategy.[27] But, on the first day of the strike (November 18, 1993), the three major national television news programs all failed to mention both the union's quick-strike strategy and federal labor law, and grossly overstated American's abilities to replace the striking flight attendants.

First, ABC's coverage, with reporter Bob Jamieson, provided inaccurate information on how many flight attendants were staying on the job:

JAMIESON: American rerouted passengers on other carriers. And it says new flight attendants would he hired to replace strikers.

TIM SMITH, AIRLINE SPOKESMAN: There is no guarantee that any flight attendant who chooses to strike will have a job to come back to.

JOHN KLINE, UNION SPOKESMAN: We know that they believe they can break our union, that they're going to get a large percentage of us to cross the picket line, but as they can see today and they will see over the next eleven days, that just is not going to happen.

JAMIESON: American claimed that half its flight attendants had crossed picket lines by evening.

Jamieson thus left the audience with the impression that the union was crumbling apart, with lots of flight attendants reporting to work, and replacements on the way. In reality, about 95 percent of the flight attendants joined the walkout.

NBC's November 18 report didn't do much better, neglecting to mention that the flight attendants' short strike strategy would undermine American's attempts to train replacements in a timely manner:

TOM BROKAW (reporting from Seattle): American Airlines and its customers are struggling tonight with the effects of a strike by the flight attendants, and it's aimed at hitting the carrier just as the holiday travel season begins. American says the strikers may not have jobs to come back to. More now from Jim Cummins.

CUMMINS (over VIDEO of pickets): The flight attendants say they plan to end their strike and return to work after the lucrative Thanksgiving holiday weekend. But the airline seems to be saying, "Don't bother."

CUMMINS (now on camera): A spokesman said American plans to replace the workers, and tomorrow it will be advertising flight attendant openings in the thirty largest markets in the country.

NBC's report also took American's threat of replacements at face value, and failed to do the math on the impossibility of American replacing nearly 21,000 workers on an eleven-day strike with new hires requiring ten days of training. Finally, CBS failed miserably in its reporting, providing incorrect information on federal laws regarding striking workers by stating that they can be fired:

CONNIE CHUNG (in Seattle): Here in Seattle and all across the country, workers in American Airlines are worried about their future tonight, as are a lot of travelers. American's flight attendants are on strike, disrupting service heading into a busy holiday week. And the airline is threatening to fire them. Correspondent Vicki Mabrey has the story.

VICKI MABREY: The eleven-day strike is meant to hurt American during Thanksgiving, the busiest travel time of the year. But company officials say striking flight attendants may be the big losers.

AL BECKER, AMERICAN AIRLINES SPOKESMAN: As we have said all along, we will permanently replace those flight attendants who choose to strike.

The news organizations' scare tactics—a sort of warning to the flight attendants and anyone else who dare to disrupt the nation's consumer economy—could have had an unintended effect. Publicizing American's exaggerated statements that most flights would still be operating and that replacement flight attendants were only days away from staffing its jets may have led many ticket holders to believe that their flights were still on schedule.

In fact, on Friday, November 19 (the second day of the strike), U.S. Secretary of Transportation Federico Peña sent a letter to Crandall reprimanding American Airlines for "numerous reports" that they had provided inaccurate information to their customers. Although jets were still flying (the pilots association voted to support the striking flight attendants by continuing to fly mostly empty jets, adding even greater cost to American), insufficient or nonexistent flight attendant crews meant that passengers could not board. Thus, by encouraging passengers to show up and then canceling flights at the last minute, American Airlines, and not the striking flight attendants, violated the consumers' interests. (Passenger outrage for this reason is directed at the airlines in the November 19 ABC package quoted earlier in this chapter.)

American Airlines' misinformation about scheduled flights resulted in the only coverage of the entire period that was clearly critical of the airline. Because the objective news position is framed around consumer interest, journalists would seem biased and unfair if they neglected to report on the airline's shortcomings in regards to the consumer. As Todd Gitlin found with the way the *New York Times* framed reports of the New Left in the 1960s, the mainstream news media's legitimacy rests on their claims of objectivity. To be completely uncritical of American Airlines would raise questions of bias. So, some disagreeable facts must be included. But, as Gitlin notes, "the *Times* incorporates discrepant information—within a frame that minimizes and muffles its significance" as it also "tends to leave out a great deal of information which would lend weight to an oppositional sense of things."[28]

Gitlin's findings hold true for the flight attendant strike story. Although the reprimand from the Secretary of Transportation was a presumably significant development, only CBS of the three major networks mentioned it, and only as a relatively minor element of its November 20, 1993, report. *USA Today* mentioned American's customer relations problems in a few lines of a November 22 story—a story primarily about how American would ultimately make consumers happy with poststrike fare reductions.[29] The *New York Times* covered the reprimand with one sentence deep

November 18, 1993, *CBS Evening News.* On the first day of the strike, the three major national television news programs all disregarded both the union's quick-strike strategy and federal labor law, and grossly overstated American's abilities to replace the striking flight attendants.

into a November 20 story and a couple sentences in a November 21 story in which American claimed the misinformation problem was solved.

As Gitlin also suggests, additional information that might make audience members more critical of American Airlines—information that would allow people to interpret the story as a class-based political narrative instead of a consumer narrative—show up in the news media, but long after the strike was over and in entirely different contexts. For example, it was not until a *USA Today* story on December 2, 1993, that a reader might have learned that flight attendants for the "model" airline Southwest (which American executives hoped to make their airline more like) earned $15,070 in starting pay and $43,150 in maximum pay, *more* than the $14,990 minimum/$32,750 maximum pay that American offered for the same hours worked per month. The omission of this detail—which did not fit the general assumption that American needed flight attendant salary savings to remain competitive—is interesting.

Similarly, it was not until December 12, 1993, that a story about the flight attendants strike reported Crandall's annual pay, totaling more than $4 million in 1992.[30] That was the same year in which the airline lost nearly $1 billion, inspiring Crandall's mission of extracting labor savings in 1993. Of course, to juxtapose Crandall's annual compensation with flight attendants' modest salaries would have raised the uncommon issue of class. And, as sociologist Warren Breed observed of the press in 1958, 'the word 'class' is almost entirely absent from the media."[31] The same still holds true more than forty years later, in a media system that finds it much more comfortable—and self-serving—to address its audience as credit-card bearing consumers and not class-bound citizens.

The flight attendants' strike ended on Monday, November 22, 1993, after a personal phone call from President Bill Clinton to Crandall and union leader Denise Hedges got both to agree to end the strike and submit to binding federal arbitration. The union readily agreed. Crandall, who had turned down the union's offer of a mediated settlement a day earlier, reportedly agreed reluctantly to the arbitration. The decision was a victory for the union because all flight attendants were reinstated and plans for replacements were canceled. Clinton's agreement helped to soothe the problems of holiday travelers and was interpreted by mainstream news outlets as a friendly gesture to labor unions, which were upset with Clinton's battle in favor of the North American Free Trade Agreement the previous week. By Wednesday, November 24, 1993, American was operating at almost full levels, transporting passengers to their destinations in time for a happy Thanksgiving.

Of any of the stories broadcast by ABC, CBS, or NBC or published by the *New York Times* or *USA Today*, only a November 24, 1993, column by *USA Today* opinion writer Julianne Malveaux dared to raise the issue of class. The short piece even recast the notion of the consumer from a class-based perspective. The column read in part:

> Some say the flight attendants are tilting against consumer demand for low-cost, no-frills travel. But all consumers aren't demanding cattle cars with packaged peanuts tossed at us periodically. Airlines like American should look at pricing policies, not flight-attendant pay (these workers start at $16,000 a year) in considering their bottom line. When full-fare passengers get the same lousy service and treatment as leisure travelers who paid a fraction of their fare, something is very wrong.
>
> Why does low cost always mean low wages for workers on the bottom (I don't see American's executives cutting their paychecks)? Do employers understand that when they cut pay, they also cut the consumer's ability to afford their products? Who will hold the line against the spiral of downward wages in our country? Who will go out on a limb to preserve "good" jobs? Cheers to the flight attendants for stepping out on a limb, for fighting for their dignity and jobs.[32]

Malveaux's column was a lone dissenting voice, one drowned out by the weight of all the traditional, consumer-based news reports and opinion pieces. For example, on the same page as the Malveaux piece was the newspaper's unsigned editorial—the official voice of the paper's editorial board—that said airlines must continue pressure to "hold down labor costs." The editorial stated flatly: "Consumers want low fares; and with deregulation, consumers must get what they want." *USA Today*'s proconsumer absurdity reached its nadir with a December 2, 1993, story that concluded that flight attendants are underpaid but then argued that perhaps consumers do not want flight attendants at all. The story, a front-page Money section feature, began:

Flight attendants, who start as low as $12,000 per year, are paid meagerly. No question.

But for all the rhetoric stirred by last month's strike against American Airlines, few have dared to breathe perhaps the key question—a 60-year-old question. Are flight attendants indispensable guardians of passengers' safety and well-being? Or, are they flying waitresses (85% are women) and waiters who are becoming less important to passengers willing to sacrifice frills for cheap fares?

The *USA Today* article illustrates a pernicious point about the dominant consumer perspective of U.S. journalism. Something is wrong—inherently unfair—in this form of objectivity when questioning the work ethic and compensation of laborers as they relate to the costs of products or services is considered good journalism and questioning the work ethic or compensation of business executives as they relate to the costs of products or services is considered taboo. As the case of the American Airlines flight attendant strike demonstrates, the consumer framing of objective-style journalism unfortunately presents to us a world that insists that we put our own individual pleasure and economic self-interest above any sense of economic justice and community interest.

NEWS FOR THE EVERYFAN

THE 1994–95 BASEBALL STRIKE

A series of Nike television ads that appeared during the first few weeks of the 1994–95 Major League Baseball (MLB) strike responded to the labor dispute by embracing the familiar perspective of the almighty consumer. Beginning on day six of the strike (August 17, 1994), Nike's rotating schedule of witty national television ads featured a frustrated adult man—the symbolic "everyfan"—keeping himself busy in an empty baseball stadium. On an ad announcing "Day 20," for example, the fan is shown pushing a squeaky chalk line machine on the empty field under the lights. As the shot pulls out, we see that he has written *HELP* in enormous letters in the outfield. With only the lonely sounds of crickets in the background, the commercial returns to the messages of three white-on-black screens:

Play ball.
Please.
Nike (with its ubiquitous swoosh logo).[1]

According to Nike's director of North American advertising, "We're not saying the owners or players are right. We just want to see baseball." The campaign's artistic director adds, "We wanted to take it from the fan's perspective."[2]

Nike's position of balancing the arguments of the owners and players—

neither party is right—and taking the fans' perspective—just play ball!—typifies the news media coverage of the 1994–95 MLB strike. Television and newspaper reports chronically framed the strike as a battle between two equally cynical and dishonorable parties. Instead of sorting through the complicated history of labor relations in MLB, news outlets applied the motto "the customer is always right" to guide their framing of conflict. Thus, the "common" people—through quotes, sound bites, survey results, and images—became the defining voice in the baseball strike story as news media used the fans/consumers to create an "objective" or "neutral" stance.

This objective stance also served the not-so-objective economic interests of Nike and television and newspapers. The Nike ad's request of "Play ball. Please" could just as well have been its own call of "HELP" as the value of its endorsements of baseball stars such as Ken Griffey Jr. and Barry Bonds plummeted with the strike. In fact, after the cancellation of the remaining 1994 baseball season, and with poor labor-management relations threatening in the National Hockey League (NHL) and the National Basketball Association (NBA), Nike announced that it would move its marketing base away from team sports and toward individual competition sports such as running and tennis, where Nike presumably has more control over an athlete's labor.[3]

The "Play ball" request could have also echoed the cry of newspaper circulation managers and television programmers. Sports news attracts 76 percent of newspaper readers, and trails only "general" news as the most popular category of interest in newspapers. Many of those sports readers apparently stopped buying newspapers when the strike eliminated baseball game reports and box scores. Leon Levitt, vice president of circulation and marketing for the Newspaper Association of America, reported that the baseball strike had a "significant" impact on newspaper sales in MLB franchise cities. Even *USA Today's Baseball Weekly*, a national publication for devoted baseball fans, saw its circulation drop from an average of 320,000 to about 200,000 by the end of March 1995.[4]

Television networks ABC and NBC, which broadcast games under their profit-sharing Baseball Network in partnership with MLB, were forced to find programming to anchor their fall schedules in the absence of the MLB League Championships and the World Series. ESPN, too, lost planned games and program content, and prematurely shut down its daily *Baseball*

Tonight program on September 14. The strike had an even more damaging effect on local television stations and regional sports cable networks that built their schedules around heavy coverage of local teams.[5] Thus, by purporting to serve the fans' cry of "Play Ball," Nike and the news media also served their own economic interests as corporate consumers of Major League Baseball.

Playing Ball in the Consumer Sphere

Civic life in the United States surely includes the professional sport that has become known as the national pastime. Just as the National Anthem is inextricably linked with the beginning of each MLB game, the players, teams, and ballparks are often enmeshed with the identity of a neighborhood and city. Imagine New York without the Yankees, Cincinnati without the Reds, or Chicago without its Cubs and Wrigley Field.

Beyond the ties of tradition, Americans are also financially involved with the private business of Major League Baseball. Of course, baseball fans who pay at the gate, the broadcast audience who attract advertisers, and shoppers who purchase MLB licensed clothing and collectibles are the mainstays of MLB revenue. But the public is also involved in the tax breaks, stadium construction, and rent subsidies that MLB enjoys. By the early 1990s, only five of MLB's then-twenty-eight teams played in privately owned stadiums, and the trend was toward more new publicly subsidized ballparks.[6]

Professional baseball has been a vital part of the American scene for more than a century and has operated as Major League Baseball since 1903.[7] But, if we should applaud MLB for its enduring ability to delight and enrich American civic life, we should also hesitate to applaud Major League Baseball's continuing missteps in its quasi-public role. For fans of professional baseball, MLB's most disappointing public moments have been when the game has stopped cold due to recurring conflicts between the players union and MLB's owners. As economist Andrew Zimbalist noted, "since 1970, each time a baseball labor contract has expired there has been a work stoppage."[8] That held true until August 2002, when owners and players forged a four-year collective bargaining agreement without interrupting the season.

In the thirty years before 2002, there were five strikes and three lock-outs. None of the work stoppages was as great as the 1994–95 strike. The strike began August 12, 1994, and forced the season to close without a World Series. The record-breaking strike ended about eight months later, when a court injunction on March 31, 1995, forced the owners to play by the provisions of the previous contract.[9]

The traditional reports on the machinations of insiders, the chronicle of the power game, and the obsession with puncturing politician's façades all figured into media coverage of the labor dispute. The news media seemed to follow every thrust and parry of Bud Selig, the then-Milwaukee Brewers owner and acting baseball commissioner; Donald Fehr, the executive director of the Major League Baseball Players Association; and the dozens of elected officials who debated the best way to deal with the work stoppage. In fact, this narrative of union-owner conflict was one of the most common stories of the baseball strike.

National news organizations also frequently told stories about issues that seemed to matter to baseball fans, the choices baseball fans faced in light of the strike, and the discussions that needed to occur to mend the wounds of the labor dispute. Journalists even made baseball fans part of the stories: fans' views on the strike were often presented via newspaper quotes, television sound bites, and public opinion polls.

But, what national news media offered to baseball fans during the 1994–95 MLB strike was largely a journalism designed to play to the consumer sphere instead of the public sphere. Instead of orienting baseball fans as full citizens who have political, economic, and social interests in the MLB strike, national coverage of the strike treated fans as mere consumers whose chief concerns were the availability, price, and quality of professional baseball.

My critical analysis of the great MLB strike is based on mainstream national television and newspaper coverage of the strike period, from July 1994—the month in which the first strike reports were broadcast or printed—through May 6, 1995—the twelfth day of the strike-delayed 1995 baseball season. I have drawn on the content of the 106 network evening news packages (39 from ABC, 29 from CBS, and 38 from NBC), as supplied by the Vanderbilt Television News Archives, to analyze the framing of baseball strike coverage. The analysis of frames also draws from a systematic sample of the 647 *New York Times* stories and 918 *USA Today* stories from the entire baseball strike coverage period. The sample represents 10 percent of each newspaper's baseball strike stories, yielding 65 reports from the *New York Times* and 92 from *USA Today*.

News coverage of the baseball strike coalesced around two major narratives. The first focused on the union-owner conflict, a traditional strike narrative that in this case served to obscure the process of production; that is, the factors behind the disputed issues of the strike. The second narrative focused on the fans of baseball, and reminded them (despite leaving them in the dark on the substantive issues of the strike) that they, the consumers, are king.

The Union-Owner Conflict Frame

The framing of the 1994–95 baseball strike was similar to the framing of other labor disputes, which are typically portrayed as a two-sided conflict involving only labor and management. These conflicts are depicted as "something of senseless origin, readily avoidable if only some good will were shown."[10] Generally, unions are blamed for recurring labor strife, as they "dredge up conflict where there would otherwise be perfect harmony."[11] The government's role in labor-management conflict is cast by the news media as a "neutral arbiter in the struggle between capital and labor, acting on behalf of the 'national interest.'"[12]

The familiar two-sided framing convention structured many of the 1994–95 baseball strike reports. Coverage focused on the intractable nature of the two parties and how both were greedy and unwilling to compromise. The stories of the union-owner conflict included the reports on insiders, power games, and politicians that, according to media critic Jay Rosen, typifies most journalistic content.[13] Thus, there were hundreds of accounts that covered the following: the negotiations and maneuverings of the baseball owners and the players union, dissension among the owners and players, the money lost by both parties as the strike continued, the proposals of salary caps and taxation systems, the mediation sessions organized by President Clinton, the response of Congress to binding arbitration legislation, the process of fielding replacement (scab) teams, and the decisions of the National Labor Relations Board and federal courts.

As W. Lance Bennett and Murray Edelman note, narrative frames of news typically specify "heroes and villains" and "deserving and undeserving people."[14] The conflict between the players and owners was most commonly cast as "millionaires vs. billionaires." This framing made the strike seem ridiculous from the onset, since it is unthinkable—in the commonsense view of news—that such wealthy players and owners could have any legitimate grievances. Although the players, with their high public visibility, often bore the brunt of public criticism, the news media generally characterized both players and owners as "villains" and the "undeserving people."

The millionaires vs. billionaires frame of the strike also had the effect of limiting the range of solutions to the disagreement. The media-approved actors in the strike were the players union, the baseball owners, and the "neutral" federal government.[15] Thus, the "union-owner conflict" served to exclude the baseball fan from any official role during the entire strike period.

The Fan Narrative Frame

If the players and owners were the villains and undeserving people of the 1994–95 strike, the deserving people—and perhaps even the heroes—were the fans who had devoted their leisure to the consumption of baseball and demanded the return of their pastime. An enduring value of the news, according to Herbert Gans, is that it takes an optimistic view of economic activity but frowns on "unreasonable profits and gross exploitation of workers or customers." Furthermore, he notes, news frequently judges strikes negatively, "especially if they inconvenience 'the public,' contribute to inflation, or involve violence."[16] Because the news interpreted no "gross exploitation" of workers in the baseball strike, players and owners were generally treated as the single entity of MLB, which gained unreasonable profits at the expense of inconvenienced, exploited fans.

Fan narratives refer to news stories that focused on the reactions of fans to the strike, directed or permitted fans to speak out in an approved forum, suggested alternative activities for baseball fans, or directly addressed fans in a dialogic manner. How does one identify a "fan narrative"? One possible approach is to count television packages with fan sound bites and newspaper articles with fan quotes. But, enumerating the frequency of one textual element such as sound bites or quotes may result in "counting the wrong things."[17] The stylistic differences between network television and newspaper reports of fans weigh against this approach. With only a few exceptions, such as sports reporters Dick Schaap and Tim McCarver of ABC and Bob Costas of NBC (who altogether filed a total of 6 of the 106 television reports) network television news used general assignment reporters to cover the baseball strike. Following the traditions of objective-style reporting, the general assignment reporters acted as "surrogate eyewitnesses" for the viewer and employed sound bites to represent the fans' view.

Newspapers, on the other hand, typically used full-time sports reporters and columnists to cover the baseball strike. They often acted as "surrogate fans" for the reader.[18] Because sports reporting is much less determined by the conventions of objectivity,[19] sports writers can afford to forgo the objective-style convention of quotes by advocating the common sense of the fans' position.[20] Newspaper sports reporters frequently address fans in a dialogic manner, using first and second person pronouns to create the sense that the reporter and fans are "in this thing together." Thus, the fan narratives used in this study represent a broader approach based on interpretation of the entire text rather than on a single feature of the text, such as sound bites or quotes.

The union-owner conflict narrative, which documented the business aspects and transactions involving the labor dispute, was the most frequent story type of the strike coverage. But the fan narrative became the most powerful story type of the strike coverage, in that it provided the "objective" or "neutral" perspective for the news media. "Eyewitness" reporters maintained their position as detached, fair observers by cloaking their evaluations of the strike in the fans' quotes and sound bites. Or, in the case of many sports reporters, the news media maintained a sense of journalistic fairness by acting as "surrogate fans" for the audience and defending the position of the "little guy," the baseball consumer.

As I'll explain below, news coverage did include other stories that addressed the news audience as people with a legal, economic, and social investment in the strike. But, these other stories, such as discussion of the MLB's antitrust exemption, the public economic impact of the strike, the many proactive fan organizations striving for real changes in MLB, and the significance of the strike to the labor movement in the United States, were given minimal time and space. Instead, mainstream news coverage of the strike was oriented to the consumer interests of baseball fans. This fan narrative evolved through four phases and lasted the duration of the strike coverage period.

Hailing the Baseball Fan

The consumer-oriented coverage of the MLB baseball strike came in four general phases during the coverage period from July 1994 to May 6, 1995. The phases reflect journalists' continuing adjustments of their consumer orientation as the issues and events of the baseball strike changed:

- Phase I: Baseball millionaires and billionaires forsake their fans
- Phase II: Baseball alternatives for the forsaken fans
- Phase III: Replacement players as a faulty consumer product
- Phase IV: The forsaken fans get their well-deserved revenge

The myths and consequences of news media stories in each frame are discussed below.

Phase I: Baseball Millionaires and Billionaires Forsake Their Fans

As the first reports of an impending strike began to filter into the national news stream in July 1994, the "millionaires vs. billionaires" story frame suggested that Major League Baseball's troubles could be solved only by the powerful insiders of the players union and the MLB owners. The strike might have been ignored by the news media, as many labor conflicts are. But, the U.S. news media, built on an ethos of consumption, were drawn to the specter of millions of threatened baseball consumers. Of course, the press rarely positioned baseball fans as citizens with any role in resolving baseball's chronic labor-management conflicts. Instead, the news media portrayed the fans as powerless, increasingly cynical, and forsaken by baseball's millionaire players and billionaire owners. Bryan Burwell of *USA Today* plainly forecast the news media's position in an August 2, 1994, column: The press would cover the "predictable chain reaction of hostility from outraged baseball fans," but, ultimately, "the fans do not matter in the resolution of this labor dispute, nor should they."[21]

The television network news reports on August 11, 1994—the last day of baseball before the strike—all told the story of the forsaken fan. Portions of the three (ABC, CBS, and NBC) network packages were remarkably similar: Each used two fan sound bites and included the image and

unquestioned logic of a little boy to dramatize the harm inflicted by striking players. Armen Keteyian's report for ABC:

KETEYIAN: As for baseball fans, they offered little sympathy for millionaire
players or millionaire owners.

BOY: I've heard that they make more than the president and, well, because
I play baseball and it's sort of an easy sport.

WOMAN: I don't think anybody's thinking about the fans. I don't think
management is, and I don't think the players are.

Bob Orr's report for CBS:

ORR: In a game that is increasingly about money, baseball is again about to
strike out.

BOY: I think it stinks. I mean, they're already making enough money.

MAN: I think the whole thing's about an obscene pursuit of wealth.

Sara James's report for NBC:

JAMES: For nine-year-old Yankees fan Dan Hopper, this was a bad day for
baseball.

BOY (Hopper): Now they're going to blow it. This is their big chance. I
don't know why they're going to strike.

JAMES: Neither does Yankees fan Larry Eizar.

MAN (Eizar): They have no respect for the fans whatsoever.

USA Today's coverage during this phase largely mimicked the networks. A
front-page story announcing the August 12 strike date featured another
angry fan:

Fans are just frustrated:

"It's the most ridiculous thing I've ever heard," says Wendy Hoffman, 37,
a business professor from Versailles, Ky.

"The players are already overcompensated, to ask for more money simply
shows greed," she says.[22]

A week before the strike was set to begin, New York Times columnist
George Vecsey told disenfranchised fans that "There is hope. We must
keep saying that."[23] But Vecsey's suggestion provided little relief for fans'
cynicism. Instead of offering fans a way to create a hopeful situation, Vecsey merely stated that if feuding U.S. ice-skating pairs champions Calla

August 11, 1994, *NBC Nightly News*. Reporter Sara James interviews a nine-year-old Yankee fan.

Urbanski and Rocky Marvel could form a truce so could owners' negotiator Dick Ravitch and union president Donald Fehr.

One of the most common myths emerging in Phase I was that overpriced players are ruining the game. As the above examples illustrate, fans alleged that all MLB players are millionaires, all players make more than the president, the players are overcompensated, and the players are asking for more money. Unfortunately, these allegations went unchecked. Many stories reminded the audience that MLB players earn an average of about $1.2 million a year, a point often made by owners' negotiator Dick Ravitch. Although $1.2 million is indeed the average salary, it is also just one way to statistically represent the salaries of MLB players. If we look at the salaries of the 746 MLB players on opening day in 1994, we find that most players (484) make less than a million. In fact, the median salary, the point at which half of the players earn more and half of the players earn less, was $410,000 that year—not exactly peanuts, but far from millions.[24] The statistical mean boosts the "average" player's salary into the millions because superstars pull up the average of those players at the bottom of the pay scale (all of whom earned the $109,000 annual minimum salary, which was less than the U.S. president's base salary of $200,000 a year in 1994)

For the record, the dramatic "millionaires vs. billionaires" frame didn't apply to most baseball owners either. Although baseball's twenty-eight owners in 1995 included billionaires Ted Turner (Atlanta Braves) and Hiroshi Yamauchi (Seattle Mariners) and large corporations such as the Tribune Co. (Chicago Cubs) and Anheuser-Busch (St. Louis Cardinals), "multimillionaire" best describes the majority of owners.[25] Although "millionaires vs. billionaires" was arguably used metaphorically and not as an accurate account of the financial status of all owners and players, the strength of this metaphor had the effect of obscuring the relevant financial details that affected the labor dispute.

Another significant yet often neglected point of the news coverage was that the players' union was not striking for more money but instead to try to prevent the owners from unilaterally imposing a salary cap during the off-season. The players union embraced a free market approach to salaries. For those players eligible for free agency, salary is limited only by what individual baseball owners are willing to pay. Thus, players' compensation is based on what the market will sustain. The proposed salary cap would take players out of a competitive bidding process through owner collusion to limit team payrolls. Players' salaries would then be limited, but—as usual—there would be no limit on the owners' potential for profits.

An offshoot of the overpaid player story is the overpriced ticket story. Although overpaid baseball players have been blamed for exorbitant ticket prices, baseball admission costs (adjusting for inflation) were actually 9 percent lower in 1990 than in 1950.[26] After the strike had ended, *USA Today* announced to fans that at least the strike had kept ticket prices "under control."[27] But the article played into the same inflationary ticket price myth and missed the point evident in the article: Baseball ticket prices in 1994 were the best bargain of all major professional team sports.

Sports economists James Quirk and Rodney D. Fort explain that player salaries have nothing to do with rising ticket prices. Instead, in the profit-oriented world of professional sports, ticket prices depend on fan demand. Thus, high public demand to attend games creates the conditions for high ticket prices. The period after the advent of free agency in 1976 illustrates baseball's pricing economics, Quirk and Fort note. Even after the trend of rising player salaries in the late 1970s, ticket prices didn't correspondingly increase, and in most cases actually fell. The quality of most teams didn't change markedly with free agency—the same players were just paid more—so there was no rise in fan demand to necessitate substantial increases in ticket prices. In some cases though, such as the New York Yankees, free agency enabled the owner to assemble a more attractive team, which increases demand and, then, ticket prices. Increased demand (in both paid attendance and television contract revenues) in turn increases revenue and the value of skilled players who attract fans.[28]

The fundamental debate between owners and players for the past few decades—indeed, since the beginning of professional baseball in 1869—has been dividing up the revenues. Should baseball's players or owners be rewarded with most of the game's revenues? After decades of severe pay restriction, free agency (begun in 1976) has allowed players to gain an increasing cut of baseball's profits. The owners' efforts to reverse this trend resulted in the labor conflict of 1994–95.

The news media's focus on players' salaries during the strike reached a level close to obsession. First, fans devalued the labor of the players. Like the little boy of ABC's August 11 report ("I play baseball and it's sort of an easy sport."), fans suggested that they could do what MLB players do, and for a lot less. In the center field bleachers of Yankee Stadium, the *New York Times* found thirteen-year-old Carmelo Vazquez, who remarked during the last game before the strike, "If I was a player, I'd be here tomorrow to play, not strike. I mean, I play baseball for nothing, for the game."[29] This fan envy/idolatry is the same phenomenon that causes the "vastly overinflated assessments" that high school and college athletes make about their chances of becoming professional athletes.[30]

Second, the news media continually tracked, evaluated, and publicized players' pay. From the first few days of the strike to the official cancellation of the season on September 14, *USA Today* ran a daily statistical feature charting the monetary losses for the owners and the players. The feature also noted the daily losses for a specific player, Bobby Bonilla of the New York Mets, MLB's highest paid player at $6.3 million for 1994.[31] *USA Today*, which had a history of publicizing an annual list of "underpaid" and "overpaid" players,[32] juxtaposed Bonilla's daily losses with the daily losses of players earning MLB's minimum annual salary of $109,000, as if to highlight the unreasonable amount Bonilla earns. CBS anchor Dan Rather, a high-priced media star in his own right, joined in on the money fascination on August 12: "Among the ballplayers, the biggest single loser in dollar terms is Bobby Bonilla of the New York Mets. Everyday the players are out, he's out thirty-one thousand dollars."

The most inane salary statistical minutiae were calculations of the costs of a player's performance as a percentage of his annual salary (e.g., the cost of each home run). *Time* magazine subjected six major league stars to such questionable figuring.[33] The magazine noted it was making an "admittedly whimsical evaluation of a few players," and then proceeded to analyze each player's salary in terms of his hits, runs, runs batted in [RBIs], home runs, stolen bases, and walks. The numbers were provocative (Did you know Andy Van Slyke's home runs were worth $88,750, whereas Frank Thomas' homers were worth $9,868?) and meaningless. In the content analyzed for this study, none of the three network news outlets or two national newspapers publicized the individual losses of a single owner or reduced an owners' performance to absurd quantifications.

Ironically, with all of the focus on players' salaries and the implications that salaries are inflationary, the greatest ticket inflation in baseball was at two locations that have been heralded as baseball's most promising and fan-friendly venues. At Baltimore, where the Orioles played in the new, critically acclaimed Camden Yards ballpark, the average ticket price rose 17.7 percent in 1995, from $11.17 to $13.14. In Denver, where the Colorado Rockies opened their first season at Coors Field in 1995, the average ticket price rose 34.2 percent in one year, from $7.90 to $10.61.[34] The rising ticket prices at both ballparks did little to deter fans. Through June 14 of the 1995 season, Baltimore led the American League and Colorado led the National League in average attendance.[35]

A frequent criticism leveled at baseball during Phase I was that baseball is a game, not a business. For example, in his August 11, 1994, report for CBS, Bob Orr charged that baseball is "a game increasingly about money." Orr might have done well to read about major league pitcher John Montgomery Ward who argued much the same thing in 1886: "What was formerly a pastime has now become a business, capital is invested from business motives, and the officers and stockholders of the different (major league) clubs include men of social standing and established business capacity."[36]

It's no wonder Orr's journalistic scoop is more than one hundred years late. Apparently, talking about baseball as a business with poor labor relations is a painful, unnatural process, especially when trying to explain it to children. On the second day of the strike (August 13, 1994), NBC anchor Brian Williams began: "Here it is, a Saturday in August, and not a single big league baseball game is to be found at the park or on the tube anywhere in the country. While it's supposed to be a game, how do you tell a ten-year-old that his or her hero in a baseball cap is on strike over a salary cap?"

The NBC report never does tell us how to explain this to a ten-year-old, but one could have started by mentioning that MLB was an approximately $2 billion-a-year industry at that time.[37] Furthermore, the history of MLB is one of profit-oriented decisions. The American League and the National League were merged into Major League Baseball in 1903 mainly to eliminate competition between the two leagues and create a baseball monopoly that could control the fortunes of any athletes who sought to play professionally. Other significant events in MLB, such as the uprooting of the Brooklyn Dodgers to Los Angeles in 1958 (and the nine other team moves from the 1950s through 2003) were not based on the best interest of the game—new franchises could have served new population centers—but in the best interest of an owner.

This "game" also involves a great deal of public financing and subsidies, as noted earlier. Chicago and the state of Illinois, for example, invested hundreds of millions of dollars in a new stadium to keep the White Sox from moving to a publicly built ballpark in St. Petersburg, Florida. The new Comisky Park called for at least $150 million to be financed by revenue bonds and a 2 percent hotel tax. The city of Chicago also had to compensate displaced neighborhood residents, and the city and the state agreed to cover up to $10 million a year in stadium operating losses. Finally, from 1991 to 2001, the state-created Illinois Sports Facilities Authority was required to pay the White Sox a $2 million maintenance subsidy and buy up to 300,000 tickets a year from the Sox if attendance in the second decade of operations fell below projections.[38] Major League Baseball has historically limited the number of its baseball franchises, which has created the condition where cities compete against each other to gain (or keep) either existing or the occasional new baseball franchises. As in the Chicago situation, the threat of a baseball franchise moving out of a public stadium amounts to public extortion. Quirk and Fort explain:

> A team can argue, persuasively, that the city should be willing to provide subsidized rental terms because of the income and jobs that the team generates for other businesses—hotels, restaurants, bars, downtown shops—by out-of-towners who are drawn into the city to see major league sports. This provides the political justification for rental contracts that often allocate as much of the costs of operating the stadium as possible to the city, and as much of the revenues from stadium operations as possible to the team.[39]

While "jobs" and "economic impact" are the political buzzwords in the news media during a campaign to keep or attract a baseball franchise, these topics were largely missing from news media coverage of the baseball strike. Only 13 of 106 (12 percent) of network television news packages covered the "public economic impact" angle of the strike. National newspapers did an even poorer job. Only 1 of the 65 sampled *New York Times* articles and 3 of 92 sampled *USA Today* articles covered the public economic impact of the baseball strike. The effect of the meager coverage of public economic issues is that the public's contribution and investment in the quasi-public business of baseball is excluded from the debate.

As a $2 billion industry that solicits cities to engage in bidding wars, MLB is certainly more like U.S. big business than a game. Perhaps the only way to accurately designate MLB as "just a game" is to refer back to a 1922 Supreme Court decision written by Justice Oliver Wendell Holmes. In a unanimous ruling that still stands today, Holmes decreed that the organization of Major League Baseball is involved primarily in "exhibitions of baseball" and not commerce.[40] This decision, which effectively exempted MLB from antitrust laws and allowed it to operate as a monopoly (an advantage that no other professional sport has), was surprisingly absent in the news rhetoric of baseball as a game not a business. In fact, of the 106 television network news packages, only 5 (about 5 percent) discussed the antitrust exemption, and only in regard to U.S. House hearings, a lawsuit against MLB, and a National Labor Relations Board decision. Newspapers provided only a slightly higher rate of coverage of the antitrust issue. The *New York Times* covered the antitrust exemption 6 times out of 65 stories sampled (9 percent), whereas *USA Today* discussed the antitrust frame in 8 of the 92 stories sampled (9 percent). The 1922 Supreme Court decision was even conspicuously missing from a *Newsweek* timeline feature that purported to list all of the important events in baseball's labor-management relations from 1869 to 1992.[41]

The Court's interpretations of the Constitution's commerce clause have since contradicted the logic of the ruling (see, *Federal Baseball Club of Baltimore v. National League of Professional Baseball Clubs*, 259 US 200 [1922]). Yet the antitrust exemption for MLB remained in place leading up to the 1994–95 strike despite several challenges. The Supreme Court, while noting the odd nature of baseball's exemption, has refused to overturn the 1922 decision. Responding to a 1971 challenge, Justice Harry Blackmun wrote "If there is any inconsistency and illogic in all of this, it is an inconsistency and illogic of long-standing that is to be remedied by the Congress and not by this Court."[42]

The antitrust exemption has aided MLB owners in controlling all professional baseball in the United States by preventing players from moving to any start-up baseball leagues. With all big-league competition eliminated, MLB essentially operates as a successful cartel. The well-managed scarcity of professional baseball has also served to make owning a base-ball franchise—even one that appears to be losing money—a reliable and lucrative investment. The value of franchises was often lost in the debate over the annual profitability of MLB clubs. Baseball economists Quirk and Fort note that the average rate of increase in franchise prices has been 7.5 percent, meaning that franchise values have doubled every nine years over the past ninety years.[43] The rate of increase has been even more rapid recently, with the New York Mets and Texas Rangers doubling in price in about three years in the 1980s.

Finally, stories about the fate of the baseball player autograph potently illustrate the change that the game of baseball is becoming a business. Such stories allege that baseball players are greedy, selfish individuals who refuse to sign autographs for children, or—worse yet—charge money for autographs.[44] Although this is true in some cases, it is worth noting (because the news media did not) that fans themselves have had a complicit role in transforming autograph-hunting from a hobby to a busi-ness. In the past few decades, baseball collectibles moved from shoe boxes and closets to trade shows, retail outlets, and online auction sites like eBay as fans began treating childhood baseball memorabilia as "investment-quality" merchandise. The gentle childhood pastime of collecting baseball cards became an enormous consumer industry worth $1.3 billion by 1991.[45]

Moreover, an increasingly popular fan pastime, "rotisserie" or "fan-tasy" baseball, encourages fans to assume the role of owner and "buy" an assortment of MLB players in a league of other fantasy owners. The team owner whose players generate the best composite season statistics totals (based on the real players' own statistics) wins the season, often with a cash award. Fantasy baseball began in 1980 at the former Manhattan restaurant La Rotisserie, where a group of friends in the publishing busi-ness invented the game and original leagues.[46] By 1995, an estimated two million people played fantasy baseball, and it grew even more popular and accessible with Internet-based leagues sponsored by ESPN, CBS, FOX, *The Sporting News*, Yahoo!, and other World Wide Web sports sites.[47] Fantasy leagues have formed around other team sports in the United States and Europe, creating a new class of international armchair sports owners.

Phase II: Baseball Alternatives for the Forsaken Fans

When the strike began on August 12, 1994, news media adjusted their consumer-oriented coverage by quickly suggesting alternatives for the presumably needy fans. Minor league baseball was the most commonly suggested alternative. Minor league players were portrayed as just a small step from the major leaguers in quality but "hungrier" than the spoiled, overpaid majors. In the minor leagues, tickets are cheap and the game is still a game, we were told. On August 13, the second day of the strike, ABC became the first network to broadcast a package devoted to minor league baseball. Anchor John Martin set up the report with an introduction that typified all other network treatments of MLB substitutes. "The parks may be smaller, the salaries nothing to brag about, and the players are hardly household names, but all across the country, baseball's romance and excitement are still evident." ABC reporter Mike von Fremd then framed minor league attendance as a wise consumer move and as an appropriate rebellious political statement for fans: "The perfect pitch, to soothe big-league withdrawal. The minor league parks are where it's all happening this weekend. These wonderful old stadiums are hosting sell-out crowds as fans come to both enjoy a game and thumb their noses at the no-show big-leaguers."

Von Fremd's report from Durham, North Carolina, peddled a nostalgic consumerism. The rhetoric implied that here, in Smalltown USA, one can buy a ticket to an earlier time, before commercialism and labor disputes contaminated the game of baseball. Of course, baseball's long history is rife with commercialism and labor disputes,[48] so the report's best evidence was a *Bull Durham* film clip, which added Hollywood's seal of approval to the nostalgia trip. Von Fremd's lead-in to a sound bite from John Simmons, a Durham Bulls pitcher, romanticizes the poor labor conditions of minor league baseball:

VON FREMD: The game may be the same, but the park has a different feel. These players aren't thinking about salaries or commercial endorsements. Right now, they're just trying to prove that they've got the right stuff.

SIMMONS: We're actually making under the poverty level, but, uh, everybody's here because we love the game and because that one-in-a million chance to make it to the big leagues.

Ironically, for all of the attractiveness of minor leaguers, von Fremd's next comment acknowledges that a great pleasure for the fan is hoping the minor leaguers make it to the big leagues: "You never know, maybe one of these guys will be tomorrow's superstar." Of course, the chance to be a superstar, the chance to get a higher (or even a reasonable) salary, and the opportunity for commercial endorsements is why most minor leaguers tolerate the minor leagues' system of poor wages. Nevertheless, nostalgic consumerism wins the day, valorizing the poverty-level wages of minor leaguers and stigmatizing major-leaguers. In the story's final scene, the Durham Bulls' catcher is shown signing autographs for children, and von Fremd approvingly concludes "minor league ego with some major league class."

If minor league baseball is an attractive nostalgic substitute, it could only be surpassed by Little League baseball, where the players play for free. NBC anchor Brian Williams introduces another network news rediscovery of "authentic" baseball in an August 25, 1994, report: "With the big leagues out of action, millions of people are discovering what everyone who ever played Little League always knew—that it's awfully close to the way the game should be played." Robert Hager filed the report from the Little League World Series games in Williamsport, Pennsylvania, "where baseball is still alive and well." At the package's most boosterish moment, Hager appeared in a stand-up shot, wearing a souvenir T-shirt that identifies him as a Little League advocate: "It's no surprise that one of the hottest souvenirs here is this T-shirt, which says this is the World Series where [Hager reads the words on his shirt front] 'players rarely STRIKE-OUT and NEVER STRIKE!' And no surprise that the big sentiment here is [Hager turns his back to the camera to reveal the words on the shirt's reverse side] no to the strike (depicted by an image of a baseball with a slash through it) and yes to the cry of PLAY BALL."

As in the minor league stories, the lack of commercialism in Little League is cherished, but, as reported, the celebration of popularity and making it to the "big time" is part of the pleasure. Hager cited the markers of Little League World Series success. The "records" include motels booked solid within a fifty-mile radius, 240 credentialed press members ("more than ever"), nine games broadcast on national television (ESPN), and more than 140,000 people in combined attendance for the first fourteen games. NBC's follow-up story on August 29, 1994, reported the lavish welcome home the Northridge, California, Little League Champions received: a Disneyland parade and rides in limousines stocked with pizza and mobile TV. Reporter Larry Carroll remarked "That is how it should be. They are, after all, the heroes of baseball."

The search for low-cost baseball options led from the nostalgic to the ludicrous. CBS anchor Dana King's introduction to a package on August 27, 1994, seemed to be missing a thread of logic: "As the baseball strike drags on, chances of a World Series this fall are looking more remote everyday. All the more reason to catch the action now in Moscow." In the Russian capital, reporter Jonathan Sanders stated that "fans in need of a fix are having to go far afield to watch the boys of summer." The trend of Americans filling up the ballpark hosting the Russian World Series apparently consisted of the one guy from Youngstown, Ohio, who was quoted. (The fan said "since they're on strike in America, I just decided to come out and catch a game.") Nevertheless, the central narrative remained the same. Sanders observed, "around here playing in the big leagues doesn't mean big bucks." The salary for the Russian players is about $150 a month, according to the report, and the players may not have American finesse, but they play with passion.

The Russian players threatened the nostalgic narrative of the story by supporting the striking U.S. major leaguers. "They should strike. No salary cap," a Russian player said. But, reporter Sanders recovered by dismissing the Russians' positions as a small slip on their way to Americanization. According to Sanders, "These former Communists still believe the baseball workers of the world must unite." Sanders' comment, of course, implicated the American players union's resistance to a salary cap as the kind of work that gains Communist sympathizers.

In all of the network television news reports on alternatives to MLB, the anchors and reporters positioned themselves as bringing relief to the disappointed or even addicted baseball consumer. NBC's Jane Pauley began her network's tale of the minor leagues on August 17 by promising that "all is not lost" for the baseball fan, while CBS's Connie Chung consoled viewers with the news that "Major League Baseball is not the only game in town" on August 19.

These news reports also failed to acknowledge their own role in creating "trends" in the minor leagues, Little League, and Russian baseball. In a report on minor league baseball, David Culhane of CBS (August 14, 1994) argued that "the game is coming back to its roots in small town America." But Culhane's discovery was not unlike Columbus' "discovering" the New World, much to the surprise of the indigenous Americans who never knew they were lost. The only thing coming back to small town America in Culhane's report was a CBS camera crew. On August 19, CBS's Bob McNamara noted that "suddenly it's a season of promise" in the minors. But again, the sudden seasonal change was the focus of CBS' strike coverage.

In the strike's coverage by ABC, CBS, and NBC, 12 of the 106 stories (11 percent) dealt with MLB alternatives. But, use of this story was concentrated early in the strike period, with all 12 MLB substitute narratives appearing between August 13, 1994 (the second day of the strike) and September 8, 1994, accounting for more than half of the 22 news packages during that period. Newspaper coverage of MLB substitute narratives was concentrated in a similar manner.

In addition to minor league and Little League baseball, the news media suggested a number of other MLB substitutes, including college and professional football[49]; hockey (until NHL suffered its own labor conflict); Ken Burns's *Baseball* documentary on PBS (the first installment of the 18.5-hour series premiered September 18, 1994)[50]; nostalgic articles about old baseball games (*USA Today* ran stories on great World Series games of the past in late October when they had planned to be reporting on the 1994 Series); nostalgic reports about the baseball's Negro League, inspired in part by Burns's documentary; the Men's Senior Baseball League World Series[51]; old movies to fill up empty slots on Ted Turner's TNT cable channel, which usually carries Braves games; computer-projected baseball (the Cincinnati Reds won this imaginary World Series)[52]; playing baseball; polo, which the *New York Times* argued was a more pure game than baseball because its rich sportsmen didn't need to think about money[53]; and even weasel races—CNN's anchor on September 28, 1994, said "baseball fans looking for diversion, take note!"

The news media's response to the forsaken fan illustrated what the mainstream commercial media do best: sell products. Major League Baseball was damaged goods, so the news media offered products X, Y, and Z. The selling angle was they're all cheaper, and they'll make you feel good, too. Unfortunately, this news strategy of "letting the marketplace settle the issue" defused public action. Fans' feelings of powerlessness were left to be resolved only through consumer choice. The American public gets this same kind of response from the news media in regard to complaints about television content. We are told "if you don't like the television show you're watching, change the channel or turn it off." The problem with this "marketplace" journalistic response is that it never leads to citizens taking an active role in changing—and improving—anything.

Instead of being a period for substitutes, the first few weeks of the strike could instead have been a period for action. A rarely publicized fact of the strike was that the Major League Baseball Players Association would have called off the strike if Congress passed a bill repealing or limiting baseball's antitrust exemption. The exemption permits MLB's owners to impose a new labor contract if they determine collective bargaining has reached an impasse. The likelihood of owners enforcing new labor conditions after the 1994 season led the players association to call the strike in August, when they still had some leverage. Without the antitrust exemption, players could take owners to court to challenge an imposed salary cap as a restraint of trade brought on by owner collusion.[54]

Thus, one course of action for baseball fans early in the strike could have been to lobby their legislators to pass such a bill. What the news audience needed, as editor and public journalism advocate Davis Merritt Jr. explains, was "mechanisms for citizens to engage in the debate beyond mere venting about it."[55] One of the most relevant mechanisms is providing mobilizing information (MI) in news stories so that people can begin to participate in civic life. James Lemert, a journalism professor at the University of Oregon, notes that the news media generally withhold MI in news of politics and controversy, while often providing it for "safe" stories.[56] For example, news organizations rarely hesitate to provide addresses or telephone numbers for charitable organizations that want to rebuild hurricane-damaged houses or supply Christmas gifts to poor children. But, in stories about politics or civic discussion where there might be "two sides" to the story, journalists often feel that they would be partisan (not "objective") by providing MI. As Lemert notes, the information itself is not partisan; it just depends what people do with it. We might want to consider, though, that withholding MI is a bias, too.

In addition to legislators, organizations such as Sports Fans United (SFU) provided another possible avenue for civic action during the baseball strike, but most people probably never heard of them. SFU, the most prominent fan organization, was established in 1992 in New York City as a lobbying force for fans interested in real change in professional sports.

SFU had been constantly fighting for the removal of MLB's antitrust exemption, but was given only cursory coverage during the 1994–95 strike. During the entire strike coverage period, only 5 of the 106 television news packages (5 percent) covered proactive fan organizations, and none of the reports provided MI (unless one counts the unintentional appearance of a banner revealing part of SFU's toll-free telephone number in an August 18, 1994, CBS package).

Newspaper coverage of proactive fan organizations was even worse. The *New York Times* only had 1 such article in the 65 sampled (1 percent), and *USA Today* had only 3 such articles of the 92 sampled (3 percent). The only story with MI was a small, six-paragraph *USA Today* story about the national petition drive combining the efforts of SFU and the Consumer Federation of America (CFA), the country's largest consumer advocacy group. The final paragraph of the *USA Today* article provided the drive's 1-800-41-FANS telephone number and its Internet mailbox. But *USA Today* also supplied harsh disincentives for fans to act. A February 10, 1995, article headline warned "Send Baseball to Washington; You'll Never See It Again." Writer Joe Urschel squelched public action with absurd anti-Clinton rhetoric and scare tactics: "[Clinton] might, for instance, just decide to lend the small-market teams, say, $40 billion of your tax money."[57]

While the announcement of the joint SFU-CFA petition drive on August 17, 1994, could have been considered a landmark event, ABC, CBS, NBC, and the *New York Times* failed to cover it. Instead of mobilizing us as citizens, mainstream national news outlets mobilized us as consumers by offering us baseball product substitutes. The news media's consumer orientation provided the American public only the most patronizing attention and excluded them from any worthwhile public discourse on the MLB crisis. In short, the national news media struck out in their efforts to involve their audience in the future of Major League Baseball, leaving baseball fans ever more cynical and even encouraging such cynicism.

Phase III: Replacement Players as a Faulty Consumer Product

As the owners began to organize and field replacement (scab) teams in February and March of 1995, a third wave of heavy news coverage emerged. Some coverage of replacement players adopted the nostalgic tone that characterized reports on the minor leagues. A March 31, 1995,

CBS package by Roger O'Neil, for example, included a fan sound bite that said "replacement players . . . go out and play for heart." But the majority of mainstream news media coverage portrayed replacement players as faulty consumer products for the discriminating baseball fan, creating what NBC's Tom Brokaw (February 17, 1995) called a "pseudo-season" for baseball. Newspaper pictures and network news video emphasized that these players were bumbling amateurs or over-the-hill, out-of-shape former pros. Images included fat, slow players and grossly inaccurate ball handling. Even some people on baseball's management side were openly critical. Detroit Tiger manager Sparky Anderson, the most senior of MLB's managers, took an unpaid leave of absence rather than coach replacements. Baltimore Orioles owner Peter Angelos, a former union lawyer, refused to field replacement players, which would have ruined shortstop Cal Ripken Jr.'s chance to break Lou Gehrig's record for consecutive games played.

ABC News sports reporter Dick Schaap did not hesitate to take up the fans' position in his assessment of scab baseball in a February 18, 1995 report: "It looks like baseball, it sounds like baseball, it even feels like baseball. But no matter how they dress it up, no matter what they call it, it isn't big league baseball." The *New York Times* argued "scabs are the ultimate owner scam,"[58] while the usually optimistic *USA Today* predicted "woeful quality of play."[59] A March 2, 1995, CBS package carried the sharpest denunciation of replacement ball. Anchor Dan Rather kicked off a report that contained no hint of nostalgia:

RATHER: On this 203rd night of the baseball strike, something advertised as quote Major League Baseball is being played once again. Whatever it is, it isn't major league. The regular players have been replaced by a collection of has-beens, never-weres, and wanna-bes, what the union calls scabs.

CBS reporter Wyatt Andrews continued the disapproving tone:

ANDREWS: The owners say replacement baseball is being put on for the fans. [VIDEO: an overweight player running to first base.] But Phillies owner Bill Giles admits the owners are also trying to pressure players to cross the picket line.

GILES: I do feel that there will be a point in time if we do play with replacement players that a lot of regular guys will come back.

ANDREWS: But so far, this is who is coming back. [VIDEO: Reds' owner Marge Schott reaches up to put a baseball cap on an overweight former

player.] Cincinnati this week signed Pedro Borbon, a forty-eight-year-old
pitcher who's missed more than fifteen seasons and very few meals.

On NBC (March 5, 1995), reporter Gary Matsumoto surveyed the spring
exhibition season and outlined the potential consumer disaster for baseball fans in 1995:

MATSUMOTO: So on opening day next month, baseball fans can now expect to be treated to more of what they've endured during the exhibition
season: error-riddled baseball, played by major league wanna-bes. At
many games this weekend, there were fewer than a thousand people in the
stands.

MAN IN STANDS: We're suffering here. We're the fans. We're suffering.

As noted earlier, one of the pleasures of watching minor league baseball—and perhaps even the Little League World Series—is the hope of
witnessing a rising superstar. Replacement baseball, as the Phase III reports argue, does not offer such pleasure, and it is thus condemned as a
faulty consumer product.

Interestingly, the rare public admission by an owner (Philadelphia
Phillies president Bill Giles) that the owners were trying to break the players union by using replacements, wasn't criticized as a despicable management strategy. Instead, the despicable act of the 1995 exhibition baseball season, as defined by the narrative of the Phase III reports, was the
fielding of substandard teams. Thus, the news media again addressed the
fans in terms of their consumer desires. Civic issues such as standards of
fairness in labor-management disputes were missing in the baseball strike
coverage.[60]

Phase IV: The Forsaken Fans Get Their Well-Deserved Revenge

In March 1995, the National Labor Relations Board (NLRB) charged
baseball's owners with unfair labor practices, ruling that they had imposed new work rules without collectively bargaining in good faith with
the players union. On March 31, 1995, U.S. District Court Judge Sonia So-
tomayer agreed with the NLRB's charges and issued an injunction that
forced MLB's owners to return to the provisions of the expired contract
with the players. With the court injunction, the players union ended the
strike, and MLB was back and just a few weeks off schedule. But, the
fans—at least the fans presented in the mainstream news media—didn't
seem satisfied. The "forsaken fan" narrative of the summer and fall of

March 2, 1995, *CBS Evening News*. Replacement players get one of their sharpest denunciations. Reporter Wyatt Andrews notes the Cincinnati Reds signing of Pedro Borbon, "a 48-year-old pitcher who's missed more than 15 seasons and very few meals."

1994 had planted the seeds for fan revenge at the return of MLB in the spring of 1995.

Revenge came not in a drive to change MLB in a substantial way, but again through media-approved consumer behavior: a consumer boycott, or demands for special consumer attention. Odetta Rogers-Clarke of NBC (April 2, 1995) established the angry fan narrative of MLB's return:

ROGERS-CLARKE: For many fans, the seven-and-a-half month strike has tarnished the image of the game.

MAN #1 IN PARK: The owners and the players basically turned their backs on the fans. You know, I will never forgive them for it.

MAN #2 IN PARK: There's nothing to it anymore. Now it's just gonna be dollars. They should just get paid by the catch now.

ROGERS-CLARKE: Winning back fan loyalty could be the toughest match yet for players and owners.

On the same day (April 2, 1995), Diane Olick of CBS publicized the mobilizing information for active fan revenge.

OLICK: Some say that even though they'll be glad to see their heroes back, perhaps a punishment is in order: a fan strike for the first week of real season play.

ED BUNKER (PRES., FAN OUT AMERICA): I want to see a one-week boycott of baseball to send a very clear message to the owners and players that fans are part of this as well.

It was not clear whether an organized, national fan boycott ever occurred, but many baseball fans were staying away from ballparks. Through June 14, 1995, average MLB attendance was down 26 percent from the previous season's average.[61]

Several stories identified the lack of a long-term agreement between the owners and players as the cause of the fans' hesitant state. An April 26 package by Peter Van Sant of CBS cited baseball's unresolved labor dispute as a central reason for many fans' reluctance to return. Yet, the solutions suggested by the story did nothing to address MLB's fundamental labor-management instability. Instead, the package promoted fan perquisites as the way to win back baseball consumers:

VAN SANT: The return of the boys of summer used to be a kind of national holiday, an escape from our problems. But not this year. With no contract between the players and owners, there's no guarantee that the season, even the World Series, will be fully played out.

Baseball is trying to win back its fans by offering special promotions and getting players to mingle with the fans. [VIDEO: Yankees player Wade Boggs signs autographs.] There's even a new TV ad campaign. [VIDEO: Clip from one of MLB's "Welcome to the show" commercials.] But, seven teams are raising ticket prices this year.

MAN IN STANDS: If they really want fan appreciation, all I'm gonna say is drop ticket prices.

Van Sant's New York Yankee–centric report (many other strike reports were centered around the Yankee fan experience) neglected to mention that twenty-one of MLB's twenty-eight clubs didn't raise prices for the 1995 season, and several clubs lowered prices. In fact, across town at the New York Mets' Shea Stadium, ticket prices remained at 1994 levels and were four dollars cheaper than a Yankees ticket.

The consumer ethos of reports like Van Sant's suggests that the best way to handle labor-management conflict is not to fix the essential problem but to assuage the consumers who are inconvenienced by it. By April 1995, the coverage of baseball's attendance problem had created a consumer sphere devoid of rational talk to resolve the long-standing labor problems of an American institution. Instead, the news media talked about appeasing the fans, and the fans began to expect it. Were there any other apparent options for baseball fans? *USA Today* published a poll that outlined the consumer-oriented agenda:

> According to the ESPN/Chilton Sports Poll, of the 82% of the USA population who follow sports, 61% say they want baseball to make the extra effort to welcome them back this season. The top five requests:
>
> 1. Ticket discounts
> 2. More promotional giveaways
> 3. Concession discounts
> 4. Welcome-back ads
> 5. More fan/player interaction[62]

Of course, missing from fan requests was a fair, long-term collective bargaining agreement that would prevent future baseball strikes.

Opening day at Detroit's Tiger Stadium on May 3, 1995, illustrated that fan-friendly strategies such as giveaways, discounts, and welcome-back messages are only cosmetic solutions to fans whose cynicism had been fueled by the news media's venting model of public discourse. The attendance was the lowest for a Tigers' home opener in more than twenty years. Even worse, though, was the large number of surly people in the stands. Fans pelted the field and players with beach balls, bottles, cigarette lighters, batteries, and thousands of souvenir Tiger schedules. More than twenty people jumped the fence and ran around the field. The projectiles and interruptions nearly resulted in the Tigers forfeiting the game. *Detroit Free Press* sportswriter Mitch Albom asked: "So what does this mean? Have we, as American sports fans, finally summoned the strength we were always told we had? Will we rise like the proletariat in the French Revolution, tossing off the yoke of oppression, fighting for our rights, demanding . . . demanding . . . What are we demanding?"[63] What could the fans demand? Excluded from any rational public discourse on the future of baseball, they were just venting, getting the revenge of the forsaken fan.

Jason Whitlock, a sports columnist for the *Kansas City Star*, demonstrated both the promise of the press's mobilizing power and the limited effectiveness of mobilizing people as mere consumers. Whitlock engaged readers in an April 6, 1995, column calling for a boycott of the Kansas City Royals' April 26 opening game. "It's time we harnessed our anger and used it to do something constructive," Whitlock argued. His column ended with a convention-breaking direct appeal to his readers: "I'll be here today from 7 A.M.–7 P.M. If you're with me, call at 234-4869, and we'll discuss the details of our war against these S.O.B.s (Stupid Offensive Baseballers)."[64]

By the next day, Whitlock told his readers that he had answered more than six hundred calls personally, and only a few were against the boycott. Local radio station KY102 joined the effort. Whitlock continued to publish his telephone number and personally answer calls. He explained "I want [the Royals] to feel your pain. As a columnist, it is my job to offer a voice to the voiceless, which in this case is you, the systematically abused baseball fan."[65]

Yet, the boycott campaign's shortcoming was its orientation to only consumer interests. On April 13, Whitlock's column announced "The Royals felt your pain." Royals President Mike Herman and other team management had met with the editorial board of the *Star* "and promised to be 'fan friendly' all season, not just on opening weekend." Whitlock withdrew the fan boycott after Herman apologized in a press release for the Royals' role in the baseball strike and promised fans "free general admission tickets to the Royals' first four home games, a free 'baseball meal' (hot dog and soda) to folks who buy tickets for seats other than general admission for the first four home games and a free open house April 22 at Kauffman Stadium."[66]

Whitlock's campaign had the potential of mobilizing people to act as citizens. In fact, in his column to withdraw the boycott, Whitlock argued that democracy had taken place and the "little" people—himself included—had been heard:

> I am a 27-year-old black man who wears an earring (left ear), sports a baseball cap to business meetings and speaks a little too much slang. Because you empowered me, and because he is a fair man, Mike Herman, one of the most intelligent men in America and one of Kansas City's most wealthy citizens, sat down with me as an equal.
> Herman listened to your complaints and responded generously.
> That's how our system was designed to work.[67]

Although Whitlock's boycott was the most successful single news media mobilization of the baseball strike, it failed to resolve any of the issues—high player salaries, the trading away of the Royals' best-paid stars, the threat of a small market like Kansas City losing its team, the possibility of another strike—that led Whitlock to be proactive in the first place. The outcome only reinforced the notion that the news audience isn't interested in the political issues associated with citizenship but only in the product issues associated with consumerism.

Imagining Fans as Citizens not Consumers

On Labor Day, September 5, 1994, NBC's David Bloom reported a story on the declining fortunes of organized labor. After surveying several ongoing but rarely covered labor disputes, he turned to the baseball strike.

> Baseball is unique. Because the sport captures the imagination, the strike captures attention.

I would argue that the imagination captured is the consumer imagination, and the visible consumer audience is what captures the attention of the news media. This is how labor disputes are covered in the United States: the consumer marketplace is defended by the news media, but the labor marketplace is not. Would the news media defend a sustainable minimum wage as quickly and actively as they have defended a fan's desire to see baseball games?

Only 1 of the 106 network television news reports (the David Bloom report) attempted to frame the baseball strike in the context of the U.S. labor movement. None of the *New York Times* stories did so, and only two *USA Today* stories did (and only by relating the strike to the experience of the football players union). It is important to note that many of the fans cited in baseball strike coverage did criticize capitalism and excessive profits. But the news media didn't permit an open discussion of this. They didn't, as good public journalism should, "position people as discussants rather than complainers."[68] In stories of fans' powerlessness and disgust, there was little discussion of the antitrust exemption and no discussion of other ways to run MLB, such as publicly owned teams, which have worked successfully with AAA minor league teams like the Rochester Red Wings, the Toledo Mud Hens, and the Columbus Clippers, and the National Football League's Green Bay Packers.[69]

The baseball strike is an example of a story where the public voice—as presented through sound bites, quotes, and public opinion polls—is at the forefront. But, these sound bites address the audience with a false sense of democratic discourse. They create a venting model for public discourse, which only encourages feelings of helplessness and cynicism. There are times when fans should be mobilized as consumers, but there are also times when they need to be mobilized as citizens. In cases like the MLB strike, we deserve news stories that mobilize us as citizens who can act to stabilize this U.S. cultural institution and could do without stories that limit our public power to the consumer complaint. If "fans will render the final verdict" on baseball's labor problems, as *Time* magazine suggests,[70] we need to know how to do it as deliberative citizens. Our public action should not be limited to deciding whether to show up at a ballpark.

Coda

In 1998, Congress passed and the president signed a piece of legislation that had great import for baseball's ongoing labor problems. The Curt Flood Act, named after the late baseball outfielder who boldly challenged MLB's antitrust exemption in the early 1970s, overturned part of baseball's antitrust exemption.[71] In the stories that covered the new law, the antitrust exemption had become the new narrative culprit for baseball's ongoing labor problems. Thus, with this one development, the heavily publicized frame of greedy "millionaires vs. billionaires" was supplanted with a legalistic frame. But, perhaps because the antitrust exemption story contradicted nearly every news frame covering the baseball strike four years earlier, the new law received very light coverage in the news media.

For example, *USA Today* completely reframed their baseball strike narrative with a short October 8, 1998, story on the new law:

> The U.S. Congress voted Wednesday to overturn part of a 76-year-old Supreme Court ruling that exempted baseball from antitrust laws on the grounds it is a game and not a business. The House passed the legislation by voice, sending it to President Clinton for his expected signature. The Senate passed the bill last July. That exemption deprived players of some of the protections enjoyed by other professional athletes *and has been blamed for baseball's many work stoppages, including the disastrous strike in 1994–95.* The bill makes clear the exemption is revoked only for labor relations, not for relocation, league expansion and the minor leagues. Both the players union and the owners support the legislation.[72]

Similarly, a *New York Times* story from the Associated Press announcing the passage of the bill stated, "The exemption deprived players of some of the protections enjoyed by other professional athletes and *has been blamed for baseball's work stoppages.*"[73] After so many stories that had been solicitous of fan opinions during the baseball strike, here, neither the *New York Times* nor *USA Today* covered the reactions of baseball fans. The major television news networks—ABC, CBS, and NBC—didn't even mention the development, which was significant given their heavy coverage of the strike.

For all of their disdain of baseball's millionaires and billionaires during the strike, the mass media have become ever more financially entwined with MLB in the poststrike period. Broadcasting contracts continue to be a major source of revenue for baseball teams (which in turn feed baseball revenues and player salaries); the news media continue to profit by reporting on baseball; and media conglomerates are increasingly the actual owners/investors in MLB teams, a very real potential conflict of interest in news coverage of MLB's labor relations. In fact, by the 2002 season, four of the five highest valued MLB teams—the New York Yankees, the Los Angeles Dodgers, the Boston Red Sox, and the Atlanta Braves—were those with media cross-ownership. For example, in 2002 the New York Yankees started the YES (Yankee Entertainment & Sports) Network, a basic cable channel in the region that charges cable systems two dollars per subscriber, the highest fee ever for a cable start-up. By comparison, CNN charges cable systems thirty-seven cents per subscriber, and Lifetime carries a fifteen cents per subscriber fee.[74] The YES Network could create $200 million in subscriber fees annually, and was already valued at more than $850 million in its first year.[75]

The key benefit to such cross-ownership is that the MLB owners can creatively assign large portions of local revenues (which can include television, radio, and cable) to the related media enterprises. The reason franchises would want to do this is to lessen the amount—potentially millions of dollars—that they kick into baseball's revenue sharing system. MLB evenly divides up its national advertising and merchandising revenue among all of the teams. But the franchises are still grossly unequal in terms of local revenue, where teams in large media markets have a much greater opportunity to sign lucrative television, radio, and cable contracts. The lack of revenue parity is evident annually on the playing field, where teams like the Yankees, Braves, and Red Sox can afford to retain star players and make late-season additions to their rosters to help increase their chances of dominating other teams.

Sharing of local revenues, in which all of the teams are required to share 20 percent of local media earnings, is designed to increase parity between large-market, high-revenue teams such as the Yankees and Red Sox and small-market, low-revenue teams such as the Montreal Expos and Kansas City Royals. In 2001, for example, baseball's richest sixteen teams ended up sharing $166.9 million with the other fourteen teams.[76] But wealthy teams with media cross-ownership are already hiding local revenues and are likely to do even more of this under a plan by the baseball commissioner's office to increase revenue sharing from 20 percent to 50 percent of local media revenue. (It may not be coincidental that Baseball Commissioner Bud Selig is the former owner of the Milwaukee Brewers, one of the small market teams. In fact, his daughter still operates the team.) As sports economist Andrew Zimbalist explained, "If you own the baseball team and the sports network, you can put the team's revenues into the sports network and not subject it to revenue sharing. The more revenue sharing you have in baseball, the more advantageous it is to a team to own its own sports network."[77]

As the baseball business becomes even more lucrative for owners, there are an increasing number of partnerships between teams and media corporations. The Atlanta Braves has long been a media property, owned by Ted Turner (now AOL Time Warner) since 1976 and used to launch the first cable superstation, TBS. The News Corporation bought the Los Angeles Dodgers in 1998 to bolster its Fox Sports Net channel. In 2002, a group led by John Henry (who had owned the Florida Marlins), which includes the New York Times Company (which also owns the *Boston Globe*) as a minority shareholder, bought the Boston Red Sox for about $700 million. The deal was more than twice the previous record sale price of $323 million for the Cleveland Indians in 2000. The Red Sox purchase also included a lucrative media partnership—an 80 percent stake in the New England Sports Network, a regional cable channel that carries the Red Sox and the NHL's Boston Bruins (who own the other 20 percent of NESN). Other corporate media owners in baseball include the Chicago Cubs (Tribune Co.), the Anaheim Angels (Disney), and the Toronto Blue Jays (Rogers Communications, Canada's largest cable operator).

When major league franchises are hiding revenues, it also affects labor relations since the owners' positions in contract negotiations are based on their reported revenues, which always seem lower than they should be. And, indeed, baseball's reportedly woeful financial situation is constantly cited by the owners and baseball commissioner as the reason for everything they do. This occurred again in baseball's scheme for "contraction," which also had implications for the players and their union. Despite being a league apparently flush with money (indeed, professional baseball is never at a loss for interested buyers, and franchise valuations climb with great consistency), on November 6, 2001, the owners, led by owner-turned-commissioner Bud Selig, voted nearly unanimously for contraction, that is, to shrink MLB's thirty teams by at least two. (This was after baseball added two teams—the Tampa Bay Devil Rays and Arizona Diamondbacks—in 1998.) The Minnesota Twins and Montreal Expos were unofficially cited as the most likely candidates for closure. Contraction would eliminate two of the lowest-revenue teams from baseball's revenue sharing plan. But, more important to the owners, it would flood baseball's monopoly labor market with fifty displaced major league players, which would likely dilute bidding for players and decrease salaries for a period. The vote for contraction came, not uncoincidentally, a day before the expiration of the collective bargaining agreement that emerged in the wake of the 1994-95 strike. The player's union was not amused and filed a grievance on the basis that contraction violated the agreement's provisions on player status.

The surprise announcement of contraction moved Senator Paul Wellstone of Minnesota and Representative John Conyers of Michigan to introduce legislation to limit baseball's antitrust exemption concerning matters of the elimination or relocation of teams.[78] The subsequent House and Senate hearings (in December 2001 and February 2002, respectively) served to generate long-overdue news media interest in the subject of baseball's financial records and the effects of its remaining antitrust exemptions. Up to this point, there had been few "truth checks" by the press. That is, the news media cynically portrayed baseball's labor situation as a struggle between the millionaires and billionaires, yet never bothered to sort through the claims and counterclaims for the benefit of the news audience and fans—even though "people really want to know" who is telling the truth.[79]

Summoned to the Capitol to explain the purpose of contraction, Commissioner Selig testified on December 6, 2001, before the House Judiciary Committee that baseball lost $519 million in the previous season and needed to eliminate at least two low-revenue teams. Initial mainstream news reports after the House hearing noted the doubts of the congressional committee members over the extent of baseball's red ink, and Selig's adamant defense of his numbers.[80] Yet, the stories never attempted to determine which side was right. The best journalism—the reports that took the time to investigate the competing claims of the owners and players' union—were not from the mainstream press but from the financial news media, particularly several reports from Chris Isidore of CNN/Money online and from *Forbes* magazine.

Isidore, a general reporter on the breaking news desk at CNN/Money, began writing an online column, SportsBiz, in June 2001.[81] The SportsBiz column is prominently linked on the CNN/Money and CNNSI Web sites, both AOL Time Warner subsidiaries, but does not appear on the CNN cable network or in *Money* magazine. (Despite the fact that AOL Time Warner owns the Atlanta Braves, Isidore says that "I've never faced any pressure within the company when writing about baseball and/or the Braves.")[82] In a December 7, 2001, report, the same day that mainstream publications such as *USA Today* and the *New York Times* provided typical narratives featuring competing claims about MLB's financial data, Isidore's column, titled "Financial Data Show Teams Owned by Broadcasters Shift Revenue," analyzed the competing claims. Where other news media failed to truth-check, Isidore did, and noted "You don't have to look any lower than the second line on the commissioner's spreadsheet—local television, radio and cable revenue—to question the legitimacy of the league's numbers, and the arguments for such significant financial help as concessions from the players, the closing of two franchises and the continuation of an exemption from antitrust laws."[83]

Isidore's analysis explained that teams such as the Los Angeles Dodgers, Chicago Cubs, and Atlanta Braves reported significantly below-market revenues from selling broadcasting rights because the clubs sold the rights to affiliated broadcasters. The effect is that these teams overstate their losses, which then supports Selig's arguments about baseball's financial woes. In a report a few weeks later, Isidore also noted that the commissioner's claims of massive financial losses were even less credible after he discovered that a central fund held hundreds of millions of dollars—money that the commissioner did not disclose in data provided to Congress. The central fund contributions, which were held back from national ad and marketing revenue that is normally distributed to all the teams, were registered by baseball's accountants as a loss for the teams (further exaggerating baseball's losses). The fund's purpose? It could serve to buy out baseball's "contracted" franchises in Minnesota and Montreal or serve as a war chest in the event of another work stoppage.[84]

A team of writers from *Forbes* magazine also reconsidered the baseball operating revenue and concluded—counter to Selig's testimony—that twenty of baseball's thirty teams were profitable in the previous year and that many franchises were hiding revenue in media properties.[85] Despite these well-researched interpretive pieces, mainstream newspapers continued their long-standing pattern of equivocating commentary about baseball's labor relations. The 2001 stories sounded like retreads from 1995. For example, even after pointing out that the $700 million sale of the Boston Red Sox didn't jibe with baseball's pleas of poverty, venerable *New York Times* sportswriter George Vecsey still concluded "The owner-commissioner is not wrong, however, about the inequities, which are at least 50 percent the fault of the ownership and 50 percent the fault of the truculent leadership of the players association."[86] Vecsey made no mention of baseball's hidden local broadcasting revenues or the massive central fund, both of which lessened revenue sharing among franchises and increased the league's inequities. Jon Saraceno of *USA Today* summed up the story with a similar tone: "Don't just blame greedy baseball owners and lead politician Bud Selig for myopic management over the years. Likewise, don't merely point a finger at greedy players and their union guru, Don Fehr. They're all responsible."[87]

Truth check, anyone?

By late August 2002, at the brink of another impasse, owners and players were able to come to an agreement. The two sides agreed to additional local revenue sharing between the most and least wealthy franchises and to higher luxury taxes for teams with the largest payrolls. The owners also agreed to drop any ideas of contraction for the duration of the four-year pact. According to Gene Orza of the players union, the rare successful agreement was a result of good faith bargaining by the owners. "The negotiations were able to go on because clubs weren't trying to undo the system or break the union—they were trying to restructure it," he said.[88]

In a fitting closure to Major League Baseball in 2002, the two low-revenue clubs that had been slated for closure had their revenge with terrific seasons. The Montreal Expos (lowest revenue of thirty teams) surpassed all expectations by finishing second place in the National League East and compiling a winning record for the first time since 1996. The Minnesota Twins (twenty-ninth in revenue) won the American League Central Division handily and reached the American League Championship Series, where they lost to the eventual World Series champions, the Anaheim Angels (twenty-third in revenue).[89]

THE UPS STRIKE, THE WTO PROTESTS, AND THE FUTURE OF LABOR IN THE NEWS

The mainstream news coverage of the 1991–94 General Motors (GM) Willow Run plant shutdown, the 1993 American Airlines flight attendant strike, and the 1994–95 Major League Baseball strike all employed the five dominant labor news frames discussed in Chapter 1. In a variety of ways, the stories told the news audience that the consumer is king; the process of production is none of their business; the economy is driven by great business leaders and entrepreneurs; the workplace is a meritocracy; and collective economic action is bad.

Mainstream news outlets in the United States continued to use these frames to structure their coverage of labor in the second half of the 1990s. But this limited approach to creating labor stories left the news media unprepared to tell the story of the decade's biggest labor strike victory and the largest mass protest against globalization ever on U.S. soil—*both* instances where the majority of U.S. citizens were on the side of labor.

The 1997 UPS Strike

The casual viewer of television in the United States in the first quarter of 2002 could have hardly missed the pervasive buzz about the color brown. The occasion celebrating this rather unsung color was the rollout of a new $45 million advertising campaign by United Parcel Service

(UPS). Breaking with their long-running promotion as "The Tightest Ship in the Shipping Business," a campaign that featured the heroic efforts of UPS delivery workers, the new ad campaign—the largest in the corporation's ninety-five-year history—obliquely asked "What Can Brown Do For You?" In the television (and print) ads, actors portraying "the mailroom guy," "the shipping manager," "the logistics manager," "the customer service manager," "the CFO," and "the CEO" talk about what "brown" does for them. Dale Hayes, the UPS vice president for brand management and customer communications, said the campaign was a "more aggressive way" to portray the company's employees "as a strong team working together, to bring solutions to customers."[1] But, strangely enough, the UPS workers who wear the brown uniforms and drive the brown trucks were absent from the ad campaign.

Perhaps the absence of worker images from UPS's most extensive corporate branding campaign ever is not so surprising. The year 2002 marked five years after the high-profile 1997 Teamsters strike against UPS, and the expiration (on July 31) of the five-year National Master Agreement that ended the strike. As talks between the union and the corporation geared up, the fact that UPS's corporate managers would aggressively seek to supplant the image of the heroic worker with the brown brand color makes sense after losing a hard-fought strike in which the majority of the United States unexpectedly—at least according to mainstream news coverage—supported the workers not management.

The success of the Teamsters' strike can be measured not only in the final contract signed between the workers and management but also in the substance of the strike coverage in the mainstream news media. The traditional frames used by the news media to cover labor reflect the consumer-oriented ideological environment in which the U.S. corporate mass media operate. In most cases, these frames result in stories that prioritize consumer objectives, obscure union messages, and disdain collective action. But, as the analysis of news coverage of the 1997 UPS strike in this chapter illustrates, the consumer-oriented frames of the news may be turned to labor's benefit with democratic social activism and a message that reveals the connection between production and consumption.

The UPS strike of August 1997 is now commonly cited as labor's greatest success of the 1990s. Through the strike, 185,000 Teamster workers brought the nation's largest parcel delivery service to a standstill and won most of their demands despite the fact that millions of consumers were touched by inconveniences. The strike was one of the top stories of 1997, with 77 *USA Today* reports, 139 *New York Times* articles, and 70 network news (ABC, CBS, NBC) packages during July and August 1997. This case study is based on a critical analysis of those reports.[2]

The UPS strike story not only received significant mainstream news coverage but also gained the nation's attention. The nonprofit Pew Research Center's monthly News Interest Index nationwide surveys asks people how closely they follow certain news stories. The UPS strike was the fifth most closely followed story (in terms of "very closely" responses) of all news stories in 1997 and the most closely followed labor story of the entire decade, with 76 percent of respondents following it closely—a combined 36 percent "very closely" and 40 percent "fairly closely."[3] But perhaps the most unique feature of the strike is that by the account of the news media's own surveys, the striking workers gained a majority of the nation's support.

On Monday, August 4, 1997, nearly 185,000 Teamsters working for UPS went on strike. The workers' primary concern was to reverse the fast growth of part-time positions, which had undercut the creation of new full-time jobs at the global parcel delivery company. The dual wage structure of the Teamster union workers at UPS was similar to that of the American Airlines flight attendants. In 1982, the Teamsters had agreed to a two-tier wage scale that paid part-timers less than half the wages of full-time workers. By 1997, with the company taking full advantage of the dual wage system, more than 60 percent of the Teamster workers at UPS were part-time (up from 42 percent in 1986), although many of them worked 35 or more hours a week.[4]

The day the Teamsters walked out, the story led all network newscasts. Even with the ever-improving economy at the time, the earliest stories on the strike featured hand-wringing consumer-oriented news frames. ABC's veteran reporter Dean Reynolds wrapped up his August 4 report from Dallas by warning, "And economists say one thing is certain. The longer this strike lasts, the higher will go the prices for everything UPS *was* shipping."

NBC's report by Mike Jensen on the same day waved an even larger red flag of inflationary fears:

JENSEN (voice-over): When all this is over, shipping charges for packages are likely to go up, says consultant William Dean.

DEAN (in office): UPS is such a dominant carrier that they're gonna have to raise their rates, and almost all the other private carriers are going to inch up at the same time.

JENSEN (voice-over): Another worry for the million-and-a-half customers who use UPS every day. For them it's only going to get worse for each day the strike goes on.

Yet, after the first day of the strike, the stories pedaling the myth of inflation had largely ended. The subsequent events of the fifteen-day UPS strike, which often couldn't be fit to typical labor news frames, seemed to genuinely baffle the consumer-oriented news media. One of the most unusual developments was the considerable public support for the striking workers. By the second week of the strike, this support was legitimized by news surveys: A *USA Today*/CNN/Gallup Poll showed that 55 percent of Americans supported the strikers, while only 27 percent supported UPS management.[5] Similarly, an ABC News/*Nightline* poll conducted in the second week found that 40 percent of respondents supported the union workers, while 30 percent supported the company (with 16 percent supporting neither, and 13 percent with no opinion).

The results of the surveys defied the news media's conventional wisdom and framing strategy—many consumers were inconvenienced, yet the bulk of Americans supported the strikers. For example, a long *New York Times* story on August 17, 1997, announcing the *USA Today*/CNN/Gallup Poll data stated:

> Even though the 13-day-old walkout by the teamsters is inconveniencing far more Americans than most strikes have, the American public strongly . . . supports the workers in this high-stakes showdown, the largest strike in the nation in two decades.
>
> That is a surprising switch because the public sided with management in most other recent work stoppages that grabbed the nation's attention, including the 1994 baseball strike, the 1982 football players' strike and the 1981 air controllers' strike.[6]

Likewise, the writer of the *USA Today* story on the proworker poll seemed rather perplexed, noting "Public support [of 55 percent] for the Teamsters comes even though 31% disapprove of unions."[7] An ABC News.com story on the ABC News/*Nightline* poll results had a similar tone, highlighting the unusual fact that although people were inconvenienced by the strike, most people didn't want President Clinton to step in and end it.[8]

The poll results undermined the potential for the disgruntled consumer to be the primary frame of the UPS strike story. In fact, the unexpected poll results created the possibility for untraditional strike narratives. For example, a *USA Today* story on York, Pennsylvania, entitled "Town finds strike is inconvenience but not calamity" took a more measured, less alarmist view of the impact on consumers.[9]

Still, there were the fairly typical consumer-problem stories: By August 5, the second day of the strike, reports focused on an electronics business hampered by missing shipments (on *CBS Evening News*), fresh flowers going unshipped (*ABC World News Tonight*), and Lobstergram and cheese-cake deliveries at a standstill (*NBC Nightly News*). Before the strike ended, the television news reports also covered the impact on fish deliveries, a wedding (an undelivered wedding dress), blood supplies, pricey Nieman Marcus department store goods, espresso, and frozen yogurt.

The news media also attempted to discredit the 185,000 striking workers by painting them as violent unionists. For example, the Big Three television networks ran seventy package reports between August 3 and 20, 1997, in their strike coverage. No fewer than ten of the reports, all between August 5 and 10, noted violence on picket lines and showed police shoving picketers back to make way for UPS trucks rolling through the UPS gate. A typical report was the August 5 lead-in by *ABC World News Tonight* anchor Diane Sawyer:

SAWYER (on camera): Tempers flared at UPS plants today, in a second day of the Teamsters strike against the shipping company.

SAWYER (voice over video of Chelmsford, Mass., police pushing picketers): Two strikers were arrested at this Massachusetts site after a scuffle with police left one person injured (shift to video of an older male UPS worker lying on the pavement, with his head cradled by an emergency medical worker).

The assumption, of course, is that the striking workers were at fault since they were the ones arrested. But there never were (and typically never are) follow-up reports to such stories that tell the consequences of the arrests, nor were there reports investigating police conduct or responsibility for the worker's injury.

In fact, the peaceful nationwide work stoppage of 185,000 workers defied the news media's typical stereotype of violent picketers. Nevertheless, during the first week of coverage, the network television news media returned again and again to the images of police physically pushing back and arresting workers attempting to nonviolently block UPS gates in a few Boston suburb locations. Even after such isolated incidences of "violence" had ended, CBS still stoked fears of more striker-induced violence by recycling the same video that CBS used earlier in the week. On August 10, 1997, CBS reporter Diane Olick filed a news package that included this content:

> OLICK (voice over video of trucks leaving UPS gates through a crowd of people): There is also growing concern that as the possibility of negotiations cools, tempers will heat up on the picket lines . . .
>
> OLICK (voice over file footage of six police officers pulling a striker away from the front of a UPS truck): . . . as they did already in Boston.
>
> RON CAREY (from *Face the Nation*): I have made it very clear that there will be no violence.
>
> UNIDENTIFIED PICKETER Some people are getting fed up—that may go violent [*sic*].

Thus, even when no violence exists (the video CBS used had nothing to do with strikers becoming inflamed by slow negotiations but instead showed police breaking a blockade with force), the news media seemed irresistibly compelled to use it as a narrative element for labor stories.

Despite the news media's hyping of a violence angle and their befuddlement over public support of the workers, in several reports the news actually did what news is supposed to do: inform the public and be a medium for the open discussion of relevant public issues. Many reports on the UPS strike presented varying opinions about the status of part-time workers in the U.S. economy, the years of downsizing at U.S. corporations, and the question of fair wages. Yet, before one concludes that the mainstream press opened up a new era of labor coverage, consider four unique factors behind the Teamsters' victory and the widespread public support of the UPS workers.

Four Factors behind the Strike's Success

1. *Democratic union reforms elicit worker support.* First, there was a new democratic environment at the International Brotherhood of Teamsters.

Under the direction of Teamster President Ron Carey and the organizational help of the Teamsters for a Democratic Union (TDU), a reform movement within the union, the Teamsters had improved democracy in decision making and maintained a high degree of solidarity among its UPS workers.[10] Almost a year in advance, the Teamsters leadership developed the kind of internal communication campaign that contrasted highly with the corrupt, secretive Teamsters leadership style of earlier decades. In advance of the contract talks, the Teamsters "hired rank and file activists from UPS centers as coordinators; mapped out an extensive one-on-one communications network; surveyed members on the issues; published flyers; prodded locals to hold before-work rallies; and put some rank and filers on the national bargaining committee. International officers and staff traveled to local meetings around the country; some attended the TDU convention [the previous] fall."[11]

So, unlike the United Automobile Workers (UAW) members at GM in Arlington who failed to support their fellow workers at Mackie (see Chapter 4), well-paid, full-time UPS workers willingly risked their positions by striking for the benefit of their fellow UPS workers who were part-time and low-paid. The Teamsters persuaded their drivers earning about twenty dollars an hour to go on the picket line to support full-time jobs for part-timers who were starting at only eight dollars an hour. UPS pilots also honored the strike, in return for support later in the year from other UPS workers when the pilots entered contract negotiations. The new democracy of the Teamsters union meant that only a few thousand union members failed to join the strike, so the public front of the Teamsters was almost completely united.[12]

2. *"Living wage" theme resonates with U.S. citizens.* The Teamsters were able to effectively turn the news media's consumer orientation to their benefit. The main issue of the strike was fairness to workers and the ability to make a living wage—one that allows workers to enjoy the fruits of their labor in the consumer economy.[13] As Jim West observed in *Labor Notes*, this was a salient issue. "Fighting for full-time jobs that can support a family resonated with workers throughout the country, many of whom have similar problems."[14] (Unfortunately, in a nation where there is still resistance to thinking of women as the chief breadwinners of families, the concept of a "family wage" may not resonate as loudly when the worker is a female flight attendant.) The work stoppage successfully struck a chord with Americans disturbed by the trend of downsizing: well-paid,

full-time, family-wage jobs being replaced with low-paying positions with no benefits and little security—while corporate profits soar. In fact, the ABC News/*Nightline* poll found that 65 percent of respondents agreed that part-time workers should get the same health insurance as full-time workers, and 82 percent felt that part-timers should get the same pay as full-timers for equal work.[15]

The idea that workers should get paid enough to be good consumers is an old one in the United States, and was popularized in 1914 by Henry Ford's offer to pay his auto plant workers at least five dollars a day, enough of a wage to be able to buy the cars they built and the new, corresponding consumer lifestyle.[16] The idea of decent living standards was renewed for labor's efforts when the new head of the AFL-CIO, John Sweeney, declared in 1996 that "America needs a raise."[17] A year late, the Teamsters had a similar slogan for the UPS strike: "Part-time America won't work." The Teamsters had prepared for nearly a year to communicate the idea of a living wage to the news media, and they trained their rank-and-file workers to speak effectively on the topic.[18] As a result, mixed in with stories exaggerating worker violence and the strike's threat to the U.S. economy were at least two network television packages that investigated the use of part-time workers in the economy.

After a story lamenting the slowdown in car parts deliveries to mechanics (on August 4, the first day of the strike), Dan Rather introduced a second report, one that provided context for one of the strike's central issues:

RATHER: We want to give you a closer look now at one of the key issues in the strike because it's one that goes beyond the Teamsters and UPS. It's the use of part-time, as opposed to full-time, workers. As CBS News economics correspondent Ray Brady reports, it's a trend in this country that is growing fast.

BRADY (voice over image of picket lines and file footage of UPS workers quickly sorting boxes along the conveyer belt lines of an immense facility): UPS employs more part-time workers than any other company—fully two-thirds of its workforce. And that's the problem. Some part-timers get just three hours of work a day, for a starting salary that hasn't been raised since 1982.

UNIDENTIFIED FEMALE WORKER (on picket line): We're guaranteed three hours. We're begging for more. We cannot live on three hours.

BRADY (voice over image of picket lines): Even part-timers who get more hours say they're paid half as much as full-timers.

UNIDENTIFIED MALE WORKER They got us working like forty hours a week and still keeping us at a part-time rate.

Brady's package for CBS continued with the story of a sixty-three-year-old woman who had worked at Woolworth's for twenty-seven years when she was fired and replaced with part-timers who earned less money and no benefits. Brady's on-camera conclusion focused on the sobering reality of business's increasing use of part-time labor: "Unions may feel that this is the time to make an issue of low-paid part-timers. As the ranks of these workers grows, more Americans may be wondering, could I be replaced by one of them?"

On the second day of the strike, August 5, NBC broadcast a package that also investigated the problem of part-time work.

TOM BROKAW (anchor): Of course, one of the issues at the heart of this strike is the practice of hiring part-time workers for long-term jobs. It's a practice in which UPS is certainly not alone in this country . . .

MIKE JENSEN (reporter, voice over picket line): Six out of ten workers at UPS are part-timers, and a lot of them want full-time jobs.

CECELIA FRETS, UPS WORKER (on picket line): I would like to make full-time, but they're not going to give it to us.

JENSEN (voice over image of picket line, shots of man on line): Anthony Diaz gets only four hours of work a day. He'd like eight.

DIAZ: I live with my three sisters and my grandmother, and help them and support them.

JENSEN: (voice over images of waitress, Wal-Mart store, and hotel doorman working): It's a sign of the times. Almost every company in America hires temporary or part-time workers in the name of efficiency—UPS because its work comes in spurts.

JIM KELLY, UPS CHAIRMAN (voice begins over shots of UPS workers sorting, then goes to a head shot of him): We have three or four hours where we have to sort packages, and there's no work before that, and no work after that, in many cases.

JENSEN: The number of temporary workers is up 400 percent in the last fifteen years. And one out of every five workers is part-time. Some labor experts defend part-time work.

PROF. JEFF SONNENFELD, EMORY UNIVERSITY: An awful lot of people got new footing into the world of work in a very important way in a critical time in their lives. And that's through part-time work.

If Jensen was a more enterprising reporter, he might have taken Kelly to task for the suggestion that there is nothing more than a few hours of work a day for workers classified as part-time at UPS. Kelly's use of *in many cases* obscured the fact that more than ten thousand UPS "part-time" workers put in over thirty-five hours a week.[19] If Jensen was also a more accurate reporter, he would have better described the background of his expert labor source Sonnenfeld, who curiously seems to be an apologist for part-time jobs. In fact, Sonnenfeld was not a "labor expert," but a management professor—one who had worked professionally as a consultant for UPS executives.[20]

Despite the report's shortcomings and inaccuracies, Jensen's package still conveyed that part-time work was damaging the full-time job market:

HECTOR PONCE, UPS WORKER (on picket line, with his young son on his shoulders): I got two kids and a wife. What I take home after taxes is about 120.

PONCE (new shot, with Jensen nodding slightly as he stands beside Ponce): You can't survive. It's impossible, impossible.

JENSEN (voice over shots of picket line, including Ponce and son): A part-time job can be a stepping stone. But if you want to work full-time and can't, part-time is more like a dead-end.

In these reports, the message planning of the Teamsters was clearly effective. Within the constraints of consumerism, the Teamsters were able to show that UPS was denying its thousands of part-time workers a living wage for them and their families and that this was part of a national trend affecting millions of workers.[21]

3. *Goodwill toward the workers in brown.* A third element that aided the success of the UPS workers in their struggle was the existing goodwill of millions of Americans. An ABC News.com timeline reflecting on the major stories of 1997 captured the American sentiment toward UPS workers: "In early August the nation learned—through sudden deprivation—just how completely dependent we have become on the armada of brown UPS vans and their ever-friendly drivers."[22] Unlike laborers in so many sectors of the U.S. economy, UPS workers have daily contact with people—a lot of people, since each UPS driver delivers up to five hundred packages a day.[23] Because UPS delivery drivers work regular routes, they build personal relationships with their customers. The *New York Times* in an August 17, 1997, story related one such anecdote: "In Brooklyn,

August 5, 1997, *NBC Nightly News*. Hector Ponce, UPS worker: "I got two kids and a wife. What I take home after taxes is about 120 ... You can't survive. It's impossible, impossible."

Michael Rodriguez, owner of Open Road Cycles, said he sympathized with the Teamster strikers partly because he was so fond of his brown-suited U.P.S. driver. 'The workers do work hard,' he said. 'I have some feelings for my regular guy. They do deserve something.' "[24]

In the consumer-based U.S. economy, most people don't have knowledge of a worker's daily life or of the process of production or a service. And, as noted in Chapter 1, the news media continually reminds the public that the process of production is not its business through the way they frame labor stories. The UPS case is unique in part because the public did not rely on the news media to communicate the experience of the worker.

4. *The economy was good.* In 1997, the U.S. economy was doing well for businesses, with high profits and low unemployment. UPS, too, was extremely successful, with 80 percent of the nation's parcel business, $1.15 billion in profits in the previous year, and a profit rate of 19.4 percent, which dwarfed competitors such as Federal Express and the U.S. Postal Service. Yet, the workers at UPS—like workers in many U.S. industries—did not share in the fruits of the economy. Given the good economy, it was hard for UPS to make the argument that they were in a precarious fiscal situation or that they were highly pressured to stay competitive.

Teamsters Successfully Engage the Five Frames

Given these four factors and with their advance planning, the Teamsters were able to turn to their favor every one of the five major frames used by the consumer-oriented news media:

1. *The consumer is king.* The Teamsters plainly showed that UPS denied their part-timers a living wage and the ability to be normal, everyday consumers.

2. *The process of production is none of the public's business.* The Teamsters trained their workers to be articulate on the issues and traded on their uniformed workers' long-term goodwill with the public and the public's knowledge of their hard work.

3. *The economy is driven by great business leaders and entrepreneurs.* Although the typical news framing of labor stories suggests that great business leaders and entrepreneurs drive the economy, the nucleus of UPS's operations is their brown-clad workers, and the company's own advertising heralded their contributions.

4. *The workplace is a meritocracy.* The Teamsters' campaign made it evident that full-time and part-time workers performed the same tasks but earned grossly disparate wages.

5. *Collective economic action is bad.* It was hard to argue that this collective action was bad. Although the strike inconvenienced some people (which the news pointed out many times), the public largely supported this strike. Moreover, since UPS held 80 percent of the parcel business and earned more than a billion dollars in profits the previous year, it was hard for the company to claim it was under attack.

Although the Teamsters were able to successfully engage the typical news frames, the limits of these consumer-oriented frames were also apparent in the UPS case. Another important issue for the Teamsters was control of the union's pension fund. UPS wanted to withdraw from the union's multiemployer pension plan and administer its own pension fund for workers. It wasn't until an August 17 report by CBS—about two weeks into the strike—that any of the television news reports attempted to explain why workers might not want their pension in the hands of their employer. As the package by correspondent Troy Roberts explained, retired Pan Am airline workers continue to suffer from underpayment of their pensions after Pan Am went bankrupt in 1991 and ceased operations. But, lacking a connection to an existing consumer-oriented frame, this story did not become a common theme of the strike coverage. (Since the collapse of Enron and other large corporations in 2002 and the subsequent loss of workers' pensions, corporate-controlled pension funds may now be a much more salient issue.)

The strike, the largest walkout since the 1983 AT&T strike, lasted fifteen days. The resulting settlement created ten thousand new full-time jobs, reduced the wage differential with raises for full-time workers and larger raises for part-timers, prohibited UPS from taking control of the workers' pension fund, and limited subcontracting of labor. Many observers hailed the Teamster victory as a victory for all of labor and a milestone that would mark labor's resurgence. On the network television news, an NBC report on August 18, an ABC report on August 19, and a CBS report on August 20 all covered the new life in the U.S. labor movement, after years of decline.

Yet, for the corporate news media, any levity that might be associated with broad public support for the Teamsters and a possible upswing in fortunes for working people was strongly tempered with worry about corporate America's bottom line. The prophets of Wall Street got the final word on whether anyone beyond the Teamsters should be pleased by the UPS settlement. On Sunday, August 17, a day before the resolution of the work stoppage, CBS News weekend anchor Russ Mitchell speculated on the causes of a stock market drop at the end of the previous week:

> MITCHELL (voice over video of Teamsters picketing): Another problem may be the UPS strike. Even though polls show most Americans are siding with workers in the dispute, some investors think labor's demands in the strike could spill over into contract talks at other companies, and cut into corporate profits.

At *ABC World News Tonight* on Tuesday, August 19, the day the strike ended, ABC carried its report on labor's new momentum. Immediately afterward, anchor Peter Jennings cheerily reported "The stock market seemed genuinely pleased with the UPS settlement" and noted the upturn in the Dow Jones index and the NASDAQ market. The same day, economics correspondent Ray Brady filed his final report on the UPS strike for the *CBS Evening News*. In his on-camera summary, Brady concluded:

> BRADY: There have been concerns this settlement might set off a whole new round of wage increases in other industries and heat up inflation. But that's not likely for now. There are no big labor contracts like rubber, autos, or steel coming up until next year.

Even after labor's biggest victory in two decades, the mainstream news media slid back into the same old consumer-oriented news frames. The good news, it would seem, is not that working people might get a well-deserved raise in an era of rising profits, but that corporate America's profits (and, of course, the prices of consumer goods) wouldn't again be threatened for at least a year.

The 1999 WTO Protests

In November 1999, fifty thousand people representing more than seven hundred organizations converged on Seattle to protest the World Trade Organization's Third Ministerial Conference. They wanted the commercial media to understand and fairly cover their major complaint: that the entire international economic system—one that is supported and controlled by major Western leaders and multinational corporations—is fundamentally flawed and undemocratic, and should be either overhauled or abolished.[25]

Background on the WTO

First, some background on the World Trade Organization (WTO). The WTO came into existence in 1995 as the successor to the General Agreement on Tariffs and Trade (GATT). GATT was a post–World War II agreement adopted in 1948 by twenty-three countries, and its main purpose was to reduce the high tariffs on the international trade of goods. The members of the GATT accord grew to more than 120 countries over the next forty years, and they met in several rounds of talks. The final round, named the Uruguay Round (because the talks began there, although trade ministers later met in Geneva and elsewhere during this round), lasted from 1986 to 1994. This round of talks continued years longer than any previous round, in part because trade ministers wanted to forge agreements on a much wider scope of international economic activity and to create a new global organization to replace GATT and coordinate and administer the new trade rules.

The WTO, which had 135 member countries by the Seattle meeting, changed the rules of global trade in significant ways. The WTO continued the GATT's dominion over the global trade of goods, but it also added oversight of international trade in services (such as telecommunications and water), and trade related to intellectual property rights (such as computer programs, recorded music, prescription drugs).

The section of the WTO that is so celebrated by the organization, and so vilified by its critics, is its Dispute Settlement Body (DSB). The DSB helps resolve trade disputes between nations at the consultative level but also has a more formal procedure for judging trade disputes. A complainant nation (representing its country's corporate interests) may initiate a three-person panel of "trade experts," who meet and deliberate in closed session and issue a decision on the dispute. Third parties may not attend the dispute panel sessions unless invited. If the panel rules that a nation has violated trade agreements, the offending country can be forced to change its trade practices or risk fines or heavy trade sanctions.

The WTO's ability to administer sanctions for violations of trade rules helps meet the organization's goals of trade arrangements "directed to the substantial reduction of tariffs and other barriers to trade and to the elimination of discriminatory treatment in international trade relations."[26] But it is the WTO's single-minded focus on trade that has led it to declare *every* environmental, health, or safety law brought before it as a trade barrier and to require those laws not be applied in a "discriminatory manner" against the complainant nation.[27] The result, labor and environmental groups explain, is a "race to the bottom," the same charge leveled at the regional North American Free Trade Agreement (NAFTA). Instead of bringing the world's nations up to equally high standards of environmental, health, safety, food, and labor protection, the WTO's dispute settlement process waters down those standards to the least common denominator.

Perhaps the most famous example of this, and one that is emblematic of the Seattle protests, is the WTO's 1998 decision regarding the Shrimp-Turtle case. In order to minimize deaths to sea turtles caught in the nets of shrimp trawlers, section 609 of the Endangered Species Act[28] requires that shrimp imported to the United States must be caught by trawlers using sea turtle excluder devices. In 1997, though, India, Malaysia, Pakistan, and Thailand brought a complaint against the United States concerning this provision of the Endangered Species Act. Both a dispute panel and a subsequent appellate panel ruled that while the United States may require turtle-safe shrimp trawlers in domestic production, it was "unjustifiable discrimination" under WTO rules to ban shrimp imports that aren't turtle-safe.[29]

The Shrimp-Turtle case illustrated how powerful an unelected body like the WTO can be at undercutting not only U.S. environmental policy but any policy that it might deem to be a trade barrier.[30] So, it was not surprising to see many protesters dressed as sea turtles among the demonstrators in Seattle.

Labor union members represented the largest group of protesters in Seattle. This should not be surprising because it was clear that the WTO saw labor as one more impediment to its trade agenda. Although buoyed by the UPS victory in 1997, labor had been sufficiently burned by NAFTA earlier in the decade to know that the stakes for unions at the WTO conference were high. NAFTA was promoted in 1993 as a boon to the economies and workers of the United States, Mexico, and Canada. The White House, the Mexican government, and the U.S. corporate elite led a multimillion-dollar public relations campaign to get Congress to adopt the accord. And, as Brian Michael Goss explains, news coverage in the *New York Times* parroted the campaign for the trade deal, with dominant story lines claiming that NAFTA would bring greater prosperity and democracy to the working people of North America and prevent Mexico from falling into the economic sphere of Japan or Europe.[31] The *Times* coverage also ignored labor sources to a large degree and (as did White House strategists) created a story line that used H. Ross Perot to represent the NAFTA opposition to the public.[32]

Since that time, the worst fears of NAFTA's critics have come true. Seven years after NAFTA's 1994 implementation, the Economic Policy Institute's review of the agreement concluded:

> NAFTA has eliminated some 766,000 job opportunities—primarily for non-college-educated workers in manufacturing. Contrary to what the American promoters of NAFTA promised U.S. workers, the agreement did not result in an increased trade surplus with Mexico, but the reverse. As manufacturing jobs disappeared, workers were downscaled to lower-paying less-secure jobs. Within manufacturing, the threat of employers to move production to Mexico proved a powerful weapon for undercutting workers' bargaining power.[33]

NAFTA's benefits for Mexican and Canadian workers have also been underwhelming, with wages for the two countries declining since 1994 and the wage gap increasing in Canada as the rich got richer. Moreover, the labor side agreement to NAFTA (the North American Agreement on Labor Cooperation [NAALC]) has been a failure. Instead of protecting workers who wish to organize in independent unions (particularly in Mexico), the side agreement's lack of an enforcement mechanism means that "neither governments nor companies take the NAALC seriously."[34] The only parties to benefit from NAFTA were the "specific set of interests" who received "extraordinary government protections," according to the Economic Policy Institute's review: "investors and financiers in all three countries who search for cheaper labor and production costs."[35]

NAFTA was approved by Congress in 1993 on a yes-or-no vote, with no possibility of amendments. That's because NAFTA was subject to "fast-track" trade authority, which gives presidents approval to negotiate trade agreements that are then voted on, but cannot be amended, by Congress.

The GATT accords that created the WTO were approved by Congress in 1994 the same way. (Presidents can negotiate trade agreements without fast-track authority, but the agreements are then subject to greater congressional debate and possible amendments.) So, when President Bill Clinton attempted in 1997 to gain fast-track approval for a proposal to expand NAFTA to cover most of the remaining Western Hemisphere (a plan called the Free Trade Area of the Americas), a newly energized AFL-CIO, with an immensely improved communications operation, mobilized rank-and-file workers to pressure Congress with more than 160,000 handwritten letters. The AFL-CIO's and affiliate unions' efforts also included an informational Web site, faxed bulletins to union activists, an anti–fast-track booklet, a video, and broadcast television and radio advertising in certain congressional districts.[36] When Clinton's fast-track agenda was stopped cold in Congress in 1997 (and again in 1998), the news media typically criticized labor for strong-arming Congress and harming the nation's future prosperity. According to Thea Lee, the AFL-CIO's assistant director for public policy, "Our message was very clear throughout: we wanted a different kind of trade agreement. But most reporters weren't prepared to hear that message. They have a script that calls for backward-looking, protectionist trade unionists. They don't even do us the courtesy of calling up to make sure their accounts are accurate."[37]

Can Fifty Thousand Citizens Be Wrong?

Labor's next opportunity to focus on global trade issues was November 30–December 3, 1999, when the WTO's Third Ministerial Conference met in Seattle. The protests of fifty thousand people—representing an enormous variety of backgrounds—against the WTO was an unprecedented event in U.S. history. Unlike the battle against NAFTA, the Seattle protests couldn't be reduced by the press to a single maligned Perot-style personality. And, unlike labor's two successful efforts against President Clinton's fast-track legislation, Seattle wasn't a behind-the-scenes policy battle in which the news media could gloss over the widespread but largely unseen action of hundred of thousands of union members.

What became clear in the news media coverage of the citizen protests is that the news lacked the ability to generate news frames to discuss it. The main problem for the mainstream consumer press is that to adequately

represent and fairly discuss the protesters' point of view would be to severely indict the entire global economic system. And that is a topic that is
tacitly out-of-bounds for the mainstream consumer news media in the
United States.

Instead, the news media resorted to its time-tested frames that support
the myth of the progressive global economy. In various ways, the news
audience was again told that the consumer is king, the process of production is none of the public's business, the economy is driven by great business leaders and entrepreneurs, the workplace is a meritocracy, and collective economic action is bad. The message of the news media,
reminiscent of the GM plant shutdown coverage, was this: Workers and
citizens should learn to adapt to corporate decisions and not be an impediment to the new global economy.

A major postmortem analysis on the WTO protests in the Sunday, December 5, 1999, *New York Times* revealed what other news coverage of the
event inferred: that the mainstream news media went to Seattle with fixed
narrative frames on what would be good and bad outcomes for the international trade meeting. Timothy Egan's article began this way:

> The biggest trade conference ever held on American soil was supposed
> to go like this: a Pacific rim city, grown wealthy on sales of software and
> planes to the global economy, would show off the fruits of unfettered com-
> merce. Meanwhile, carefully choreographed street protests would enable
> President Clinton to nudge the delegates into taking action against such
> excesses of the global economy as child labor and pollution.
>
> In this narrative, Seattle was able to play the hero, while its companies
> and citizens were cast as bit players. Here was a dynamo full of dot.com
> millionaires. A port full of ships with goods from every nation. A region
> that provides half the world's commercial jets. Protesters who behave
> while walking on stilts.
>
> But the cast refused to follow the script.
>
> Instead, the world saw neighborhoods choked by tear gas, homegrown
> Starbucks stores looted and more than 500 people arrested by a police
> force that looked, at times, like Ninja Turtles.
>
> Perhaps, more significantly, the weeklong Battle of Seattle left many
> participants with a sense that the transition to a new economic order
> might not be so easy or so smooth.[38]

As in other major labor news events of the 1990s, reports on the WTO protests upheld the five dominant frames used by the consumer-oriented news media for telling stories about labor. Two in particular, "the economy is driven by great business leaders and entrepreneurs" and "collective economic action is bad," prevailed in nearly all of the mainstream news media coverage of the WTO meeting.

Egan's article hints at the major narrative streams built around these frames. First, the press treated the WTO—a largely faceless institution in all of the stories (with the regular exception of U.S. Trade Representative Charlene Barshefsky, President Clinton, and WTO Director-General Mike Moore)—as the standard-bearer for a progressive globalization driven by great business leaders and entrepreneurs (including Egan's references to Microsoft, Boeing, and scores of dynamic dot.com millionaires). Many reports either implicitly or explicitly stated that critics of global trade should stop grousing and get out of the way because globalization's momentum is fierce and its success inevitable.

Second, few accounts were supportive of protests or even bothered to accurately explain why the thousands of people were there. The news media should have known what labor's position was. Less than two weeks before the meeting in Seattle, the National Press Club in Washington, D.C., invited AFL-CIO President John Sweeney to speak before them. In his speech, Sweeney unequivocally stated labor's support for trade and for the push to admit China to the WTO, but with a different set of rules:

> Editorials pose a choice between free trade and protectionism, between engaging China and isolating it, between embracing the global market and turning our backs on it. Opponents are being dismissed as part of the past, and as obstacles to the prosperous future of the new economy.
>
> This is nonsense. The debate isn't about free trade or protectionism, engagement or isolation. We all know we're part of a global economy. And we're so engaged that we're already running a $60 billion trade deficit with China.
>
> The real debate is not over whether to be part of the global economy, but over what are the rules for that economy and who makes them—not whether to engage China, but what are the terms of that engagement, and whose values are to be represented . . .

. . . In Seattle, working people from across the world will call on the WTO to review its record and reform its rules before taking on new areas for negotiation. Our objectives are simple.

Every worker deserves protection of basic human rights—prohibitions against child labor, slave labor, discrimination, and the freedom to join together with others in a union. The WTO must incorporate rules to enforce workers' rights and environmental and consumer protections, and compliance should be required for any new member. WTO proceedings must be opened up to give citizens a meaningful voice. National and state laws and regulations concerning public health and the environment must be safe from global veto. And the ability of governments to safeguard their people from devastating import surges or product dumping must be strengthened. Until the WTO addresses these important issues, there will be no support for a major new round of trade negotiations.[39]

Despite the fact that Sweeney took labor's message directly to the press, the news media continued to cast labor as a barrier to globalization (as if there was only one possible structure for a global economy) and habitually misrepresented the Seattle protesters as short-sighted protectionists, naïve 1960s-style poseurs, and violent rioters.

Globalization's Inevitability

Even though David Stockman debunked the "trickle down" economic theory of his boss Ronald Reagan in the 1980s, and profits of free trade gushed in a one-way torrent to the nation's wealthiest in the 1990s, NBC's Tom Brokaw didn't hesitate to sell free trade as a "trickle down" populist tool in his introduction of a November 29, 1999, package on the *NBC Nightly News*:

BROKAW: What does all of this mean to you? Well, NBC's chief financial correspondent Mike Jensen explains tonight how these talks could trickle down to every family in America.

Jensen's subsequent report sounded like an invitation drafted by the U.S. Chamber of Commerce to jump on the free trade bandwagon. Jensen acknowledged some problems of free trade—child labor and pollution—but told the audience that the United States would get those under control. Other problems, such as the freedom to join an independent union, were not mentioned. And labor's concern for manufacturing jobs in the United

States? Never mind, Jensen seemed to say, blithely noting that "most experts" think the WTO's work is a "good thing." And besides, Jensen concluded, you can't stop the WTO anyway. So there.

JENSEN: The first of 3,000 officials from 135 countries arrive in Seattle. Why should Americans care when our own economy is already booming? [cut to VIDEO of U.S. manufacturing assembly lines] Because trade with other countries is one reason why it's booming. Twelve million American jobs, fully 10 percent of our workforce—a direct result of exports. [cut to VIDEO of man looking at pants at the Gap] We also love to buy all of those low-priced imports. Economist Steven Roche:

ROCHE: It's a win-win situation.

JENSEN (over slow-motion VIDEO of crowded Chinese street and graphic that says "1.25 Billion Consumers"): Most analysts say there will be even more jobs if China, with its staggering one and a quarter *billion* consumers, becomes a member of the World Trade Organization. Right now, it's just an observer. Who would benefit? American companies like Kodak, which salivates at the thought of selling a camera or film to one out of a hundred Chinese.

CHRIS PADILLA, EASTMAN KODAK DIR. OF INT'L TRADE RELATIONS: We expect that it could increase our exports to China by two or three times in the next few years.

JENSEN (over VIDEO of WTO protesters): But there's concern on the part of many Americans because some of the imports we buy are made by children. [VIDEO: Asian children in garment factory] The U.S. wants to ban that, worldwide. Same thing with pollution. [VIDEO: smokestacks] Some of the countries we buy from have no rules. The U.S. wants uniform standards. American unions and some industries like textiles also have another issue. Josh Hamilton, president of a South Carolina textile company, worries that if China is allowed in the trade organization, it will flood the world with cheap cloth and yarn.

HAMILTON: It just knocks us right out of the market.

JOHN SWEENEY, PRESIDENT OF AFL-CIO: It's bad for our economy, bad for workers.

JENSEN (on camera in an electronics shop): But most experts say getting rid of trade barriers on both sides is a good thing, for American workers and consumers. That no matter what comes out of this four-day meeting, and a lot of analysts don't think it will be much, world trade has such momentum, almost nothing will get in its way.

Jensen's report demonstrates tight control over the debate. Even the sound bites are just three-second slogans to season Jensen's corporate party-line appraisal of the WTO and free trade in general. Although the story celebrates exports, it doesn't mention the growing U.S. trade deficits under NAFTA and the country's $60 billion deficit with China.

The news is so enamored with the business-oriented New Economy from which it reaps great financial benefits (NBC and its corporate parent General Electric were also likely salivating over 1.25 billion Chinese consumers) that it fails to cover issues that concern the working class. Just a year before the Seattle protests, and eight years into the nation's economic expansion, NBC's own *Wall Street Journal*/NBC News Poll indicated that 58 percent of U.S. citizens said foreign trade hurts the economy, whereas only 32 percent said it was good for the economy. But NBC seemed unworried about the concerns of working people.[40] Instead, it wanted to get consumers salivating over more of those low-priced imports they love to buy.

Mike Jensen wasn't the only free trade advocate. NBC colleague Claire Shipman concluded on December 1, 1999, that the demonstrators were "no match for the relentless battle to tear down trade barriers," which meant that even if the demonstrators' arguments had any merit, it's pointless to pay any attention to them. Likewise, movie critic-cum-conservative pundit Michael Medved wrote in a column for *USA Today* that "the WTO demonstrators face certain failure . . . no sane observer believes that the march toward international trade suddenly will halt. In this new millennium, a global economy isn't debatable—it's inevitable."[41]

NBC's Andrea Mitchell (who, for fair disclosure for this story's subject matter, should have reminded viewers that she is married to Federal Reserve chairman Alan Greenspan, who has a great interest in boosting corporate profits through unfettered trade) paused for a slight measure of sympathy for unionized workers in a November 30 report. From a Seattle textile shop floor, Mitchell noted "The promise of long-term economic benefits doesn't mean much to garment workers here in the U.S. They worry about the short term, about losing their jobs to cheap labor overseas." Mitchell summarized, "Anger and fear among the older industries, as the world economy moves in new directions. And whatever is accomplished here in Seattle, many workers are afraid they will be left behind." Mitchell both echoes the inevitability of free trade and blames the worker-casualties for failing to see the long-term economic benefits of the "New Economy." (Mitchell never does explain the benefits or who will reap them, though.)

Others went one step further and claimed free trade is essentially the cure to all of the world's ills. Free trade's biggest booster, the *New York Times* columnist Thomas Friedman, stated that "Every country and company that has improved its labor, legal and environmental standards has done so because of more global trade, more integration, more Internet—not less. These are the best tools we have for improving global governance."[42] And a December 3 editorial by *USA Today* asserted, "If anything, the global flow of money, goods and workers—the 'globalization' that the WTO has come to symbolize—is among the most powerful forces raising up the world's poor and disenfranchised."[43]

According to social critic Thomas Frank, this characterization of trade as humanitarianism recasts laborers, environmentalists, and other protesters as phony populists who are blocking the truly liberating market populism delivered by free trade and the New Economy. Media coverage of the Seattle protesters thus pits "the old populist subject, the American working class" against the corporate invention of market populism, which equates free markets with freedom and democracy: "In the clash of populisms [in Seattle] that inevitably resulted, friends of the corporate way sought again and again to trump the workerist populism with the even higher octane populism of the market, charging protesters with seeking to deprive the vastly more numerous people of the Third World of the ability to make a decent living."[44] Of course, for journalists to buy into this rosy notion of market populism required that they disregard one of labor's main points in Seattle—that the WTO had, since its inception, rejected all labor rules that would ensure basic human rights and a decent living for the world's workers.

Protectionists, Poseurs, Rioters

In the days leading up to the November 30, 1999, opening of the Seattle conference, the mainstream press accorded the gathering Seattle protesters with a modicum of professional respect. Like all of "us" in the United States, protesters were regular citizens and had the right to free speech. Yet after the protesters came out in numbers fifty-thousand strong and used nonviolent street theater, marches, and civil disobedience to criticize the WTO and delay or shut down many proceedings of the trade meeting's official first day, fair treatment for the protesters in the news took a long vacation. Instead of "us," protesters were cast as short-sighted protectionists or naïve 1960s-style poseurs, labels that allowed protesters to be treated as deviant outsiders. Moreover, after a few dozen of the protesters vandalized some downtown shops, such as Starbucks, Niketown, the Gap, and Nordstrom, the news media indiscriminately painted *all* protesters as rioters. The city's subsequent suspension of free speech and the violent police crackdown on protesters was then matter-of-factly reported by the mainstream press as a necessity. Free trade trumped free speech. Bob Hasegawa, secretary-treasurer of Teamsters Local 174 in Seattle during the 1999 demonstrations, best summed up the attitude of the WTO, Seattle officials, and the consumer news media toward the anti-WTO demonstrators: "What they're telling us is that it's OK for you to protest if you're small in numbers and weak, but once you grow into a mass movement, it's not OK to protest."[45]

The initial reports from the days leading up to the WTO meeting illustrate the official acceptance and unofficial nervousness about the large number of protesters. A November 12 *USA Today* article began: "Billboards are going up. Giant street puppets have been constructed. Teach-ins are being organized. A downtown march is set. Civil disobedience training has begun, and hotel rooms are scarce."[46] The article later noted that "[Washington Council on International Trade Head Patricia] Davis, who is leading local planning for WTO, is skeptical of reports of WTO protests in Seattle with upward of 50,000 people. 'It's getting cold,' she says. 'I think they're throwing out the big numbers to scare people.'"[47] On Sunday, November 28, the *New York Times* echoed this sentiment in a front-page article: "In Seattle, which finds itself gearing up for large street protests, the celebratory mood that accompanied the city's selection as host site is clearly tempered by nervousness. Protesters say they expect 50,000 people, possibly many more. Publicly, at least, city leaders insist that the groups are welcome and that Seattle, site of the nation's first general strike in 1919, will be a model host for ministers and dissenters alike."[48]

In the next day's *New York Times* (November 29), the newspaper of record granted near-respectability to the protesters arriving in Seattle. The *Times'* Steven Greenhouse wrote, "Ten years ago, trade ministers' meeting attracted only a handful of protesters who were largely seen as cranks, but the protests have mushroomed and include many mainstream groups. The protests have been fueled by the Internet, anxiety about globalization and anger with World Trade Organization rulings."[49] The implicit key to respectability is being *mainstream*, and, as we shall see, the key to later discrediting the protesters is for the news media to portray them as *not mainstream*, that is, not one of us normal WTO-loving consumers.

Prior to the opening day of the trade summit, there were some news efforts to explain the critical issues surrounding the WTO, an organization that few had ever heard of before the Seattle talks. For example, CBS anchor Dan Rather on November 29 rhetorically asked "Just what is the World Trade Organization?" and then answered somewhat awkwardly, "It is a big powerful, business-oriented international institution, dedicated primarily to elimination, if possible, otherwise reducing tariffs on international trade [*sic*]." He then explained that the WTO had ruled on disputes such as steel dumping, U.S. hormone-treated beef, and commercial fishing. But, as media analyst Seth Ackerman noted, this CBS report "obscured the core criticisms of the WTO." Rather "failed to explain that the WTO has ruled *against* environmental restrictions in every case that has come before it. Indeed, Rather's reference to the WTO's ruling on 'fishing restrictions aimed at saving endangered species' might have misled viewers into thinking that the WTO was intervening *on behalf* of threatened animals, instead of ruling that such restrictions are an unacceptable restraint on free trade."[50]

What might have helped the overall news coverage of the WTO protests would have been reports on the many well-attended talks held by WTO critics in Seattle before the trade summit began. One such event, a two-day teach-in at Benaroya Hall in downtown Seattle, addressed globalization issues the weekend before the conference began. More than twenty-five hundred people packed the hall, and as many were turned away.[51] Although journalists from ABC, CBS, NBC, the *New York Times*, and *USA Today* were in town, none covered the event.

Reports on the protesters became breaking news by the beginning of the summit. But the stories were not the kind of publicity the protesters wanted. In a prescient comment published at the end of a November 29 *New York Times* article, Michael Dolan, of the advocacy group Public Citizen and one of the protest coordinators, said, "I'm scared that if one anarchist throws a brick through a store window downtown, that will become the big story, and our whole critique of the WTO is going to get lost."[52] The next day, Dolan's fears were realized.

On November 30, the mainstream news media shifted their focus from the WTO meetings to the protests after some shop windows were broken and Seattle responded with armored police wielding tear gas, pepper spray, rubber bullets, and clubs; all-night curfews; a hastily created fifty-block no-protest zone where even peaceful protesters were prohibited; and two units of the National Guard. A front-page December 1 *New York Times* article was right to point out that only a tiny fraction of the protesters were violent and that their vandalism wasn't supported by others: "A small group of men, dressed in black clothing and masks and ignoring cries of 'Shame on you!' from other protesters, smashed windows and spray-painted graffiti at downtown stores like Nordstrom, Niketown, Starbucks, and the Gap."[53] By not making this important point, *USA Today*'s front-page story on December 1 seemed to indict all protesters as violent: "Mayor Paul Schell declared a civil emergency Tuesday and imposed an all-night curfew on downtown Seattle after protesters shut down an international trade summit and clashed with police who seemed surprised by the ferocity of the crowds."[54] The *USA Today* story further failed to note that the protesters it described as ferocious were also unarmed and practiced passive, nonviolent civil disobedience, making the "clash" with police a decidedly uneven affair.

News commentary further separated the protesters from the normal "us" of the news audience. Columnist Friedman of the *New York Times* disparaged the protesters as "a Noah's ark of flat-earth advocates, protectionist trade unions and yuppies looking for their 1960's fix."[55] A *USA Today* editorial simultaneously identified all protesters as "not us" and obfuscated police responsibility for the ever-present clouds of tear gas. "When the tear gas cleared in downtown Seattle—thanks to the National Guard and massive arrests Wednesday—the toll of environmental and labor protests became clear: Starbucks and Nordstrom suffered smashed windows; regular citizens were deeply shaken."[56]

Worth remembering is that the fifty thousand or more protesters were all "regular citizens," too, and were likely shaken as well. In fact, many were physically shaken, as the major broadcast networks began to illustrate with brief video clips of police brutality, including an armored Seattle police officer kicking an unarmed young man in the groin and several

officers clubbing a lone female medic (who had been assisting injured protesters) as she sat on a street curb. Yet the interpretation of such images
tread lightly on the question of brutality, and instead worried why the
Seattle Police Department didn't take control earlier. Indeed, the crux of a
December 2, 1999, NBC News In Depth package by reporter Pete Williams
titled "Taking Control" centered on William's statement that "many of the
nation's police departments wonder 'What if the same thing happened to
us?' "

In their excited reports on the "Battle in Seattle," the mainstream news
media's focus on law-and-order issues often overlooked that the vast majority of demonstrators were having their right of free speech violated.
Following the WTO convention, the Seattle City Council appointed a citizen's panel, the Accountability Review Committee, to investigate the violence and the undemocratic treatment of protesters. The committee re-
viewed local news coverage and conducted interviews of those involved
in the WTO protests. Their September 2000 report confirmed the story
that the national news media coverage missed:

> It would be reckless to assert that there was any intention to infringe on in-
> dividual civil liberties. Nevertheless, several city activities had the effect of
> abridging those constitutional guarantees. Initially, poor planning sent a
> woefully inadequate police force on to the streets. Police were unable to
> perform their implied promise to arrest those doing acts of civil disobedi-
> ence. Once overwhelmed, police resorted to chemical irritants that im-
> pinged equally on law-abiding demonstrators and bystanders, and did not
> substantially deter the law-breakers they were intended to disperse. . . .
> The declaration of a limited curfew, while it might have met legal scrutiny
> on paper, resulted in actions that were explicitly intended to limit protest.
> Thus, poor communication and execution turned a legitimate strategy into
> a series of actions by police that impinged on a citizen's right of expres-
> sion.[57]

Interestingly, this angle on the protests—that is, the experience of the
vast majority of peaceful protesters—could have been easily discovered in
the independent media, such as the Independent Media Center's indy-
media.org Web site, which carried stories from hundreds of grassroots
correspondents wielding notepads, tape recorders, and video cameras.

ABC's Brian Rooney did report on the Independent Media Center on December 5 as an example of the kind of "new media" that was developed for the WTO meeting, but the report didn't contrast indymedia's coverage with ABC's or that of any other mainstream media.[58]

But, overall, the mainstream news media covering Seattle seemed much less concerned with the impact of the WTO on the lives of Americans than with the image of the conference as a grand schmoozefest for President Clinton and international government and business leaders. In other words, journalists seemed to say the WTO meeting in Seattle had a public relations problem, not a democracy problem.

For example, on December 1, the day after thousands of protesters had shut down the talks by clogging the streets, the *New York Times* reported that "It was an embarrassing beginning to negotiations that the administration had once been reluctant to hold at all."[59] On December 2, another *New York Times* story began, "If Seattle had wanted to use the World Trade Organization meeting as a postcard demonstrating its idiosyncratic charms to the rest of the world, it would surely have hoped for some better pictures."[60] On the same day, *NBC Nightly News* anchor Tom Brokaw began his newscast with a gloomy-voiced story of embarrassment for the U.S. president's administration:

BROKAW: When the World Trade Summit was planned for Seattle, the administration obviously hoped it would be a triumph for Bill Clinton in the closing months of his presidency. Instead, it's been a nightmare of protests and demonstrations in the streets, absentee dignitaries in the conference halls, and a cool reception for the president's speech.

All of these reports viewed the protests through the eyes of two familiar frames—that collective economic action, such as protests, is bad, and that the economy is driven by great business leaders and entrepreneurs, who should be able to go about their work without having to deal with embarrassing intrusions by people who aren't "regular" citizens.

John Cochran's December 1 package for ABC's *World News Tonight* demonstrates how these consumer-oriented frames for labor news heighten concerns for official subjects and turn a deaf ear toward the concerns of protesters.

COCHRAN (on camera stand-up): For a city that welcomes world trade, that expected the WTO conference could shine a positive light here, the past two days have been a crushing disappointment. (Continues with voice over VIDEO of boarded-up shop windows.) Anyone walking through what should be streets thronged with Christmas shoppers found only destruction. (Continues with voice over VIDEO of young people scrubbing graffiti from building.) Peaceful protesters helping with the clean-up said they, too, were disappointed.

YOUNG WOMAN: I don't want the statement that we had to get clouded by the violence that occurred yesterday, so I think this is a good way to help remedy that.

Unfortunately, the violence did cloud the protesters' message, as Cochran then concluded his package with the following:

COCHRAN (voice over VIDEO of National Guard troops on Seattle street, with clubs in hand): Tonight, city officials are breathing a little easier, but Seattle is still in a state of shock.

Perhaps the worst reportage resulting from consumer-oriented labor frames was the December 1 package for ABC by Deborah Wang. After mentioning Microsoft and Boeing, and interviewing Scott Miller of the US Alliance for Trade Expansion (who, of course, wants to expand trade), a representative of DaVinci Gourmet (who wants to export more flavored coffee syrups), and a representative of Oneanta Trading Co. (who wants to export more Washington State apples), Wang concluded that "so many people here are on the side of President Clinton and the WTO, and not on the side of all the protesters in the streets."

Again, a report misrepresented the protesters as opponents of all trade (despite the voluminous evidence to the contrary) and further characterized them as out of step with the presumed silent majority of trade officials, big and small businesses, and corporate lobbyists who represent "so many" people in Seattle. Wang's conclusions ignore the more reliable evidence of a nonpartisan nationwide survey conducted earlier in the year (and carried in a guest column in the *New York Times* on December 3) which indicated the majority of Americans are critical of unfettered global trade. Andrew Kohut, director of the Pew Research Center for People and the Press, wrote

In a Pew Research Center nationwide survey in April [1999], 43 percent of the respondents said that in the future a global economy would help average Americans, while 52 percent said it would hurt them. But these overall results mask a yawning gap.

Among Americans in families earning $75,000 or more, 63 percent see globalization as positive. That falls to just 48 percent for those with household income of $50,000 to $74,999. And among half of American adults in families earning less than $50,000, the positive view of globalism is held just by 37 percent.[61]

More specifically, a national *Business Week* poll conducted just a few days after the end of the WTO meeting in Seattle verified that the majority of Americans supported the Seattle protesters. Fifty-two percent of respondents said they were sympathetic toward the protesters at the summit, compared to 39 percent who said they were not sympathetic. Like the case of the striking UPS workers, the mainstream corporate news media stumbled in its efforts to get beyond its typical news frames and tell this remarkable (and for them, unexpected) story.[62]

So, despite the consumer-oriented coverage, why did the majority of U.S. citizens sympathize with the protesters? The most important factor is that amidst the characterizations of the protesters as protectionists, poseurs, and rioters, some news narratives and images that communicated the experience and message of the protesters did get through, due to the numbers and persistence of the demonstrators.[63] In other words, unable to ignore what had become a major news event in the streets (instead of the conference rooms) of Seattle, the mainstream news media had to alter their coverage.

A December 2, 1999, "In Their Own Words" interview on *NBC Nightly News* illustrated the almost begrudging way some mainstream reports shifted their framing of the story to include criticism of the WTO and police. Despite anchor Tom Brokaw's introduction, the interview with a theology professor/protester provided an alternative view of what was happening on Seattle's streets.

BROKAW: Now to a view from a veteran demonstrator who found himself in the unusual position of defending places like Niketown and Starbucks from the anarchists' rampage. Ken Butigan is a theology professor at Berkeley who also teaches peaceful protest tactics. His experience tonight, in his own words.

BUTIGAN (head shot): Unprovoked, the police used massive force, including [Cut to slow-motion VIDEO of armored police firing tear gas canisters point-blank at protesters.] unnumbered rounds of tear gas, pepper spray, and rubber bullets on hundreds, or maybe thousands, of nonviolent protesters. [Cut to close-up of man wiping eyes of another.] I saw in the eyes of young people a great deal of trauma and panic in the face of what was really a war zone. [Cut to young man wearing backpack being swung down hard to the sidewalk by an armored police officer.] . . . The way we're going to make significant and deep change in this world is through active, powerful, creative, mobilized, nonviolence.

Butigan's interview ended with his repudiation of the anarchists' activities, but his overall message was evident in both his words and the images. It was the police who were violent and who used a disproportional amount of force in response to the cracked windows and graffiti caused by a relatively few vandals.

Likewise, a *CBS Evening News* report by correspondent John Roberts on December 2, 1999, represented its most open coverage of the critics of the WTO and contained one of the few instances of network television news coverage that quoted a representative of labor, as illustrated in this excerpt:

> ROBERTS (voice over VIDEO of protesters): Demonstrators claim that it [the WTO] is undemocratic, cloaked in secrecy, and panders to the interests of big business at the expense of labor and the environment.
>
> RON JUDD, EXECUTIVE DIRECTOR, SEATTLE LABOR COUNCIL: I don't think a lot of us realized that when they were creating this organization that it would be so closed down, that it was going to be so secretive, and that there wasn't going to be an ability for people to have input through their respective organizations.

Roberts's conclusion even echoed the voice of the protesters, as he signed off, "Now, the whole world *is* watching."

Long before the WTO meeting in Seattle, the majority of Americans were not impressed with the new economic order of the 1990s (as evidenced by the UPS case and the April 1999 Pew Research Center poll). So, although stories and images that were critical of the WTO and free trade were not as common as stories that were framed to discredit the protesters, those critical moments were likely much more salient with the majority of the people. Indeed, the protests generated two great dissonant images that were hard for the world to ignore: (1) the disproportional violence wielded by police on the demonstrators and (2) the disproportional communication between the demonstrators in the streets and the delegates behind closed doors.

Two other factors contributed to the protesters' popular success. First,

December 2, 1999, *NBC Nightly News*. Professor Ken Butigan: "Unprovoked, the police used massive force, including unnumbered rounds of tear gas, pepper spray, and rubber bullets on hundreds, or maybe thousands, of nonviolent protesters."

the protests had the effect of pushing President Clinton's agenda, one of the few ways their message was carried directly into the meetings. In a speech to the WTO that reflected some of the concerns of those protesting in the streets, Clinton said "The public must see and hear and, in a very real sense, actually join in the deliberations."[64] Second, the fact that the WTO talks themselves fell apart, with reports of squabbling and disagreement by the delegates, seemed to confirm criticisms and doubts: The economy was being driven by less-than-great business leaders and entrepreneurs.

Citizens of the United States were not the only ones suspicious of elite business and political leaders who would attempt to engineer the global economy without their input. Seattle helped to mobilize a more international movement of Internet-connected protesters around the world. Subsequent gatherings by the World Bank and International Monetary Fund in Washington, D.C., and Prague; the G8 summit of leaders from the world's leading industrial nations in Genoa; and the private, clubby World Economic Forum in Davos, Switzerland were greeted with thousands of protesters. Even Nobel Prize–winning economist Joseph Stiglitz, who in the 1990s had served on President Clinton's Council of Economic Advisors and as chief economist of the World Bank, agreed that the three main institutions of globalization—the World Bank, the International Monetary Fund, and the WTO—were undemocratic and secretive and had exploited poorer nations and their people for the benefit of the rich.[65]

Although the WTO conference in Seattle ended in failure for the trade delegates, Seattle was a victory for the protesters, who gained great organizational momentum and communicated their message despite the misframed media coverage. So, it was not surprising that the WTO's next meeting (in 2001) was located in Doha, Qatar, a tiny sheikdom on the Persian Gulf, which *USA Today* reported had a "tight visa policy," a "docile media," and "no labor unions, no political parties and no domestic anti-globalization groups." Instead of finding Qatar to be a troubling location for a trade organization that already had a poor record of responding to labor unions, social justice groups, and environmental activists, *USA Today* proved it could be docile as well, describing Qatar as "the perfect antidote to Seattle."[66]

The Future of Labor in the Corporate News

The case studies of GM's Willow Run plant closing, the American Airlines flight attendant strike, the Major League Baseball strike, the UPS strike, and the protests at the WTO meeting in Seattle all illustrate how the news media cover labor relations news by reporting from a consumer perspective. In a far-too-predictable fashion, the mainstream corporate news media in the 1990s continually resorted to the same five news frames to structure stories about labor relations. These consumer-oriented stories framed labor both literally and figuratively—shaping news reports that misrepresented worker's motives, obscured the issues, lionized business executives, and impugned collective action—and often leaving labor groups falsely "framed" for crimes such as violence, inflation, protectionism, and anti-Americanism. In other words, the news media have given labor a bum rap, one that, despite labor's sometime internal problems, it doesn't deserve.

It is through the inventiveness of some labor groups and social activism organizations that they have been able to harness the corporate media's consumer news frames to improve labor news coverage. Some of the most powerful news stories of recent years have developed when the fruits of consumption get linked back to often-invisible means of production. Of course, the mainstream news media, which don't regularly cover a labor beat and seldom use investigative reporters, rarely shed light on production and labor. The impetus for such stories usually begins with social activism by labor or other organizations. For example, the production-consumption link was visible in much of the UPS story. In some ways, it was undeniable, since many people were personally acquainted with the 185,000 striking UPS workers across the United States. In other words, the citizens/consumers knew the people who did the work and identified them as regular people with valid concerns—not as the faceless, potentially demonized members of organized labor. The reform-minded Teamsters also did an excellent job of communicating their message of a living wage to the media and the people.

Protesters of the WTO in Seattle also helped to lay bare the operations of the unelected international trade body and its decisions that impact a wide range of global concerns, including the endangerment of sea turtles, the proliferation of genetically modified foods, and the horrors of sweatshop and child labor. The exposé of Wal-Mart's use of sweatshop labor—which used the narrative "hook" of Kathie Lee Gifford's sweatshop-made Wal-Mart clothing line—was another major news story that linked the unseen process of production to consumption. And, as historian Lawrence Glickman explains, campaigns for a living wage demonstrate ways in which labor has advantageously linked consumerism—that is, the ability to earn a wage so that one can live in a comfortable fashion—to production.[67] The recent wave of living wage campaigns since 1994 has resulted in more than one hundred local living wage ordinances in the United States by 2003. The ordinances—in cities such as Baltimore, Boston, Detroit, Los Angeles, Milwaukee, Minneapolis, St. Louis, and Tucson—generally require that city service contractors pay a living wage, usually enough to lift a family of four above the poverty line. The point of the campaigns is that public dollars should be used for public good and should support only companies that are committed to compensating their employees with fair wages.[68]

The news media, though, generally don't portray the link between consumption and production, often because the production process and treatment of labor doesn't reflect favorably on their advertisers or own corporate parents. In fact, it scares the hell out of businesses when they can't control the image of production (witness the discomfort of Nike and its CEO Phil Knight over charges of sweatshop labor). Businesses don't want to call attention to production, which is exactly what labor and social advocates do. Corporations often fight to control or hide the image of production through public relations and advertising. GM's efforts to make Saturn a "different" people-friendly auto company and Wal-Mart's advertised "Buy American" policy are both approaches (rather transparent approaches to the keen observer) that try to mask the true modes of production. Recent books from the left (e.g., Thomas Frank's *The Conquest of Cool: Business Culture, Counterculture, and the Rise of Hip Consumerism*) and the right (e.g., David Brooks' *Bobos in Paradise: The New Upper Class and How They Got There*) detail how corporations, through advertising and PR, now sell consumption as hip and countercultural, and business entrepreneurialism as equally radical.[69] This is only possible, though, by obscuring labor and class relations and genuine radical social action.

Thus, there is a constant battle between corporate interests defining consumerism in one fashion—buy, buy, buy, and let business do as it wishes—versus labor, which asks for a living wage to participate in a consumer economy (both in the United States and abroad) and for fair, safe modes of production. The major news media are commercial, corporate media, and they generally frame news stories in ways that favor corporate interests. But, in cases of widespread democratic (and nonviolent) public activism by labor and other social groups, news cannot afford to be *seen* as acting on behalf of corporate capitalism. So, in these instances, the news media are unable to adequately frame labor news from their typical consumer economy perspective and must report at least some criticism of the production side of the economy to sustain their own credibility. In other words, the mainstream news media won't cover labor news, especially with favorable frames, unless the stories are thrust on them. Then, of course, corporate damage control teams go to work, to reestablish corporate-friendly framing of news events. The UPS "brown" branding campaign of 2002 is an example of this effort, publicizing the corporate processes and obscuring the company's former symbol—the people who do the work. Even Kathie Lee Gifford hired a public relations firm to transform her image from being the namesake for sweatshop-produced Wal-Mart clothing to (briefly) the nation's most visible crusader for garment workers' rights.[70]

The relentless and well-financed nature of such corporate communications, which continually refine and redefine their stories to fit the dominant frames of the news and gloss over indiscretions, overwhelms most labor communication efforts. But, as we have seen, savvy labor and socially progressive groups can turn this same strategy back on socially irresponsible corporations and organizations.

The question we are left with at the end of this book is the problem posed in the beginning: How does labor get the news media to go beyond their typical consumer-oriented frames and tell fair and compelling stories about people's lives at work? Given the lessons of case studies, four recommendations are in order.

1. Workers and allies must protest visibly, vigorously, and strategically.
2. Labor unions must use a multifaceted approach.
3. Labor unions should utilize nonmainstream media.
4. Labor unions should seek to maintain and encourage diversity in media ownership.

First, workers and their allies must protest visibly, vigorously, and strategically. The protests in Seattle illustrate that no how matter distasteful the message may be to the corporate news media, fifty thousand passionate demonstrators cannot be ignored. Even though the protesters were often maligned by the news media, they became the story of Seattle, and they redefined the WTO conference. The protests were successful only because the many groups—representing labor, environmentalism, human rights, sustainable agriculture, and other causes—worked together weeks in advance under the coordination of the Direct Action Network.[71] The WTO protests showed that successful mass protests can, at least for a short time, shake up the mainstream news media's traditional framing of stories and make it act more like a public sphere than a consumer sphere.

Second, labor unions need to recognize that protests are only part of the battle against corporations and organizations with a global reach. As labor scholar Howard Kimeldorf has noted, communicating labor's story takes a multifaceted approach.

> Deindustrialization and accelerated capital mobility have redrawn traditional battle lines, pulling labor and its supporters away from the trenches of the shop floor to the court of public opinion where the new multinational corporations appear increasingly vulnerable. Sophisticated "corporate campaigns" directed at shareholders, mass protests and boycotts aimed at consumers, and highly publicized legal challenges to corporate decision making have placed organized labor on a more solid footing as it heads into the next century.[72]

This same "corporate campaign" approach, used by locked-out steelworkers at the Ravenswood Aluminum plant in West Virginia to combat elusive international owners and emerge victorious in 1992, has been called "the Ravenswood model" by labor scholars Tom Juravich and Kate Bronfenbrenner. The approach of the Ravenswood workers, like that of UPS workers just a few years later, required "the research, the strategies, and the full participation of the members and the broader community, locally, nationally, and internationally."[73]

Third, labor unions should not hesitate to go outside the mainstream mass media to communicate their stories. The debate in the early 1990s was "should labor sponsor a national newspaper"?[74] The Internet has now made that a moot question, as it has created an inexpensive alternative mass medium with more than 182 million online in the United States and Canada and more than 605 million online worldwide by September 2002.[75] In fact, the increasing worldwide accessibility of the Web enables Web publications to have the same reach as global capitalism. A high-profile daily labor publication on the Web has yet to emerge.

Still, there are models of how this might be done. The AFL-CIO maintains an information-rich labor Web site (www.aflcio.org); the Independent Media Center (www.indymedia.org) offers grassroots media coverage from the left; and MediaChannel (www.mediachannel.org) serves as a clearinghouse for media-related news from more than nine hundred affiliate Web sites worldwide. There are also a number of city-or regional-based Web publications, such as KC Labor from Kansas City (www.kc labor.org) and Los Angeles Labor News (www.lalabor.org). Perhaps the best general labor movement news portal on the Web is LaborNet (www.labornet.org), but neither this nor the other labor sites are as current or as well designed as the top commercial daily news media sites on the Web. In an era when Fox News Channel is able to successfully carve out a niche for itself as the "conservative" cable news channel in the United States (as if CNN was liberal?), it seems reasonable and justifiable that labor could sponsor a nationally and internationally known comprehensive labor news Web site for working people, at a cost far less than media such as newspapers or television.

Finally, though, for all of the shortcomings of the mainstream news media, labor should not give up on it. Increasing consolidation of the news media into a handful of corporations is bad for both labor unions and citizens. Thus, labor unions should ally themselves with organizations and citizens who seek to maintain limits on media ownership in the United States and around the world and should encourage diversity in ownership. The Newspaper Guild, a union of more than thirty-four thousand media workers, knows this firsthand; it has been involved in combating not only labor difficulties at individual newspapers but also further deregulation of the media.

The most recent chapter of deregulation is Federal Communications Commission Chairman Michael Powell's move toward the elimination of the cross-ownership rule, which since 1975 has prohibited a single company from owning a broadcast station and newspaper in the same market. The idea behind the rule was to maximize the number of voices in a community and prevent one corporation from dominating public discourse in a region. Journalism historian Douglas Gomery explains that without the rule, "a local television station owned by a newspaper company can simply televise a summary of the paper's content, offering no benefits to the consumer, yet it will still be able to dominate the local political and cultural discourse."[76]

In its condemnation of the proposed deregulation, the Newspaper Guild cited the Canadian government's elimination of a cross-ownership ban in 2000. In the following year, a single television company, CanWest Global, acquired 80 percent of daily newspapers across Canada. Can-West's news monopoly in Canada did little but serve the company's bottom line, as it instituted layoffs, increased workloads, exercised censorship of news critical of CanWest, and required all of its newspapers to publish its new conservative national editorials.[77]

CanWest Global's Orwellian corporate motto—"If you can watch it, read it, hear it, or download it, we want to be the source"—might be appreciated by a stockholder, but it should gravely concern every champion of democracy and social justice.[78]

There could be a similar fate for the news media in the United States. From a consumer perspective, it would make little difference. Large media corporations can tell consumer-oriented news stories as well as anyone can. But, from the standpoint of workers and citizens, it makes all the difference. In this book I have argued that the corporate media already march lockstep in most of their coverage of labor relations. To concentrate the control of the news media in even fewer hands would further decrease the number of editorial voices in the news and, correspondingly, further decrease the potential for alternative viewpoints and frames.

As the FCC voted in 2003 to allow television networks to acquire even more stations and to eliminate the cross-ownership ban (which, not surprisingly, barely received mention in the U.S. corporate news media), citizens and grassroots organizations from the left and right mobilized to send Washington nearly two million messages in opposition. Although the voting majority of the FCC was unmoved, Congress could not ignore the groundswell of criticism and voted to roll back at least part of the deregulatory ruling. The FCC case is instructional in again illustrating not only how the mainstream news media ultimately serve their own bottom line (in the near-blackout of news about the sweeping deregulation that their corporate owners supported with heavy lobbying) but also the power of collective action. Thus, labor unions must be ever vigilant and must seek to frame news stories—and sometimes even work to reframe the structure of the news industry—before the news media frames labor.

APPENDIXES

Appendix A ABC, CBS, and NBC Packages on the GM Willow Run Shutdown

Date	Network	Reporter	Subject*
1991.12.18	ABC	Chris Bury	GM reorganization
1991.12.18	ABC	Linda Patillo	Arlington, TX plant
1991.12.18	NBC	Mike Jensen	GM cutbacks
1991.12.18	NBC	Jim Cummins	Arlington/UAW
1992.01.24	ABC	Chris Bury	Ypsilanti vs. Arlington
1992.02.23	NBC	Jim Cummins	GM plant closing tomorrow
1992.02.24	NBC	Jim Cummins	GM plant closing announced
1992.02.24	ABC	Jim Hickey	Reaction in Ypsilanti
1992.02.24	ABC	Chris Bury	Reaction in Arlington
1992.02.24	ABC	Jim Bitterman	GM's success in Europe
1992.10.07	CBS	Richard Threlkeld	NAFTA/Willow Run workers
1993.01.11	NBC	Fred Briggs	Ypsilanti Township lawsuit
1993.02.09	NBC	Mike Boettcher	Ypsilanti township lawsuit
1993.02.09	CBS	Jacqueline Adams	Lawsuit/similar situation in NY
1993.08.04	CBS	Linda Taira	Court ruling in favor of GM

*The Subject listings of Appendixes A–E are taken from the Vanderbilt Television News Archive, http://tvnews.vanderbilt.edu. The Archive Web site contains abstracts for each story; video copies of news packages may be ordered from the Archive.

Appendix B ABC, CBS, and NBC Packages on the American Airlines Flight Attendant Strike

Date	Network	Reporter	Subject
1993.11.18	ABC	Bob Jamieson	American Airlines strike
1993.11.18	CBS	Vicki Mabrey	American Airlines strike
1993.11.18	NBC	Jim Cummins	American Airlines strike
1993.11.19	ABC	Bob Jamieson	American Airlines strike
1993.11.19	CBS	Vicky Mabrey	American Airlines strike
1993.11.19	NBC	Jim Cummins	American Airlines strike
1993.11.20	CBS	Vicky Mabrey	American Airlines strike
1993.11.20	CBS	Monica Gayle	American Airlines strike
1993.11.20	NBC	Gary Matsumoto	American Airlines strike
1993.11.21	ABC	Erin Hayes	American Airlines strike
1993.11.21	CBS	Vicky Mabrey	American Airlines strike
1993.11.21	CBS	Linda Taira	American Airlines strike
1993.11.22	ABC	Bob Jamieson	American Airlines strike
1993.11.22	CBS	Vicky Mabrey	American Airlines strike
1993.11.22	CBS	Rita Braver	American Airlines strike
1993.11.22	NBC	Andrea Mitchell	American Airlines strike
1993.11.22	NBC	David Bloom	American Airlines strike
1993.11.23	NBC	David Bloom	American Airlines strike

Appendix C ABC, CBS, and NBC Packages on the Major League Baseball Strike

Date	Network	Reporter	Subject
1994.07.11	CBS	Wyatt Andrews	Possible strike
1994.07.12	ABC	Armen Keteyian	Possible strike
1994.08.04	NBC	Robert Hager	Players' response
1994.08.04	ABC	Armen Keteyian	Players' response
1994.08.06	CBS	Anthony Mason	Strike set
1994.08.07	NBC	Larry Carroll	Issues examined
1994.08.10	NBC	Mike Jenson	Risks to both sides
1994.08.10	ABC	Armen Keteyian	Great season lost
1994.08.11	CBS	Bob Orr	Economic impact
1994.08.11	NBC	Sara James	Strike set to start
1994.08.11	NBC	Mike Jensen	Economic impact
1994.08.11	ABC	Armen Keteyian	Impasse
1994.08.11	ABC	Jeff Greenfield	Owner revenues
1994.08.12	ABC	Armen Keteyian	Impact on businesses
1994.08.12	NBC	Sara James	Break in owners' ranks?
1994.08.12	CBS	Bob Orr	Baseball finances
1994.08.12	CBS	Diana Gonzalez	Colebrunn's lost season
1994.08.13	NBC	Rehema Ellis	Day 2 of strike
1994.08.13	CBS	David Culhane	Day 2/possible fan protest
1994.08.13	ABC	Mike von Fremd	Minor leagues
1994.08.14	ABC	Armen Keteyian	Day 3 of strike
1994.08.14	CBS	David Culhane	No talks/minor leagues
1994.08.17	NBC	David Bloom	Minor leagues
1994.08.18	CBS	Giselle Fernandez	Talks planned
1994.08.19	CBS	Bob McNamara	Minor leagues
1994.08.20	NBC	Sara James	Economic impact
1994.08.25	ABC	Jim Hickey	Talks break down
1994.08.25	NBC	Robert Hager	Little League World Series
1994.08.27	NBC	Kelly O'Donnell	No foodbank donations
1994.08.27	CBS	Jonathan Sanders	Russian baseball
1994.08.27	ABC	Jim Angle	Fans' lament
1994.08.29	NBC	Larry Carroll	Little League baseball
1994.09.02	CBS	James Hattori	Japanese baseball
1994.09.05	NBC	Robert Hager	Rotisserie baseball
1994.09.05	NBC	David Bloom	Decline of unions
1994.09.08	ABC	Tom Foreman	Minor leagues
1994.09.08	NBC	Sara James	Luxury tax proposal
1994.09.08	NBC	Mike Jensen	Projected business losses
1994.09.08	CBS	Jacqueline Adams	Latest meeting
1994.09.09	ABC	Armen Keteyian	Talks break down
1994.09.09	NBC	Bob Costas	Talks break down
1994.09.14	CBS	Jaqueline Adams	Season ends
1994.09.14	ABC	Armen Keteyian	Season ends
1994.09.14	NBC	Bob Costas	Season ends
1994.09.22	NBC	Bob Costas	House hearings
1994.09.22	ABC	Armen Keteyian	House hearings
1994.10.22	NBC	Dawn Fratangelo	Profile of player Jim Czajkowski

Appendix C (continued)

Date	Network	Reporter	Subject
1994.12.15	ABC	Armen Keteyian	Business of baseball
1994.12.23	NBC	Rehema Ellis	Talks break down
1994.12.23	ABC	Tom Foreman	Talks break down
1994.12.23	ABC	Armen Keteyian	Baseball's future
1994.12.23	CBS	Frank Currier	Talks break down
1995.02.01	NBC	Bob Dotson	Replacement player dreams
1995.02.04	ABC	Bill Greenwood	Prospects for talks
1995.02.05	CBS	Bob Orr	Prospects for Clinton's solution
1995.02.05	NBC	Tom Pettit	Clinton threatens intervention
1995.02.06	ABC	Armen Keteyian	Republicans oppose plan
1995.02.06	ABC	Mark Potter	Impact on Florida economy
1995.02.06	NBC	Brian Williams	White House deadline
1995.02.07	ABC	Brit Hume	Clinton's efforts
1995.02.07	NBC	Brian Williams	Clinton's efforts
1995.02.07	CBS	Bob Orr	Clinton's efforts
1995.02.14	CBS	John Blackstone	Trujillo's lawsuit
1995.02.14	ABC	Brian Rooney	Trujillo's lawsuit
1995.02.16	CBS	Diana Gonzalez	Spring training
1995.02.17	NBC	Bob Dotson	Impact on Dunedin, FL
1995.02.18	NBC	Kenley Jones	Replacement player dreams
1995.02.18	ABC	Dick Schaap	Replacement players
1995.02.20	ABC	Mark Litke	American players in Japan
1995.02.25	CBS	Diana Olick	Replacement players
1995.03.02	ABC	Mark Potter	Replacement players
1995.03.02	CBS	Wyatt Andrews	Replacement players
1995.03.04	ABC	Armen Keteyian	Breakthrough in talks
1995.03.04	NBC	Gary Matsumoto	Player-owner talks/replacements
1995.03.04	CBS	Bob Orr	Player-owner talks
1995.03.05	CBS	Bob Orr	Latest talk issues
1995.03.05	ABC	Armen Keteyian	Latest talk issues
1995.03.05	NBC	Gary Matsumoto	Latest talk issues
1995.03.06	ABC	Jeff Greenfield	Status of strike
1995.03.09	ABC	Bob Jamieson	Financial scenario of strike
1995.03.26	NBC	Odetta Rogers-Clarke	NLRB sends dispute to court
1995.03.26	ABC	Bob Jamieson	NLRB sends dispute to court
1995.03.27	CBS	Bob Orr	Struggle for solution
1995.03.28	CBS	Bob Orr	Owners' proposal
1995.03.29	ABC	Tim McCarver	Angelos profile
1995.03.31	CBS	Diana Olick	Court injunction
1995.03.31	ABC	Bob Jamieson	Court injunction
1995.03.31	NBC	Rehema Ellis	Court injunction
1995.03.31	NBC	Roger O'Neil	Fan reaction to Rockies
1995.03.31	NBC	Tom Brokaw	Live discussion with Costas
1995.04.01	ABC	Bob Jamieson	Confusion over opening day
1995.04.01	NBC	Odetta Rogers-Clarke	Dispute ending
1995.04.01	NBC	Kenley Jones	End for replacement player
1995.04.02	CBS	Diana Olick	Prospects for new season

Appendix C (continued)

Date	Network	Reporter	Subject
1995.04.02	NBC	Mike Boettcher	Prospects for new season
1995.04.02	NBC	Odetta Rogers-Clarke	Fan reaction
1995.04.02	ABC	Bob Jamieson	Preparing for new season
1995.04.03	ABC	Armen Keteyian	Preparing for new season
1995.04.03	ABC	Mark Potter	Impact on Dunedin, FL
1995.04.03	CBS	Richard Threlkeld	Problems in new season
1995.04.04	ABC	Mark Potter	Problems in new season
1995.04.15	ABC	Dick Schaap	First real game
1995.04.23	NBC	Jon Frankel	MLB's need to woo fans
1995.04.26	CBS	Peter Van Sant	Opening day/fans missing
1995.04.27	ABC	Armen Keteyian	MLB's struggle to win back fans
1995.04.29	CBS	Jerry Bowen	Legendary baseball

NLRB = national labor relations board; MLB = major league baseball.

Appendix D ABC, CBS, and NBC Packages on the United Parcel Service (UPS) Strike

Date	Network	Reporter	Subject
1997.08.03	CBS	Frank Currier	UPS strike
1997.08.03	NBC	Andrea McCarren	UPS strike
1997.08.04	ABC	Aaron Brown	UPS strike
1997.08.04	ABC	Dean Reynolds	UPS strike
1997.08.04	CBS	Frank Currier	UPS strike / part-time workers
1997.08.04	CBS	Ray Brady	UPS strike / part-time workers
1997.08.04	NBC	Jim Avila	UPS strike / part-time workers / mail-order business
1997.08.04	NBC	Mike Jensen	UPS strike / part-time workers / mail-order business
1997.08.05	ABC	Tom Foreman	UPS strike
1997.08.05	CBS	Frank Currier	UPS strike / businesses
1997.08.05	NBC	Jim Avila	UPS strike / businesses / part-time workers
1997.08.05	NBC	Mike Jensen	UPS strike / businesses / part-time workers
1997.08.06	ABC	Bill Redeker	UPS strike
1997.08.07	ABC	Tom Foreman	UPS strike
1997.08.07	CBS	Frank Currier	UPS strike
1997.08.07	CBS	Ray Brady	Eye on America (UPS strike / part-time workers)
1997.08.07	NBC	Jim Avila	UPS strike
1997.08.08	ABC	Bill Redeker	UPS strike / post office
1997.08.08	ABC	Judy Muller	UPS strike / post office
1997.08.08	CBS	Frank Currier	UPS strike
1997.08.08	CBS	Jacqueline Adams	UPS strike
1997.08.09	ABC	Bill Redeker	UPS strike
1997.08.09	CBS	Byron Pitts	UPS strike
1997.08.09	NBC	Andrea McCarren	UPS strike
1997.08.09	NBC	Scott Cohn	UPS strike
1997.08.10	ABC	Bill Redeker	UPS strike
1997.08.10	CBS	Diana Olick	UPS strike
1997.08.10	NBC	Andrea McCarren	UPS strike
1997.08.10	NBC	Kenley Jones	UPS strike
1997.08.11	ABC	Jackie Judd	UPS strike
1997.08.11	CBS	Diana Olick	UPS strike / driver killed
1997.08.11	NBC	Andrea Mitchell	UPS strike / driver killed
1997.08.12	ABC	Jackie Judd	UPS strike
1997.08.12	ABC	Bob Jamieson	UPS strike
1997.08.12	CBS	Diana Olick	UPS strike
1997.08.12	CBS	Ray Brady	UPS strike
1997.08.12	NBC	David Gregory	UPS strike
1997.08.12	NBC	David Bloom	UPS strike
1997.08.13	ABC	Mike von Fremd	UPS strike / Louisville, KY
1997.08.13	CBS	Ray Brady	UPS strike
1997.08.13	CBS	John Blackstone	UPS strike
1997.08.13	NBC	David Bloom	UPS strike

Appendix D ABC, CBS, and NBC Packages on the United Parcel Service (UPS) Strike

Date	Network	Reporter	Subject
1997.08.14	ABC	Bill Redeker	UPS talks / labor movement
1997.08.14	CBS	Bill Whitaker	UPS strike talks
1997.08.14	CBS	Bob Orr	UPS strike talks
1997.08.15	ABC	Jackie Judd	UPS strike
1997.08.15	CBS	Diana Olick	UPS strike
1997.08.15	CBS	Jerry Bowen	UPS strike
1997.08.15	NBC	Claire Shipman	UPS strike
1997.08.16	NBC	Jim Avila	UPS strike
1997.08.16	ABC	Bill Redeker	UPS strike
1997.08.17	CBS	Wyatt Andrews	UPS strike
1997.08.17	ABC	Bill Redeker	UPS strike
1997.08.17	CBS	Byron Pitts	UPS strike / pension plans
1997.08.17	CBS	Troy Roberts	UPS strike / pension plans
1997.08.17	CBS	Russ Mitchell	Stock market / Friday's drop
1997.08.17	NBC	Andrea McCarren	UPS strike / Taft-Hartley
1997.08.17	NBC	John Palmer	UPS strike / Taft-Hartley
1997.08.18	ABC	Bill Redeker	UPS strike
1997.08.18	CBS	Diana Olick	UPS strike
1997.08.18	NBC	Claire Shipman	UPS strike / industry vs. labor
1997.08.18	NBC	Pat Dawson	UPS strike / industry vs. labor
1997.08.19	ABC	Bill Redeker	UPS strike / settlement / union
1997.08.19	ABC	Peter Jennings	UPS strike / settlement / union
1997.08.19	ABC	Bob Jamieson	UPS strike / settlement / union
1997.08.19	CBS	Diana Olick	UPS strike / settlement / union
1997.08.19	CBS	Ray Brady	UPS strike / settlement / union
1997.08.19	NBC	Claire Shipman	UPS strike / settlement / union
1997.08.20	CBS	Diana Olick	*Eye on America* (UPS / unions)
1997.08.20	CBS	Sandra Hughes	*Eye on America* (UPS / unions)

Appendix E ABC, CBS, and NBC Packages on the World Trade Organization (WTO) Protests

Date	Network	Reporter	Subject
1999.11.28	NBC	John Palmer	Seattle / WTO / conference
1999.11.28	NBC	George Lewis	Seattle / WTO / conference
1999.11.29	ABC	Deborah Wang	Seattle / economy /WTO /demonstrations
1999.11.29	CBS	John Roberts	Seattle / WTO meeting
1999.11.29	NBC	George Lewis	Seattle / WTO summit
1999.11.29	NBC	Mike Jensen	Seattle / WTO summit
1999.11.30	NBC	George Lewis	Seattle / WTO meeting / protests
1999.11.30	NBC	Andrea Mitchell	Seattle / WTO meeting / protests
1999.11.30	ABC	John Cochran	Seattle / WTO conference / protests
1999.11.30	ABC	Deborah Wang	Seattle /WTO conference / protests
1999.11.30	CBS	John Roberts	Seattle / WTO / violence
1999.12.01	ABC	John Cochran	Seattle / WTO / protests / Clinton address
1999.12.01	ABC	Terry Moran	Seattle / WTO / protests / Clinton address
1999.12.01	ABC	Deborah Wang	Seattle / WTO / protests / Clinton address
1999.12.01	CBS	John Roberts	Seattle / WTO meeting / protests
1999.12.01	CBS	John Blackstone	Seattle / WTO meeting / protests
1999.12.01	NBC	Claire Shipman	Seattle / WTO summit / protests
1999.12.01	NBC	George Lewis	Seattle / WTO summit / protests
1999.12.02	ABC	Judy Muller	Seattle / WTO / demonstrations / the anarchists
1999.12.02	CBS	John Blackstone	Seattle / WTO meeting / protests
1999.12.02	CBS	John Roberts	Seattle / WTO meeting / protests
1999.12.02	NBC	George Lewis	Seattle / WTO meeting / protests
1999.12.02	NBC	Kelly O'Donnell	Seattle / WTO meeting / protests
1999.12.02	NBC	Tom Brokaw	Seattle / WTO meeting / protests
1999.12.02	NBC	Pete Williams	*In Depth* (law enforcement / crowd control)
1999.12.03	ABC	John Cochran	Seattle / WTO Clinton Statement
1999.12.03	CBS	John Blackstone	Seattle / WTO / violence
1999.12.04	CBS	John Blackstone	Seattle / WTO / demonstrations
1999.12.04	NBC	George Lewis	Seattle / WTO / demonstrations
1999.12.05	ABC	Brian Rooney	Seattle / WTO / demonstrations / new media
1999.12.07	ABC	Deborah Wang	Seattle / WTO / violence
1999.12.07	CBS	John Blackstone	Seattle / police chief resigns
1999.12.28	CBS	Bill Whitaker	Seattle / WTO / Y2K celebrations canceled

NOTES

Chapter 1. How Labor Gets Framed

1. Jürgen Habermas, *The Structural Transformation of the Public Sphere*, trans. Thomas Burger (Cambridge: MIT Press, 1989).

2. In a similar vein, when an ad campaign sponsored by the Health Care Reform Project in 1994 accused Pizza Hut of covering its European workers with health insurance but only a small percentage of its American employees, Pizza Hut's savvy response in the news media appealed directly to the consumer. The pizza chain claimed that health care coverage for its workers would hike pizza prices, increasing an eleven-dollar pizza to twenty dollars. The *New York Times*, in a bold editorial, used Pizza Hut's own costs in figuring that a proposed federal health insurance requirement would add only about forty cents to an eleven-dollar pizza. Regardless, the national debate over health care ended in 1994 with little hope for medical benefits for poorly paid fast-food workers. See Editorial, "Pizza Hut's Double Standard," *New York Times*, 22 July 1994, p. A26.

3. Julie Schmit, "'A Disaster' for Travelers: Planes Fly, But Without Passengers," *USA Today*, 19 November 1993, p. 1A.

4. Adam Bryant, "A Strike at American Airlines Disrupts Travel of Thousands," *New York Times*, 19 November 1993, p. A1.

5. From October through December 1993, *USA Today* ran thirty-three stories and the *New York Times* ran thirty stories on the flight attendant strike.

6. Graef S. Crystal, *In Search of Excess: The Overcompensation of American Executives* (New York: W.W. Norton, 1992), 179.

7. Ibid., 179. The data on Crandall's compensation is from pages 179–81.

8. Bryant, "Strike at American Airlines," p. A1.

9. See Michael Parenti, *Inventing Reality: The Politics of Mass Media* (New York: St. Martin's Press, 1986); William J. Puette, *Through Jaundiced Eyes: How the Media View Organized Labor* (Ithaca: Cornell University Press, 1992); and Jonathan Tasini, "Lost in the Margins: Labor and the Media," *Extra!* 3, no. 7 (1990): 2–11. See also Herbert J.

Gans, *Deciding What's News: A Study of* CBS Evening News, NBC Nightly News, Newsweek, and Time (New York: Pantheon, 1979), 46.

10. James W. Carey, *Communication as Culture: Essays on Media and Society* (Boston: Unwin Hyman, 1989), 21.

11. Lance Bennett and Murray Edelman, "Toward a New Political Narrative," *Journal of Communication* 35, no. 4 (1985): 159.

12. Todd Gitlin, *The Whole World is Watching* (Berkeley: University of California Press, 1980), 7.

13. Peter Golding and Graham Murdock, "Culture, Communications, and Political Economy," in *Mass Media and Society*, ed. James Curran and Michael Gurevitch (London: Edward Arnold, 1991), 27.

14. Ralph Miliband, *The State in Capitalist Society* (London: Weidenfeld and Nicolson, 1969), 238.

15. Jimmie L. Reeves and Richard Campbell, *Cracked Coverage: Television News, the Anti-Cocaine Crusade, and the Reagan Legacy* (Durham: Duke University Press, 1994), 59.

16. Juliet B. Schor, "Towards a New Politics of Consumption," in *The Consumer Society Reader*, ed. Juliet B. Schor and Douglas B. Holt (New York: The New Press, 2000), 452.

17. See Robert Goldman and Stephen Papson, *Sign Wars* (New York: Guilford Press, 1996).

18. See Diana B. Henriques, "Business Reporting: Behind the Curve," *Columbia Journalism Review*, November/December 2000: 18–21. On the rise of business news, see Thomas Frank, *Commodify Your Dissent* (New York: W.W. Norton, 1997), especially pages 23–28 on the "Culture Trust." Also see Gary Andrew Poole, "'Wealth Porn' and Beyond," *Columbia Journalism Review*, November/December 2000: 22–23.

19. Andrew Hill, "A Year of Scandal, Public Opprobrium and Stiff Legislation. But Has Corporate America Truly Mended Its Ways?" *Financial Times*, 30 December 2002, p. 9.

20. Michael Oneal, "Coming up Roses in a Downcast Year," *New York Times*, 29 December 2002, sec. 3, pp. 1, 11.

21. See Elizabeth A. Fones-Wolf, *Selling Free Enterprise: The Business Assault on Labor and Liberalism, 1945–60* (Urbana: University of Illinois Press, 1994).

22. See Freeman and Rogers, *What Workers Want*.

23. See AFL-CIO Committee on the Evolution of Work, *The Changing Situation of Workers and Their Unions* (Washington: AFL-CIO, 1985).

24. Tasini, "Lost in the Margins." Also see Sara Douglas, Norma Pecora, and Thomas Guback, "Work, Workers, and the Workplace: Is Local Newspaper Coverage Enough?" *Journalism Quarterly* 62, no. 4 (1985): 855–60. For more on the news media's preference for business news, see Michael Hoyt, "Downtime for Labor," *Columbia Journalism Review* 22 (1984): 36–40; Jo-Ann Mort, "How the Media 'Cover' Labor," *Dissent* 39 (1992): 81–85.

25. Parenti, *Inventing Reality*. The list of seven generalizations paraphrases Parenti's list.

26. Puette, *Through Jaundiced Eyes*, 154–55.

27. Richard B. Freeman and James L. Medoff, *What Do Unions Do?* (New York: Basic Books, 1984), 20.

28. See Puette, *Through Jaundiced Eyes*.

29. Robert McChesney, "Why We Need *In These Times*," *In These Times*, 18 January 2002. http://www.inthesetimes.com/issue/26/06/feature1.shtml (25 January 2002).

30. See Douglas, Pecora, and Guback, "Work, Workers"; Hoyt, "Downtime for Labor"; Mort, "How the Media 'Cover' Labor"; and Jo-Ann Mort, "The Case for a National Labor Paper: Rejoinder II," in *The New Labor Press: Journalism for a Changing Union Movement*, ed. Sam Pizzigati and Fred J. Solowey (Ithaca: Cornell University Press, 1992), 218–33.

31. William Serrin, foreword to *Three Strikes: Labor's Heartland Losses and What They Mean for Working Americans*, by Stephen Franklin (New York: Guilford Press, 2001), x. Maureen Williams suggests that the "flat, lifeless journalism" about labor "leads to perceptions of a flat, lifeless social movement." See Maureen Williams, "Marginality and Invisibility in Newspaper Construction of the Labor Movement: Metaphor Kept Hostage," (Ph.D. diss., University of Massachusetts at Amherst, 1992) vi.

32. Jerry Rollings' report of the Machinists Union Media Monitoring Project states that "union issues that receive the most attention are strikes." See Jerry Rollings, "Mass Communications and the American Worker," in *Labor, The Working Class, and the Media*, vol. 1 of *The Critical Communications Review*, ed. Vincent Mosco and Janet Wasko (Norwood, N.J.: Ablex, 1983), 138.

33. Leila Sussman, "Labor in the Radio News: An Analysis of Content," *Journalism Quarterly* 22, no. 3 (1945): 207–15.

34. See Yorgo Pasadeos, "Sources in Television Coverage of Strikes," *Journal of Broadcasting & Electronic Media* 34, no. 1 (1990): 77–84; Hayg Oshagan and Christopher Martin, "When a Plant Dies: Coverage of Labor and Management in the Willow Run Assembly Plant Shutdown" (paper presented at the annual meeting of the International Communication Association, Sydney, Australia, July 1994); Paul Walton and Howard Davis, "Bad News for Trade Unionists" in *Trade Unions and the Media*, ed. Peter Beharrell and Greg Philo (London: Macmillan, 1977). Also see Sussman, "Radio News," and Tasini, "Lost in the Margins."

35. See Walton and Davis, "Trade Unionists."

36. Rollings, "Mass Communications," 135.

37. See Glasgow University Media Group, *Bad News*, vol. 1 (London: Routledge and Kegan Paul, 1976); Glasgow University Media Group, *More Bad News*, vol. 2 (London: Routledge and Kegan Paul, 1980); Glasgow University Media Group, *Really Bad News*, vol. 3 (London: Readers and Writers, 1982).

38. Glasgow, *More Bad News*, 401, italics added. Also see David Morley, "Industrial Conflict and the Mass Media," *Sociological Review* 24, no. 2 (1976): 245–68; Walton and Davis, "Trade Unionists."

39. In Mike Haggerty and Wallace Rasmussen, *The Headline vs. The Bottom Line: Mutual Distrust Between Business and the News Media* (Nashville: The Freedom Forum First Amendment Center, 1994), 59. The Freedom Forum survey did not address the issue of labor coverage.

40. S. Robert Lichter, Stanley Rothman, and Linda S. Lichter, *The Media Elite* (Bethesda, Md.: Adler & Adler, 1986), 29. The survey was conducted in 1979–1980 with 238 journalists at the *New York Times, Washington Post, Wall Street Journal, Time, Newsweek, U.S. News and World Report,* and ABC, CBS, NBC, and PBS news divisions. The 216 surveyed business leaders came from only six different major corporations.

41. The elite journalists ranked the media, blacks, intellectuals, consumer groups, business leaders, and feminists all above labor in regard to which groups should have social influence.

42. David Croteau, "Challenging the 'Liberal Media' Claim," *Extra!* II, no 4 (1998), 4–9. This issue of *Extra!* is titled "The Myth of the Liberal Media."

43. For an analysis of the Pittston strike, see Tasini, "Lost in the Margins," and Puette, *Through Jaundiced Eyes.*

44. For an account of the historic Flint sit-down, see Sidney Fine, *Sit-down: The General Motors Strike of 1936–37* (Ann Arbor: University of Michigan Press, 1970).

45. Tasini, "Lost in the Margins," 6.

46. Arthur B. Shostak and David Skocik, *The Air Traffic Controllers' Controversy: Lessons from the PATCO Strike* (New York: Human Sciences Press, 1986), 109.

47. Edward S. Herman and Noam Chomsky, *Manufacturing Consent* (New York: Pantheon, 1988), 31.

48. Fred Weir, "McUnion Busting," *In These Times*, 22 August 1999. http://www.inthesetimes.com/weir2319.html (3 October 1999).

49. Barbara Ehrenreich broadly defines *working class* as "not only industrial workers in hard hats, but all those people who are not professionals, managers, or entrepreneurs; who work for wages, rather than salaries; and who spend their working hours variously lifting, bending, driving, monitoring, typing, keyboarding, cleaning, providing physical care for others, loading, unloading, cooking, serving, etc. The working class so defined makes up 60 to 70 percent of the U.S. population." See Barbara Ehrenreich, "The Silenced Majority," in *Gender, Race and Class in Media*, ed. Gail Dines and Jean M. Humez (Thousand Oaks, Calif.: Sage, 1995), 40–42.

50. Thomas McCarthy, introduction, in Jürgen Habermas, *Public Sphere*, xii.

51. *Television news packages* are reports that typically range between 1 minute, 30 seconds and 3 minutes in length, and are prepackaged in a self-contained report by a correspondent in the field. The news anchor introduces a package, and the pre-edited packaged report plays through its entirety before the news anchor again appears on camera. For this study, I have limited my analysis of network news to packages that appear in the news because they are the most fully developed narratives of network newscasts. Thus, the short twenty-second "reader" reports (typically with a "topic box" graphic over the anchor's shoulder) and slightly longer VO (voice-over) and VOSOT (voice-over, sound-on-tape) reports that include some video and perhaps a sound bite are not included in this study although they are elements of television newscasts.

52. Peyton M Craighill, e-mail to the author, 15 August 2001. Craighill, Project Director of The Pew Research Center for the People and the Press, supplied News Interest Index data for all labor stories in their surveys from the 1990s.

53. See Puette, *Through Jaundiced Eyes;* Tom Zaniello, *Working Stiffs, Union Maids, and Riffraff: An Organized Guide to Films about Labor* (Ithaca: Cornell University Press, 1996).

Chapter 2. Labor at the Millennium

1. A *major work stoppage* is defined as one involving one thousand or more workers. See Commission on the Future of Worker-Management Relations, *Fact-Finding Report* (Washington, D.C.: GPO, 1994), 24. See also Bureau of Labor Statistics, "A Few More Work Stoppages in 1998." http://stats.bls.gov/opub/ted/1999/feb/wk2/art05.htm (22 June 1999).

2. John M. Broder, "The Trial of the President: The President; Economy, Long a Friend, Brings Clinton More Help," *New York Times*, 9 January 1999, p. A11.

3. Richard B. Freeman and Joel Rogers, *What Workers Want* (Ithaca: Cornell University Press, 1999), 13–14.

4. Department of Labor, Bureau of Labor Statistics, *Highlights of Women's Earnings in 2000*, Report 952 (Washington, D.C.: GPO, August 2001). http://www.bls.gov/cps/cpswom2000.pdf (7 July 2000).

5. Department of Labor, Bureau of Labor Statistics, "Employment Status of the Civilian Population by Race, Sex, Age, and Hispanic Origin." http://stats.bls.gov/webapps/legacy/cpsatab2.htm (7 July 2000).

6. Louis Uchitelle, "The American Middle, Just Getting By," *New York Times*, 1 August 1999, sec. 3, pp. 1, 13.

7. Lawrence Mishel, Jared Bernstein, and John Schmitt, *The State of Working America, 2000/2001* (Ithaca: Cornell University Press, 2001), 113.

8. Ibid., 3.

9. Ibid., 4.

10. International Labor Organization, "U.S. Lead Industrialized World in Hours Worked, Productivity." http://us.ilo.org/news/focus/0110/FOCUS-6.HTML (4 November 2001).

11. Juliet Schor, *The Overworked American: The Unexpected Decline of Leisure* (New York: Basic Books, 1992), 29.

12. Mishel, Bernstein, and Schmitt, *Working America*, 8. Italics in original.

13. Ibid., 257, 261–62.

14. Ibid., 5, 9.

15. Ibid., 4.

16. Commission, *Fact-Finding Report*, 26.

17. Robert Reich, "Press Conference of Dunlop Commission on Worker-Management Relations," C-Span, 2 June 1994. Reich served as secretary of labor during Bill Clinton's first term as president. After Clinton's reelection in 1996, Reich resigned from the position. Despite what Reich felt the administration and his office had accomplished for labor, he lamented that by late 1996 "nothing fundamental" had changed in the growing class inequalities and increasing job insecurity in the United States. See Robert Reich, *Locked in the Cabinet* (New York: Knopf, 1997), 331.

18. U.S. Bureau of the Census, *Statistical Abstract of the United States* (Lanham, Md.: Bernan Press, 1993). See also Department of Labor, Bureau of Labor Statistics, "Union Members in 2000." ftp://ftp.bls.gov/pub/news.release/union2.txt (3 September 2001).

19. See Michael Goldfield, *The Decline of Organized Labor in the United States* (Chicago: University of Chicago Press, 1987); Robert H. Zieger, *American Workers, American Unions, 1920–1885* (Baltimore: Johns Hopkins University Press, 1986).

20. Commission, *Fact-Finding Report*, 18, 24.

21. Freeman and Rogers, *What Workers Want*, 4, 7.

22. See Barry Bluestone and Bennett Harrison, *The Deindustrialization of America: Plant Closings, Community Abandonment, and the Dismantling of Basic Industry* (New York: Basic Books, 1982), chap. 5.

23. David Harvey, *The Condition of Postmodernity* (Cambridge, Mass.: Blackwell, 1989), 135.

24. For a sample of reports on America's socioeconomic exclusions in terms of race and gender, see the Kerner Commission Report: Commission on Civil Disorders, *The Report of the National Advisory Commission on Civil Disorders* (Washington, D.C.: GPO, 1968); August Meier and Elliott Rudwick, *Black Detroit and the Rise of the UAW* (New York: Oxford University Press, 1979); George Lipsitz, *Class and Culture in Cold War America: A "Rainbow at Midnight"* (New York: Praeger, 1981); Alice Echols, *Daring to Be Bad: Radical Feminism in America, 1967–1975* (Minneapolis: University of Minnesota Press, 1989).

25. Mike Davis, *Prisoners of the American Dream: Politics and Economy in the History of the U.S. Working Class* (London: Verso, 1986), 197.

26. Bluestone and Harrison, *Deindustrialization of America*, 17.

27. See Charles F. Sabel, *Work and Politics: The Division of Labor in Industry* (Cambridge: Cambridge University Press, 1982), and Michael J. Piore and Charles F. Sabel, *The Second Industrial Divide: Possibilities for Prosperity* (New York: Basic Books, 1984).

28. Piore and Sable, *Second Industrial Divide*, 195.

29. See Bluestone and Harrison, *Deindustrialization of America;* Kim Moody, *An Injury to All: The Decline of American Unionism* (London: Verso, 1988).

30. Weld Royal, "Spotlight on the Maquiladora: An Award-Winning Border Plant Has Been Transformed into a Lean Role Model," *Industry Week*, 16 October, 2000, p. 91. Delphi maintains it headquarters in Troy, Michigan; in 2000, its production workers in Mexico earned $1.47 an hour.

31. Moody, *Injury to All*, 113.

32. Ibid., 112.

33. Piore and Sabel, *Second Industrial Divide*, 17.

34. See ibid., 249.

35. Saturn. "Our History, 1982–1990." http://www.saturnbp.com/company/our story/history/1982–1990.jsp (6 May 2000).

36. Jane Slaughter, "'Partnership' Takes a Hit at Saturn," *Labor Notes* (April 1999): 1, 11.

37. Harvey, *Condition of Postmodernity*, 150.

38. Piore and Sabel, *Second Industrial Divide*, 277.

39. Goldfield, *Decline of Organized Labor*, 116.

40. Also known as the Wagner Act, after its chief sponsor U.S. Senator Robert F. Wagner of New York.

41. *National Labor Relations Act, U.S. Statutes at Large* 49, pt. 1 (1936): 449–57.

42. Robert H. Zieger, *American Workers, American Unions, 1920–1885* (Baltimore: Johns Hopkins University Press, 1986), 40. See also Elizabeth A. Fones-Wolf, *Selling Free Enterprise: The Business Assault on Labor and Liberalism, 1945–1960* (Urbana: University of Illinois Press, 1994), and Chapter 3 of this book.

43. Zieger, *American Workers*, 108.

44. See ibid.; Melvyn Dubovsky, *The State and Labor in Modern America* (Chapel Hill: University of North Carolina Press, 1994); James R. Green, *The World of the Worker: Labor in Twentieth-Century America* (New York: Hill and Wang, 1980).

45. Goldfield, *Decline of Organized Labor*, 185.

46. Howard Kimeldorf, *Reds or Rackets: The Making of Radical and Conservative Unions on the Waterfront* (Berkeley: University of California Press, 1988), 160.

47. Moody, *Injury to All*, 133.

48. Ibid., 134, 139.

49. Bluestone and Harrison, *Deindustrialization of America*, 18–19.

50. See Barbara Presley Noble, "At the Labor Board, New Vigor," *New York Times*, 4 September 1994, national edition, p. 21.

51. Court Gifford and Jim Skovron, "Striker Replacements: House Committee Approves Measure to Nullify Clinton Executive Order," *Daily Labor Report*, 15 June 1995, p. D3.

52. See Mishel, Bernstein, and Schmitt, *Working America*, 172–79, for the effects of global trade on wages.

53. Taylor E. Dark, *The Unions and the Democrats: An Enduring Alliance*, rev. ed. (Ithaca: Cornell University Press, 1999), 21, 201.

54. AFL-CIO, "Brief Facts on Fast Track." http://www.aflcio.org/global economy/ft_quickfacts.htm (8 August 2002).

55. Dark, *Unions and the Democrats*, 203.

56. Zieger, *American Workers*, 66.

57. See Bluestone and Harrison, *Deindustrialization of America;* Moody, *Injury to All.*

58. Goldfield, *Decline of Organized Labor,* 189, 190. Elizabeth Fones-Wolf also presents an excellent history of U.S. business strategies against labor. See Fones-Wolf, *Selling Free Enterprise.*

59. See Moody, *Injury to All,* 140.

60. Ken Silverstein, *Washington on $10 Million a Day: How Lobbyists Plunder the Nation* (Monroe, Maine: Common Courage Press, 1998), 90.

61. Ruth Marcus and Sarah Cohen, "The Loophole Lesson in 'Soft Money': Campaign Reformers Confront History of Unintended Results," *Washington Post,* 18 March 2001, p. A01.

62. See AFL-CIO Committee on the Evolution of Work, *The Changing Situation of Workers and Their Unions* (Washington, D.C.: AFL-CIO, 1985), 10.

63. Commission, *Fact-Finding Report,* 70.

64. Aaron Bernstein, "All's Not Fair in Labor Wars," *Business Week,* 19 July 1999, 43.

65. David Brody, *Workers in Industrial America: Essays on the 20th Century Struggle* (New York: Oxford University Press, 1980).

66. Martin Jay Levitt and Terry Conrow, *Confessions of a Union Buster* (New York: Crown, 1993).

67. Kirkland quoted in David Brody, "The Future of the Labor Movement in Historical Perspective," *Dissent* 41, no. 1 (1994): 57.

68. Moody, *Injury to All,* 15, xiv. See also Harold Meyerson, "A Second Chance: The New AFL-CIO and the Prospective Revival of American Labor," in *Not Your Father's Union Movement,* ed. Jo-Ann Mort (London: Verso, 1998)

69. See, e.g., Zieger, *American Workers.* Philip S. Foner's *History of the Labor Movement in the United States,* 10 vols. (New York: International Publishers, 1947–1994) is also an excellent source for early U.S. labor history, from colonial times through 1929.

70. See Roger Keeran, *The Communist Party and the Auto Workers Union* (Bloomington: Indiana University Press, 1980). See also August Meier and Elliott Rudwick, *Black Detroit and the Rise of the UAW* (New York: Oxford University Press, 1979).

71. Howard Kimeldorf and Judith Stepan-Norris, "Historical Studies of Labor Movements in the United States," *Annual Review of Sociology* 18 (1992): 495–517.

72. Zieger, *American Workers,* 126.

73. See Goldfield, *Decline of Organized Labor,* 238–40.

74. See Peter Rachleff, *Hard-Pressed in the Heartland: The Hormel Strike and the Future of the Labor Movement* (Boston: South End Press, 1993); Barbara Kopple, *American Dream* (New York: HBO Video, 1992), film. Kopple's documentary won the 1991 Academy Award for best documentary. See also Moody, *Injury to All,* 314–27, and Stanley Aronowitz, *False Promises: The Shaping of American Working Class Consciousness* (Durham: Duke University Press, 1992), 412.

75. Kimeldorf, *Reds or Rackets,* 162.

76. John J. Sweeney and David Kusnet, *America Needs a Raise* (Boston: Houghton Mifflin, 1996). See also Jeremy Brecher, *Strike!* (Cambridge, Mass.: South End Press, 1997).

77. See Stephen Franklin, *Three Strikes: Labor's Heartland Losses and What They Mean for Working Americans* (New York: Guilford Press, 2001).

78. Sweeney and Kusnet, *America Needs a Raise,* 107. Taylor Dark suggests that union threats to go independent of a political party are "truly idle threats, intended more to assuage internal union constituencies and perhaps scare a few gullible Democrats than to foreshadow a real change in union strategy." See Dark, *Unions and the Democrats,* 207.

79. For a more recent appraisal of labor's national trajectory, see Hal Leyshon, "AFL-CIO Stays the Course," *Labor Notes* (January 2002): 1, 12–13.

80. See 9 to 5: National Association of Working Women. http://www.9to5.org/.

81. See Marc Cooper, "Unions 101: Organized Labor Sparks a New Wave of Campus Radicalism," *Detroit Sunday Journal,* 20 June 1999, pp. 1, 5, 7. See also National Labor Committee, http://www.nlcnet.org/.

82. Goldfield, *Decline of Organized Labor,* 35.

83. AFL-CIO Committee on the Evolution of Work, *The Changing Situation of Workers,* 12–13.

84. Ibid.

85. See AFL-CIO, "Labor Day 1999: Americans' Attitudes Toward Unions." http://www.aflcio.org/labor99/am_attitude.htm (10 September 1999). The survey was conducted March 1999 by Peter D. Hart Research Associates Inc. Another 15 percent responded "depends," while 11 percent answered "not sure."

86. Richard B. Freeman and Joel Rogers, *What Workers Want* (Ithaca: Cornell University Press, 1999).

Chapter 3. The Consumer Media Emerges

1. Pew Research Center for the People and the Press, "Self Censorship: How Often and Why," 30 April 2000, http://www.people-press.org/reports/display.php3?ReportID=39 (4 May 2000). See also the May/June 2000 issue of the *Columbia Journalism Review.*

2. Lawrence C. Soley and Robert L. Craig, "Advertising Pressures on Newspapers: A Survey," *Journal of Advertising* 21, no. 4 (1992): 1–10; quote appears p. 7.

3. Warren Breed, "Mass Communication and Socio-Cultural Integration," *Social Forces* 37 (1958): 112, 114.

4. Upton Sinclair, *The Brass Check: A Study of American Journalism* (Pasadena, Calif.: The author, 1920), 353.

5. Editor & Publisher, *Editor & Publisher International Yearbook* (New York: Editor & Publisher, 1997).

6. John Morton, "Chains Swallowing Other Chains," *American Journalism Review,* July/August 1997, 52.

7. Davis Merritt, *Public Journalism and Public Life: Why Telling the News Is Not Enough* (Hillsdale, N.J.: Lawrence Erlbaum, 1995).

8. John McManus, *Market-Driven Journalism: Let the Citizen Beware?* (Thousand Oaks, Calif.: Sage, 1994).

9. Phillip Meyer, "Learning to Love Lower Profits," *American Journalism Review,* December 1995, 40.

10. Bill Moyers, "Journalism and Democracy: On the Importance of Being a 'Public Nuisance,'" *The Nation,* 7 May 2001, 11–17. See also Committee of Concerned Journalists, "Changing Definitions of News," 6 March 1998, http://www.journalism.org/resources/research/reports/definitions/default.asp (10 May 2003).

11. Martin A. Lee and Norman Solomon, *Unreliable Sources: A Guide to Detecting Bias in the News Media* (New York: Lyle Stuart, 1990).

12. James Ledbetter, "Look Who's Talking, Too," *Village Voice,* 15 March 1994, 7.

13. See Christopher R. Martin, "The Limits of Community in Public Journalism," in *Communication and Community,* ed. Gregory J. Shepherd and Eric W. Rothenbuhler (Mahwah, N.J.: Lawrence Erlbaum, 2001), 235–50.

14. Jim West, "Unions Focus on Advertiser/Circulation Boycott as Detroit Newspapers Reject Peace Offer," *Labor Notes* (November 1995): 5, 14.

15. Ibid. See also Richard McCord, *The Chain Gang: One Newspaper Versus the Gannett Empire* (Columbia: University of Missouri Press, 1996).

16. See Aaron Bernstein, " 'Disaster' for Motown Papers?" *Business Week*, 4 August 1997, 38–40; Mark Fitzgerald, "Feeling the Effects of the Strike," *Editor & Publisher*, 28 September 1996, 11, 36.

17. Daniel Howes, "Analysis: Back to Work Offer Reflects Strike's Reality," *Detroit News*, 16 February 1997, http://detnews.com/1997/metro/9702/16/02160088.htm (21 May 1997).

18. "Newspaper Struggle Enters Fifth Year," *Labor Notes* (August 1999): 2.

19. Bill Carter, "Urging Union Viewers to Boycott NBC's Shows," *New York Times*, 2 May 1994, p. C7.

20. John Nerone, *Violence Against the Press: Policing the Public Sphere in U.S. History* (New York: Oxford University Press, 1994), 192–93.

21. Robert Manor, "ABC Ends Union Lockout," *Chicago Sun-Times*, 16 January 1999, p. 30.

22. Ellen Cohn, "Firing Line," *Village Voice*, 12 July 1994, p. 39.

23. Ralph Miliband, *The State in Capitalist Society* (London: Weidenfeld and Nicolson, 1969), 221.

24. James Curran, "Mass Media and Democracy," in *Mass Media and Society*, ed. James Curran and Michael Gurevitch (London: Edward Arnold, 1991), 88.

25. Edward S. Herman and Noam Chomsky, *Manufacturing Consent: The Political Economy of the Mass Media* (New York: Pantheon, 1988), 1.

26. Louis Althusser, *Lenin and Philosophy and Other Essays*, trans. Ben Brewster (London: NLB, 1971).

27. Graham Murdock and Peter Golding, "Information Poverty and Political Inequity: Citizenship in the Age of Privatized Communications," *Journal of Communication* 39, no. 3 (1989): 180–95.

28. See, e.g., Mike Haggerty and Wallace Rasmussen, *The Headline vs. The Bottom Line: Mutual Distrust Between Business and the News Media* (Nashville: The Freedom Forum First Amendment Center, 1994); S. Robert Lichter, Stanley Rothman, and Linda S. Lichter, *The Media Elite* (Bethesda, Md.: Adler & Adler, 1986).

29. See Richard Campbell, *60 Minutes and the News: A Mythology for Middle America* (Urbana: University of Illinois Press, 1991).

30. An episode of the PBS investigative series *Frontline* titled "Smoke in the Eye" and broadcast 2 November 1999, analyzed the *60 Minutes* scandal in detail.

31. Unusual labor dispute situations can summon a distinct set of narrative frames. For example, physical violence usually results in the stereotypical characterization of unions as corrupt mob institutions. However, Puette notes that less than 1 percent of union locals have even been suspected, much less convicted, of organized crime. See William J. Puette, *Through Jaundiced Eyes: How the Media View Organized Labor* (Ithaca: Cornell University Press, 1992), 29.

32. James S. Ettema and D. Charles Whitney, *Audiencemaking: How the Media Create the Audience* (Thousand Oaks, Calif.: Sage, 1994), 5.

33. Piers Brendon, *The Life and Death of the Press Barons* (London: Secker & Warburg, 1982), 9–10.

34. Jürgen Habermas, *The Structural Transformation of the Public Sphere*, trans. Thomas Burger (Cambridge: MIT Press, 1989), 27. See also Michael Warner, *The Letters of the Republic: Publication and the Public Sphere in Eighteenth-Century America*

(Cambridge: Harvard University Press, 1990), for a full account of the precommercial press.

35. Michael Schudson, "Was There Ever a Public Sphere? If So, When? Reflections on the American Case," *Habermas and the Public Sphere*, ed. Craig Calhoun (Cambridge: MIT Press, 1992), 160.

36. For a full account of the penny press, see chapter 1 of Michael Schudson, *Discovering the News: A Social History of American Newspapers* (New York: Basic Books, 1978).

37. Gerald J. Baldasty, "The Rise of News as a Commodity: Business Imperatives and the Press in the Nineteenth Century," in *Ruthless Criticism: New Perspectives in U.S. Communication History*, ed. William S. Solomon and Robert W. McChesney (Minneapolis: University of Minnesota Press, 1993), 98–121. See also Gerald J. Baldasty, *The Commercialization of News in the Nineteenth Century* (Madison: University of Wisconsin Press, 1992).

38. Baldasty, "Rise of News," 114.

39. Ibid., 111.

40. Christopher P. Wilson, "The Rhetoric of Consumption: Mass-Market Magazines and the Demise of the Gentle Reader, 1880–1920," in *The Culture of Consumption: Critical Essays in American History, 1880–1980*, ed. Richard Wightman Fox and T. J. Jackson Lears (New York: Pantheon, 1983), 39–64.

41. David Brody, *Workers in Industrial America: Essays on the 20th Century Struggle* (New York: Oxford University Press, 1980), 31.

42. David Montgomery, *The Fall of the House of Labor: The Workplace, the State, and American Labor Activism, 1865–1925* (Cambridge: Cambridge University Press, 1987), 255.

43. Jon Bekken, "The Working Class Press at the Turn of the Century," in *Ruthless Criticism: New Perspectives in U.S. Communication History*, ed. William S. Solomon and Robert W. McChesney (Minneapolis: University of Minnesota Press, 1993), 151–75.

44. Melvyn Dubovsky, *Industrialism and the American Worker, 1865–1920* (Arlington Heights, Ill.: AHM, 1975), 42–43.

45. Bekken, "Working Class Press," 154.

46. Sinclair, *Brass Check*, 346.

47. Bekken, "Working Class Press," 151.

48. Sam Pizzigati and Fred J. Solowey, *The New Labor Press: Journalism for a Changing Union Movement* (Ithaca: Cornell University Press, 1992), xii.

49. See Nerone, *Violence Against the Press*, 181. Nerone notes that "the World War I years saw the destruction of a large chunk of the radical network that had been built over the past two decades. By the end of the war, fifteen hundred of the more than five thousand Socialist party locals—about one-quarter of the organizational base—had been eliminated. Most of the lost locals were in small communities. The attrition rate for Socialist newspapers was similar; losses there were likewise concentrated in small towns."

50. See Bekken, "Working Class Press."

51. Stuart Ewen, *Captains of Consciousness: Advertising and the Social Roots of the Consumer Culture* (New York: McGraw-Hill, 1976), 24–26.

52. See Richard Wightman Fox and T.J. Jackson Lears, eds., *The Culture of Consumption: Critical Essays in American History, 1880–1980* (New York: Pantheon, 1983).

53. Roland Marchand, *Advertising the American Dream: Making Way for Modernity, 1920–1940* (Berkeley: University of California Press, 1985), 218.

54. Ewen, *Captains of Consciousness*, 28.

55. Joe Arena, "The Information Society under Construction: Retail Credit and the

Mythos of Technology," (paper presented at the annual meeting of the Association for Education in Journalism and Mass Communication, Atlanta, Georgia, August 1994). See also Schudson, *Discovering the News*, 132–34; Fox and Lears, *Culture of Consumption*.

56. Marvin Olasky, "The Development of Corporate Public Relations, 1850–1930," *Journalism Monographs* 102 (1987).

57. Robert W. McChesney, *Telecommunications, Mass Media, and Democracy: The Battle for Control of U.S. Broadcasting, 1928–1935* (New York: Oxford University Press, 1994), 264.

58. *National Labor Relations Act, U.S. Statutes at Large* 49, pt. 1 (1936): 449–57.

59. Stuart Ewen, *PR! A Social History of Spin* (New York: Basic Books, 1996), 307.

60. Elizabeth A. Fones-Wolf, *Selling Free Enterprise: The Business Assault on Labor and Liberalism, 1945–60* (Urbana: University of Illinois Press, 1994), 287.

61. See, e.g., David Harvey, *The Condition of Postmodernity* (Cambridge, Mass.: Blackwell, 1989).

62. Lawrence B. Glickman, *A Living Wage: American Workers and the Making of Consumer Society* (Ithaca: Cornell University Press, 1997), 3.

63. George Lipsitz, "The Meaning of Memory: Family, Class, and Ethnicity in Early Network Television," in *Gender, Race and Class in Media*, ed. Gail Dines and Jean M. Humez (Thousand Oaks, Calif.: Sage, 1995), 47.

64. Jennie Tunkieicz and Joel Dresang, "Racine Labor Paper's Death Tied to Globalization, Experts Say," *JSOnline/Milwaukee Journal Sentinel*, 29 December 2001, http://www.jsonline.com/news/racie/dec01/8857.asp (3 January 2002).

65. See Pizzigati and Solowey, *New Labor Press*.

66. Roger Keeran, *The Communist Party and the Auto Workers Union* (Bloomington: Indiana University Press, 1980), 258–59.

67. Dan Schiller, *Objectivity and the News: The Public and the Rise of Commercial Journalism* (Philadelphia: University of Pennsylvania Press, 1981), 186.

68. Editorial, "The Wolves are Howling," *Los Angeles Times*, 3 September 1910, p. 4, quoted in Nerone, *Violence Against the Press*, 173.

69. Editorial, "When a Newspaper Is Struck," *Chicago Tribune*, 21 July 1985, p. 2.

70. A. W. Phillips, "The Relation between Unemployment and the Rate of Change of Money Wage Rates in the United Kingdom, 1861–1957," *Economica* 25, no. 100 (1985): 283–99.

71. See Bruno Jossa and Marco Musella, *Inflation, Unemployment and Money: Interpretations of the Phillips Curve* (Cheltenham, UK: Edward Elgar, 1998).

72. Also called the lowest sustainable unemployment rate. See Paul A. Samuelson and William D. Nordhaus, *Economics*, 16th ed. (Boston: McGraw-Hill, 1998).

73. Samuelson and Nordhaus, *Economics*, 593–94.

74. Glenn Burkins, "Organized Labor Is Seeking Big Pay Gains—Successes by Some Unions Are Leading to Worries about Wage Inflation," *Wall Street Journal*, 3 September 1999, p. A2.

75. David Friedman, "Out of Steps?; The Teamsters–UPS Strike Is Over, but Its Issues Point to Trouble Ahead for the Continued Rise of U.S. Prosperity," *Los Angeles Times*, 24 August 1997, p. M1.

76. Steven Greenhouse, "U.A.W. Deal Doesn't Pack the Wallop It Once Did," *New York Times*, 23 September 1999, p. C1.

77. "Is the Phillips Curve Losing Its Allure?" *Business Week*, 28 April 1973, p. 88.

78. Thomas J. Sargent, "Economic Scene; Back to Basics on Budgets," *New York Times*, 10 August 1983, p. D2.

79. Joel Kurtzman, "Prospects: Will Lower Unemployment Fuel Inflation?" *New York Times*, 13 March 1988, sec. 3, p. 1.

80. Louis Uchitelle, "The Nation; Inflation Is Tied to Unemployment, but How?" *New York Times*, 1 May 1988, sec. 4, p. 5.

81. Charles Stein, "Job Reports Boost Markets; July Employment Figures Suggest Economy Growing Steadily without Inflation," *Boston Globe*, 3 August 1996, p. F1.

82. J. Bradford DeLong, "Economic Scene; Is the Relationship between Inflation and Unemployment a Curve or More of an Economics Hardball?" *New York Times*, 9 March 2000, p. C2.

83. Jared Bernstein, "Slowing Economy Threatens Earnings of Low-wage Workers, Risks Increase in Inequality," *Quarterly Wage and Employment Series*, Fourth Quarter, 2000, Washington, D.C.: Economic Policy Institute, http://www.epinet.org (5 July 2001).

84. Italics added. Steven Vames, "Growth in Wages Moderates, but Orders for Durable Goods Surge 10%." *New York Times on the Web*, 27 July 2000, http://www.nytimes.com (27 July 2000).

85. Roberto Chang, "Is Low Employment Inflationary?" *Economic Review*, Federal Reserve Bank of Atlanta, First Quarter, 1997, 4–13. See also Douglas Staiger, James H. Stock, and Mark W. Watson, "The NAIRU, Unemployment, and Monetary Policy," *Journal of Economic Perspectives* 11, no. 1 (1997): 33–50.

86. Gregory D. Hess and Mark E. Schweitzer, "Does Wage Inflation Cause Price Inflation?" *Policy Discussion Paper Number 10*, Federal Reserve Bank of Cleveland, April 2000, p. 2. http://www.clev.frb.org/Research (29 June 2002).

87. Bernard Corry, "Politics and the Natural Rate Hypothesis," in *The Natural Rate of Unemployment: Reflections on 25 Years of the Hypothesis*, ed. Rod Cross (Cambridge: Cambridge University Press, 1995), 371.

88. See, e.g., Adam Bryant, "American Pay Rattles Foreign Partners," *New York Times*, 17 January 1999, sec. 4, pp. 1, 4.

89. Sarah Anderson and John Cavanaugh, "Living Well at Workers' Expense: The Top Three Executives at the Firms Studied Each Earned, on Average, More Than $2.6 Million," *New York Times*, 14 May 1995, p. M5.

90. Vames, "Growth in Wages Moderates."

91. Hess and Schweitzer, "Does Wage Inflation," p. 1.

92. Kevin Boyle, *The UAW and the Heyday of American Liberalism* (Ithaca: Cornell University Press, 1995), 30.

93. James Yountsler, *Labor's Wage Policies in the Twentieth Century* (New York: Twayne, 1956), 183–84.

94. Bill Goode, *Infighting in the UAW: The 1946 Election and the Ascendancy of Walter Reuther* (Westport, Conn.: Greenwood Press, 1994), 74.

95. Youtsler, *Labor's Wage Policies*, 184.

96. Sara U. Douglas, *Labor's New Voice: Unions and the Mass Media* (Norwood, N.J.: Ablex, 1986), chap. 5.

97. James Ledbetter, "Ad Hoc Censorship," *Village Voice*, 31 May 1994, p. 9.

98. See Jon Bekken, "The Portrayal of Labor in Reporting Textbooks: Critical Absences, Hostile Voices" (paper presented at the annual meeting of the Association for Education in Journalism and Mass Communication, Atlanta, Georgia, August 1994).

99. Henry H. Shulte and Marcel P. Dufresne, *Getting the Story: An Advanced Reporting Guide to Beats, Records and Sources* (New York: Macmillan, 1994), 335.

100. See Schudson, *Discovering the News*, for a social history of objectivity in the news.

101. Robert Goldman and Arvind Rajagopal, *Mapping Hegemony: Television News Coverage of Industrial Conflict* (Norwood, N.J.: Ablex, 1991), 11.

102. Schudson, *Discovering the News*, 185.

103. J. Herbert Altschull, *Agents of Power: The Media and Public Policy* (White Plains, N.Y.: Longman, 1995), 63.

104. Gaye Tuchman, "Objectivity as a Strategic Ritual: An Examination of News-men's Notions of Objectivity," *American Journal of Sociology* 5, no. 4 (1972): 660–79. See also Gaye Tuchman, *Making News: A Study in the Construction of Reality* (New York: Free Press, 1978).

105. McManus, *Market-Driven Journalism*, 85.

106. Ad Age Dataplace, "100 Leading National Advertisers," *Advertising Age*, 1 March 2001, http://adage.com/dataplace/lna/index.html (6 April 2001).

Chapter 4. Upholding Corporate Values and Downsizing General Motors

1. Raymond Serafin, " 'Heartbeat': New Ads Pump Life into Chevy's 'American' Image," *Advertising Age*, 12 January 1987, 3.

2. Micheline Maynard, "With Bold Stroke, GM Turns a Page/Goal: Save $5 Billion by Mid-Decade," *USA Today*, 19 December 1991, p. 1B.

3. See Kim Moody, *An Injury to All: The Decline of American Unionism* (London: Verso, 1988), 182–85.

4. See, e.g., Stanley Aronowitz, *False Promises: The Shaping of American Working Class Consciousness* (Durham: Duke University Press, 1992); David Harvey, *The Condition of Postmodernity* (Cambridge, Mass.: Blackwell, 1989); Michael Goldfield, *The Decline of Organized Labor in the United States* (Chicago: University of Chicago Press, 1987); Barry Bluestone and Bennett Harrison, *The Deindustrialization of America: Plant Closings, Community Abandonment, and the Dismantling of Basic Industry* (New York: Basic Books, 1982); David M. Gordon, *Fat and Mean: The Corporate Squeeze of Working Americans and the Myth of Managerial "Downsizing"* (New York: Free Press, 1996).

5. Willis F. Dunbar, *Michigan: A History of the Wolverine State* (Grand Rapids, Mich.: William B. Eerdmans Publishing, 1980). See also Marion F. Wilson, *The Story of Willow Run* (Ann Arbor: University of Michigan Press, 1956).

6. Tony Marcano, "Famed Riveter in War Effort, Rose Monroe Dies at 77," *New York Times*, 2 June 1997, p. B13. See also Amy Kesselman "Rose Will Monroe: The Rise of Rosie the Riveter," *The Guardian* (London), 5 June 1997, p. 19.

7. Sara Rimer, "American Dream Put on Hold at Car Plant Doomed to Shut," *New York Times*, 7 September 1992, sec. 1, p. 1. See also Paul Hoversten, " 'Real People, Real Blood' in Mich," *USA Today*, 24 February 1992, p. 3A.

8. Robert M. Entman, "Framing: Toward Clarification of a Fractured Paradigm," *Journal of Communication* 43, no. 4 (1993): 53.

9. See Patricia Edmonds, "GM Troubles Put Plants at Odds/Ypsilanti Has Fought War before," *USA Today*, 20 December 1991, p. 3A; Thomas C. Hayes, "Tug of War over G.M. Plant Closing." *New York Times*, 19 December 1991, p. D1.

10. Davis Merritt, *Public Journalism and Public Life: Why Telling the News Is Not Enough* (Hillsdale, N.J.: Lawrence Erlbaum, 1995), 100.

11. Edmonds, "GM Troubles Put Plants," 3A.

12. See, e.g., Gaye Tuchman, *Making News: A Study in the Construction of Reality* (New York: Free Press, 1978).

13. Michael Schudson, *Discovering the News: A Social History of American Newspapers* (New York: Basic Books, 1978).

14. Theodore L. Glasser, "Objectivity Precludes Responsibility," *The Quill*, February 1994, 13–16.

15. Herbert J. Gans, *Deciding What's News: A Study of* CBS Evening News, NBC

Nightly News, Newsweek, *and* Time (New York: Pantheon, 1979), 339–40. See also Robert Goldman and Arvind Rajagopal, *Mapping Hegemony: Television News Coverage of Industrial Conflict* (Norwood, N.J.: Ablex, 1991).

16. Robert W. McChesney, *Corporate Media and the Threat to Democracy* (New York: Seven Stories Press, 1997), 14.

17. Gordon, *Fat and Mean*, 207, 7.

18. Michael R. Kagay, "From Coast to Coast, from Affluent to Poor, Poll Shows Anxiety over Jobs," *New York Times*, 11 March 1994, p. A14.

19. Robert Reich, *Tales of a New America* (New York: Vintage, 1987), 148.

20. Bluestone and Harrison, *Deindustrialization of America*, 78–80.

21. Gordon, *Fat and Mean*, 35.

22. See Graef S. Crystal, *In Search of Excess: The Overcompensation of American Executives* (New York: W.W. Norton, 1992).

23. Doron P. Levin, "Making a Difference; Playing Rough with GM," *New York Times*, 29 December 1991, sec. 3, p. 12.

24. Hayg Oshagan and Christopher Martin, "When a Plant Dies: Coverage of Labor and Management in the Willow Run Assembly Plant Shutdown" (paper presented at the annual meeting of the International Communication Association, Mass Communication Division, Sydney, Australia, July 1994).

25. Micheline Maynard, "GM: Deals Won't Be Cut to Keep Plants Open," *USA Today*, 13 January 1992, p. B2. Stempel's message was repeated in Donna Rosato, "GM Rebuffs Bids," *USA Today*, 6 February 1992, p. 1B.

26. David Sedgwick, "The Numbers Give Willow Run the Edge," *Detroit News*, 20 December 1991, p. E1.

27. Thomas C. Hayes, "Making a Difference; Saving 3,727 G.M. Jobs in Texas," *New York Times*, 1 March 1992, sec. 3, p. 10.

28. Doron P. Levin, "The G.M. Cutbacks; G.M. Picks 12 Plants to Be Shut As It Reports a Record U.S. Loss," *New York Times*, 25 February 1992, p. A1.

29. See David Sedgwick and Noreen Seebacher, "Willow Run Aftershocks Run Deep," *Detroit News*, 26 February 1992, p. C1.

30. Bluestone and Harrison, *Deindustrialization of America*, 78–79.

31. Institute for Social Research, "Stress and Unemployment," *ISR Newsletter* 17, no. 3 (1992): 3.

32. Jeffrey Schmalz, "The 1992 Campaign: Voters; Hurt and Angry Car Workers Say Brown Speaks for Them," *New York Times*, 13 March 1992, p. A1.

33. Robert B. Westbrook, "Politics as Consumption: Managing the Modern American Election," in *The Culture of Consumption: Critical Essays in American History, 1880–1980*, ed. Richard Wightman Fox and T. J. Jackson Lears (New York: Pantheon, 1983), 143–73.

34. Sara Rimer, "A Caprice That Chevy Couldn't Sell," *New York Times*, 24 October 1992, sec. 1, p. 35.

35. Sara Rimer, "American Dream Put on Hold at Car Plant Doomed to Shut," *New York Times*, 24 September 1992, p. 1.

36. Sara Rimer, "Hard Times Change Many Minds," *New York Times*, 2 October 1992, p. D1.

37. Merritt, *Public Journalism*, xii.

38. Jürgen Habermas, *The Structural Transformation of the Public Sphere*, trans. Thomas Burger (Cambridge: MIT Press, 1989).

39. For an account of how news stories might be framed from a labor point of view, see Karen Keiser, "Framing the Fight," *Labor Research Review* 21 (1993): 71–79.

40. *Township of Ypsilanti v. General Motors Corp.*, No. 92-43075-CK 8 (Washtenaw County Cir. Ct., 9 February 1993).

41. Robert Reich, *The Work of Nations: Preparing Ourselves for 21st Century Capitalism* (New York: Vintage, 1992), 281.

42. Doron P. Levin, "G.M. Blocked from Closing Auto Plant," *New York Times*, 10 February 1993, p. D1.

43. Steve Marshall, "Judge: GM Can't Close Plant," *USA Today*, 10 February 1993, p. 3A.

44. Associated Press, "G.M. Papers Detail Costs in Plant Shift," *New York Times*, 18 December 1992, p. D3.

45. *Township of Ypsilanti v General Motors Corp.*, 20–21.

46. Ibid., 2–3.

47. *Township of Ypsilanti v. General Motors Corp.*, 201 Mich. App. 128 (Mich. Ct. App. 1993).

48. Doron P. Levin, "Court Backs G.M. on Plant Closing," *New York Times*, 5 August 1993, p. D4.

49. See Donna Rosato, "Saturn Expansion?" *USA Today*, 23 June 1992, p. 1B, and "G.M. Plant May Reopen," *New York Times*, 18 February 1994, p. D4.

50. Steven M. Barkin and Michael Gurevitch, "Out of Work and On the Air: Television News of Unemployment," in *Critical Perspectives on Media and Society*, ed. Robert K. Avery and David Eason (New York: Guilford, 1991), 306–28.

51. James Bennet, "Company News; G.M. Settles Suit over Plant Closing," *New York Times*, 15 April 1994, p. D3.

52. Michael Clements and Judith Schroer, "Good Times Roll; Perseverance Pays Off for Autoworkers," *USA Today*, 29 April 1994, p. 1B.

53. Clements and Schroer, "Good Times," 2B.

54. See, e.g., Keith Naughton, "Caught Short: Why Detroit Can't Build Enough Cars," *Detroit News and Free Press*, 28 August 1994, p. 1A, 8A.

55. Helen Fogel, "Willow Run Not Flexible Enough for GM," *Detroit News*, 28 August 1994, p. 9A.

56. Dean Braid, "Strike Wins Reluctant New Jobs from a Reluctant General Motors," *Labor Notes* (November 1994): 1, 14.

57. Gregg Jones, "GM to Keep Arlington Plant Open: Local Effort Had Effect, Analysts Say," *Dallas Morning News*, 25 February 1992, pp. 1A, 9A.

58. "Texas Workers Helped Save Arlington GM Plant," *Houston Chronicle*, 25 February 1992, p. A10.

59. See Mike Parker and Jane Slaughter, *Choosing Sides: Unions and the Team Concept* (Boston: South End Press, 1988); Elizabeth A. Fones-Wolf, *Selling Free Enterprise: The Business Assault on Labor and Liberalism, 1945–60* (Urbana: University of Illinois Press, 1994).

60. Chris Payne and Darrin Schlegel, "Change Called Necessary to Avoid Plant Shutdown," *Dallas Morning News*, 9 December 1996, p. 1A.

61. Editorial, "Old Reliable; GM Retrofit Is a Sign of Company's Ability to Change," *Dallas Morning News*, 13 December 1996, p. 11A.

62. Editorial, "Sign on the Dotted Line; Union Members Should OK GM Contract," *Dallas Morning News*, 28 February 1997, p. 7A.

63. Jeane Graham, "National Semiconductor Wants $1 Million Break; Partial Abatement Sends Wrong Signal, Manager Says," *Fort Worth Star-Telegram*, 12 August 1997, p. 1.

64. Kevin Shay, "Closing the Tax Gap; Local Firms Gain Speed as GM Hits the

Brakes," *Dallas Morning News*, 21 September 1997, p. 9A. See also City of Arlington, "Tax Abatement Agreements, 1989–1997," http://www.ci.arlington.tx.us/business /agreements_1989_1997.html (5 January 1998).

65. Jennifer Autrey, "Saving a Community; East Arlington Has Sounded an Alarm: Help Us Stop the Decline," *Fort Worth Star-Telegram*, 21 September 1997, p. 1.

66. Lonnie Morgan, telephone conversation with author, 13 February 1998.

67. Anonymous, letter to Deno Castillo, UAW Local 129, Fort Worth, Tex., December 1997.

68. David Welch, "Tensions Building in No-Progress Mackie Strike," *Fort Worth Star-Telegram*, 24 January 1998, p. 1.

69. David Welch, "Mission Asked to Stop Taking Workers to Mackie," *Fort Worth Star-Telegram*, 15 January 1998, p. 3.

70. Sean Wood, "Most Workers Won't Return to Texas Automotive Plant, Union Says," *Fort Worth Star-Telegram*, 20 January 1999. See also Bill Swindell, "Strikers Feel Slighted by UAW; Union Members at GM Plant Say They've Been Supportive During Mackie Standoff," *Arlington Morning News*, 26 April 1998, p. 9A.

71. David Welch, "Texas Plant Given New Life: GM Plans to Invest $400 Million in Its Arlington Facility," *Detroit News*, 13 April 1999, p. B1. See also Dow Jones, "G.M. to Lift Texas Output," *New York Times*, 25 September 1999, p. C4. The assembly plant was assigned to build the next generation of two of the company's full-size sport utility vehicles—the Chevrolet Tahoe and GMC Yukon—beginning in 2000.

72. Gans, *Deciding What's News*, 46.

73. Steve McLinden, "Arlington, Texas-Based Automotive Supplier Expands to Match GM's Plans," *Fort Worth Star-Telegram*, 18 September 1999. On 18 January 2002, TDS Logistics of London, Ontario, Canada, acquired Mackie Automotive Systems. At the time, Mackie had approximately 2,200 employees in fifteen facilities in four countries, including about 600 employees in the Arlington area. See Press Release, TDS Automotive, "TDS Completes Purchase of Mackie Automotive Systems," 18 January 2002, http://www.tdsautomotive.com/tdsindex.htm. See also Steve McLinden, "2 Auto Dealers to Build, Expand along I-20," *Dallas-Ft. Worth Star Telegram*, 5 March 2002, http://www.dfw.com/mld/startelegram/business/columnists/steve_mclinden/2793974.htm.

74. Kathleen Kerwin, "The Shutdown GM Needs? It's a Chance to Clean House and Downsize," *Business Week*, 13 July 1998, 35.

75. Keith Bradsher, "A New Route for General Motors" *New York Times*, 9 August 1998, sec. 1, p. 21.

76. "G.M. Removes Itself from Industrial Pedestal" *New York Times*, 30 May 1999, sec. 3, p. 4.

77. Larry Weiss, "Auto Makers Test Labor-Cutting Strategy in Brazil" Resource Center of the Americas, August 1999. http://www.americas.org/news/ (9 August 1999).

Chapter 5. The Eagle Is Stranded

1. William J. Puette, *Through Jaundiced Eyes: How the Media View Organized Labor* (Ithaca: Cornell University Press, 1992), 154.

2. Georgia Panter Nielsen, *From Sky Girl to Flight Attendant: Women and the Making of a Union* (Ithaca: Cornell University Press, 1982), 13.

3. Nielsen, *Sky Girl*, 117.

4. Quote in Barbara Sturken Peterson and James Glab, *Rapid Descent: Deregulation and the Shakeout in the Airlines* (New York: Simon & Schuster, 1994), 193.

5. Thomas Petzinger Jr., *Hard Landing: The Epic Contest for Power and Profits that Plunged the Airlines into Chaos* (New York: Times Books, 1995), 131. Also see Robert J. Serling, *Eagle: The Story of American Airlines* (New York: St. Martin's/Marek, 1985), 462.

6. Petzinger, *Hard Landing*, 132.

7. See chapter 4 of Paul Stephen Dempsey and Andrew R. Goetz, *Airline Deregulation and Lassez-Faire Mythology* (Westport, Conn.: Quorum Books, 1992).

8. Judith Schroer, "Passengers Forced to Wing It/Plenty of Grumbling on the Ground," *USA Today*, 22 November 1993, p. 3A.

9. Dirk Johnson, "American Airlines' Pilots Decide to Fly Empty Jets to Back Strike," *New York Times*, 20 November 1993, sec. 1, p. 1.

10. See "Corrections," *New York Times*, 5 May 1998, p. A2.

11. See Rhonda Richards, "What to Do if You're Flying During the Strike," *USA Today*, 19 November 1993, p. 2A; Julie Schmit, "Advice, Refunds, Options," *USA Today*, 22 November 1993, p. 3A; Julie Schmit, "Playing It Smart with Your Ticket," *USA Today*, 23 November 1993, p. 2A; Edwin McDowell, "Advice for Travelers During the Strike," *New York Times*, 19 November 1993, p. D5.

12. On the myth of the free press, see W. Lance Bennett, *The Politics of Illusion*, 3d ed. (White Plains N.Y.: Longman, 1996).

13. Michael Schudson, *The Good Citizen: A History of American Civic Life* (Cambridge: Harvard University Press, 1998), 313.

14. This is an example of Reeve's and Campbell's notion of "policing the boundaries" of reason and nonsense, an idea discussed in Chapter 1. See Jimmie L. Reeves and Richard Campbell, *Cracked Coverage: Television News, the Anti-Cocaine Crusade, and the Reagan Legacy* (Durham: Duke University Press, 1994).

15. Del Jones, "Airline Strike May Bring a New Fare War," *USA Today*, 22 November 1993, p. 1B.

16. Adam Bryant, "Airline Sees Strike as a Test of Industry," *New York Times*, 20 November 1993, sec 1, p. 7.

17. Bryant, "Airline Sees Strike," 7.

18. Del Jones and Doug Carroll, "Labor's Stormy Skies/Appetite for Low Fairs is One Culprit," *USA Today*, 19 November 1993, p. 1B.

19. Ibid.

20. Doug Carroll, "Fare Cuts Leave Analysts Skeptical," *USA Today*, 17 April 1992, p. 3B.

21. Editorial, "Who Wins in Air Fare Wars?" *St. Louis Post-Dispatch*, 8 June 1992, p. 2B.

22. AMR Corporation, *1996 Annual Report* (Dallas: AMR Corporation), 10.

23. Paul Stephen Dempsey and Andrew R. Goetz, *Airline Deregulation and Lassez-Faire Mythology* (Westport, Conn.: Quorum Books, 1992), 110.

24. Ibid., 111.

25. Ibid., 110–11.

26. From Wire Reports, "Lorenzo Knows the Woes of Crandall," *USA Today*, 24 November 1993, p. 10B.

27. See Jack Hovelson, "Airline: Strikers's Jobs Gone," *USA Today*, 19 November 1993, p. 1A; Dirk Johnson, "American Airlines Say It's Trying to Relay Flight Data to Customers," *New York Times*, 21 November 1993, sec. 1, p. 32; "New Attendants' Training Focuses Solely on Safety," *New York Times*, 22 November 1993, p. A8. Even after reporting that the flight attendants would return after eleven days, *USA Today*'s 19 November story still played up the airline's spokesman's threats, as noted in the title.

28. Todd Gitlin, *The Whole World Is Watching* (Berkeley: University of California Press, 1980), 52.

29. Del Jones, "Airline Strike May Bring a New Fare War," p. 1B.

30. Barbara Presley Noble, "At Work: Helping a Union Find Its Way," *New York Times*, 12 December 1993, sec. 3, p. 23. This was also the last story about the strike in the five media outlets analyzed in this study.

31. Warren Breed, "Mass Communication and Socio-Cultural Integration," *Social Forces* 37 (1958): 109–16.

32. Julianne Malveaux, "Don't Gouge Workers," *USA Today*, 24 November 1993, p. 18A.

Chapter 6. News for the Everyfan: The 1994–95 Baseball Strike

1. I viewed this Nike "Day 20" commercial while watching *The Late Show with David Letterman* on 31 August 1994. For a description of the campaign, see Scott Kaufmann, "Just Settle It: 'Play Ball' Advertising Campaign Puts Nike in Fans' Shoes," *USA Today Baseball Weekly*, 7–13 September 1994, p. 12.

2. Ibid.

3. See Bruce Horovitz, "Pro Teams Are About to Strike Out with Advertisers," *USA Today*, 31 October 1994, p. 7B.

4. Elizabeth Sanger, "Newspapers Bunt on Baseball Coverage," *Newsday*, 30 March 1995, p. A57.

5. Robert Silverman, "Stations Prime Pinch Hitters," *Variety*, 8–14 August 1994, 27.

6. Andrew Zimbalist, *Baseball and Billions* (New York: Basic Books, 1992).

7. See ibid. See also David Quentin Voight, *American Baseball: From Gentleman's Sport to Commissioner System* (Norman: University of Oklahoma Press, 1966).

8. Zimbalist, *Baseball and Billions*, xix.

9. For a review of the major events of the strike, see Paul D. Staudohar, "The Baseball Strike of 1994–95," in *Diamond Mines: Baseball and Labor*, ed. Paul D. Staudohar (Syracuse: Syracuse University Press), 48–61.

10. Michael Parenti, *Inventing Reality: The Politics of Mass Media* (New York: St. Martin's Press, 1986), 85.

11. William J. Puette, *Through Jaundiced Eyes: How the Media View Organized Labor* (Ithaca: Cornell University Press, 1992), 155.

12. Parenti, *Inventing Reality*, 85–86.

13. See, e.g., Jay Rosen, *What Are Journalists For?* (New Haven: Yale University Press, 1999).

14. Lance Bennett and Murray Edelman, "Toward a New Political Narrative," *Journal of Communication* 35, no. 4 (1985): 159.

15. By *federal government* I mean the U.S. government, although the Montreal Expos and the Toronto Blue Jays teams gave the Canadian provincial governments a small role.

16. Herbert Gans, *Deciding What's News: A Study of* CBS Evening News, NBC Nightly News, Newsweek, *and* Time (New York: Pantheon, 1979), 46.

17. See Brian Winston, "On Counting the Wrong Things," in *Labor, the Working Class, and the Media*, vol. 1 of *The Critical Communications Review*, ed. Vincent Mosco and Janet Wasko (Norwood, N.J.: Ablex, 1983), 167–86.

18. My thanks to Richard Campbell for the "surrogate eyewitness" and "surrogate fan" descriptions of reporters.

19. See Bruce Garrison, *Sports Reporting*, 2d ed. (Ames: Iowa State University Press, 1993), 9–10.

20. Because television is more effective at instantly communicating the objective information of sporting event outcomes, newspaper sports writing has evolved into a more interpretive journalism.

21. Bryan Burwell, "Fan's Voice Shouldn't Carry Any Say," *USA Today*, 2 August 1994, p. 3C.

22. Hal Bodley, "Players Call Strike Aug. 12," *USA Today*, 29 July 1994, p. 1A.

23. George Vecsey, "Baseball Is Skating on Thin Ice," *New York Times*, 5 August 1994, p. B7.

24. See David Finkel, "Strike, Called," *Labor Notes* (September 1994): 1, 13.

25. Walter Shapiro, "Bummer of '94," *Time*, 22 August 1994, 68–74.

26. Zimbalist, *Baseball and Billions*, 51. See also Gerald W. Scully, *The Business of Major League Baseball* (Chicago: University of Chicago Press, 1989), 105–7.

27. Michael Hiestand and Gary Mihoces, "Strike's Silver Lining: Ticket Prices Stabilize," *USA Today*, 25 April 1995, p. 13C.

28. James Quirk and Rodney D. Fort, *Pay Dirt: The Business of Professional Baseball* (Princeton: Princeton University Press, 1992).

29. Francis X. Cline, "In the Bleachers, Fans Cling to Dwindling Outs," *New York Times*, 12 August 1994, p. B7.

30. Quirk and Fort, *Pay Dirt*, 214.

31. See, e.g., "The Losses Mount," *USA Today*, 13 September 1994, p. 7C. Most sources listed Bonilla's 1994 salary at $6.3 million; *USA Today* listed his salary at $5.7 million.

32. See Kenneth M. Jennings, *Balls and Strikes: The Money Game in Professional Baseball* (New York: Praeger, 1990), 222.

33. Shapiro, "Bummer," 70.

34. Hiestand and Mihoces, "Strike's Silver Lining," 13C.

35. "Attendance," *Detroit Free Press*, 16 June 1995, p. 5F.

36. In Ralph Andreano, *No Joy in Mudville: The Dilemma of Major League Baseball* (Cambridge, MA: Schenkman, 1965), 47. Montgomery's original article appeared in *Lippincott's Magazine* in August, 1886.

37. See Zimbalist, *Baseball and Billions*.

38. Ibid., 129.

39. Quirk and Fort, *Pay Dirt*, 145.

40. Ibid., chap. 5.

41. Mark Starr, "We Was Robbed," *Newsweek*, 22 August 1994, 46–54.

42. Justice Blackmun's comments in *Flood v Kuhn*, 407 US 258 (US Sup Ct 1971). See Quirk and Fort, *Pay Dirt*, 193–4.

43. Quirk and Fort, *Pay Dirt*, 56–57. Also, see Scully, *Business of Major League Baseball*, 129–130.

44. See, for example, Editorial, "Baseball's Kid-Gougers," *USA Today*, 21 February 1995.

45. Richard Sandomir, "The Players Are Back, but Are Card Collectors?" *New York Times*, 13 April 1995, p. B11.

46. Zach Wolff, "The Virtual Field of Dreams," *Netguide*, March 1995, p. 50–55.

47. Ronald Grover, "Confessions of a Fantasy Baseball Junkie," *Business Week*, 27 July 1998, 81.

48. See, for example, Voight, *American Baseball*.

49. See, for example, Larry Weisman, "NFL to End Sports Fans' Withdrawal," *USA Today*, 2 September 1994, pp. 1A-2A.

50. Matt Roush, "Documentary May Be New Fall Classic," *USA Today*, 16 September 1994, pp. 1A-2A.

51. *World News Tonight*, reporter Dick Schaap, ABC, 13 November 1994.

52. See, for example, Mike Wise, "Where Did the Baseball Season Go? Cyberspace," *New York Times*, 17 August 1994, pp. B1, B9.

53. Harvey Araton, "Strikes? Salary Caps? Hey, There's Always Polo," *New York Times*, 25 September 1994, p. 21.

54. For rare coverage of this topic, see "Senate Action Would End Part of Antitrust Exemption," *New York Times*, 15 September 1994, p. B8; and Editorial, "Change Law on Baseball," *USA Today*, 19 September 1994, p. 12A. Both articles were published after the season was officially called off on September 14, 1994.

55. Jay Rosen and Davis Merritt, Jr., *Public Journalism: Theory and Practice* (Dayton: Kettering Foundation, 1994), 27.

56. James Lemert, "Effective Public Opinion," in *Public Opinion, the Press, and Public Policy*, ed. J. David Kennamer (Westport, CT: Praeger, 1994). 41–61.

57. Joe Urschel, "Send Baseball to Washington; You'll Never See It Again," *USA Today*, 10 February 1995, p. 11A.

58. George Vescey, "Scabs Are the Ultimate Owner Scam," *New York Times*, 5 February 1995, p. 23.

59. Editorial, "Spring Dreaming," *USA Today*, 14 February 1995, p. 14A.

60. One editorial loosely linked the baseball strike to the issue of replacement workers. See Editorial, "After the Strike: Fairness," *New York Times*, 23 February 1995, p. A14.

61. "Attendance," *Detroit Free Press*, 5F.

62. Michael Hiestand, "Baseball Marketing Schemes Tardy but on Target," *USA Today*, 27 April 1995, p. 3C.

63. Mitch Albom, "Rudely Welcomed; Anger Over Strike Isn't Baseball's Only Problem," *Detroit Free Press*, 3 May 1995, p. 1A.

64. Jason Whitlock, "Save KC Baseball . . . or Else," *Kansas City Star*, 6 April 1995, p. D1.

65. Jason Whitlock, "It's Time to Send a Message," *Kansas City Star*, 7 April 1995, p. D1. See also Jason Whitlock, "Protest Is Message to Baseball," *Kansas City Star*, 9 April 1995, p. C1.

66. Jason Whitlock, "Apology Accepted: No Boycott," *Kansas City Star*, 13 April 1995, p. D1.

67. Ibid., p. D1.

68. Jay Rosen, *Public Journalism as a Democratic Art* (New York: Project on Public Life and the Press, 1994) n. pag.

69. See Zimbalist, *Baseball and Billions*, 137–40.

70. Paul E. Witteman, "A Resounding Victory for Stupidity," *Time*, 26 September 1994, 71.

71. See Larry G. Bumgardner, "Baseball's Antitrust Exemption," in *Diamond Mines: Baseball and Labor*, ed. Paul D. Staudohar (Syracuse: Syracuse University Press), 83–95.

72. Don Cronin, "Baseball Antitrust Laws," *USA Today*, 8 October 1998, p. 1C. Italics added.

73. AP, "Congress Votes Baseball Bill," *New York Times*, 8 October 1998, p. D4. Italics added.

74. Richard Sandomir, "YES Says No to Cablevision Proposal," *New York Times*, 27 March 2002, p. D5.

75. Kurt Badenhausen, Cecily Fluke, Lesley Kump, and Michael K. Ozanian, "Double Play," *Forbes*, 15 April 2002, 92–98.

76. Chris Isidore, "Financial Data Show Teams Owned by Broadcasters Shift Revenue," *CNN/Money*, 7 December 2001, http://money.cnn.com/2001/12/07/news/column_sportsbiz/index.htm (7 December 2001).

77. Badenhausen, Fluke, Kump, and Ozanian, "Double Play," 94. The luxury tax lasted from 1997 to 1999, but was expected to be a part of future baseball agreements because the lack of revenue parity between franchises remains a big issue.

78. Hal Bodley, "Talking Contraction," *USA Today*, 6 February 2002, p. 6C.

79. Paul Irvin, "Campaign Coverage" (presentation at the annual meeting of the Iowa Broadcast News Association Convention, Cedar Rapids, Iowa, April 2002). Thanks to Paul Irvin, a project director of the Radio and Television News Directors Foundation in Washington, D.C., whose talk on campaign coverage helped me to think of the strike coverage in its similar lack of truth checks on the claims and counterclaims.

80. See Hal Bodley, "Selig: Baseball in a Pickly; MLB Commissioner to Reveal Financial Woes Today," *USA Today*, 6 December 2001, p. 1C, http://www.usatoday.com/usatonline/20011206/3678082s.htm (6 December 2001). See also Richard Sandomir, "Baseball Teams Lost Half a Billion, Selig Says," *New York Times*, 6 December 2001, http://www.nytimes.com/2001/12/06/sports/baseball/06BASE.html (6 December 2001); Richard Sandomir, "Selig Defends Contraction to Congress," *New York Times*, 7 December 2001, http://www.nytimes.com/2001/12/07/sports/baseball/07BASE.html (7 December 2001). The television networks ABC, CBS, and NBC did not broadcast a report on either hearing. Reports on the war in Afghanistan dominated their programs at that time.

81. See Isidore's columns at http://money.cnn.com/commentary/column_sportsbiz/.

82. Chris Isidore, e-mail correspondence with author, 29 April 2002.

83. Isidore, "Financial Data Show."

84. Chris Isidore, "Cries of Poverty Are Undercut by Hundred of Millions in Central Fund," *CNN/Money*, 7 December 2001, http://money.cnn.com/2001/12/21/news/column_sportsbiz/index.htm (7 December 2001).

85. Badenhausen, Fluke, Kump, and Ozanian, "Double Play."

86. George Vecsey, "After the Sale of the Red Sox, Baseball Must Get Story Straight," *New York Times*, 23 December 2001, sec. 8, pp. S1, S4.

87. Jon Saraceno, "Players, Owners Both to Blame," *USA Today*, 9 November 2001, p. 3C.

88. Michael Silverman, "Let's Play Ball! Baseball Owners, Union Reach Deal," *Boston Herald*, 31 August 2002, p. 1.

89. Financial data from Badenhausen, Fluke, Kump, and Ozanian, "Double Play," p. 96.

Chapter 7. The UPS Strike, the WTO Protests, and the Future of Labor in the News

1. Stuart Elliott, "Going Big on Brown," in Advertising Newsletter, *New York Times on the Web*, 19 February 2002, http://www.nytimes.com/email. The TV ads were scheduled to also run during broadcasts of the NCAA men's basketball tournament, the Academy Awards, and on CNN, CNBC, Fox News Channel, and Discovery. The print ads appeared in the *Wall Street Journal*, *Business Week*, *Forbes*, *Fortune*, *Newsweek*, *Sports Illustrated*, and *Time*.

2. Network news stories were acquired through the Vanderbilt Television News

Archive. Newspaper reports were obtained via the Nexis full text database, and supplemented with microfilm copies.

3. Peyton M. Craighill, e-mail to author, 15 August 2001. Craighill, Project Director of The Pew Research Center for the People and the Press, supplied News Interest Index data for all labor stories in their surveys from the 1990s.

4. Jeremy Brecher, *Strike!* (Cambridge, Mass.: South End Press, 1997), 358–59.

5. David Field, "Poll: 55% Support Strikers at UPS," *USA Today*, 15 August 1997, p. A1. See also Steven Greenhouse, "Strikers at U.P.S. Backed by Public," *New York Times*, 17 August 1997, pp. A1, A16.

6. Greenhouse, "Strikers at U.P.S. Backed," p. A1. The story's assertion that "the public sided with management in most other recent work stoppages that grabbed the nation's attention, including the 1994 baseball strike, the 1982 football players' strike and the 1981 air controllers' strike" is also a gross simplification of public sentiment regarding these strikes.

7. Field, "Poll: 55% Support Strikers," p. 1A.

8. Gary Langer, "Poll: Keep Clinton Out of U.P.S.," *ABC News.com*, 12 August 1997, http://more.abcnews.go.com/sections/us/upspoll812/index.html (12 August 1997).

9. Laura Parker, "Town Finds Strike Is Inconvenience but Not Calamity," *USA Today*, 15 August 1997, p. 6A.

10. See Jim West, "Big Win at UPS!" *Labor Notes* (September 1997): 1, 14–15.

11. Ibid., 14.

12. For an overview of the Teamster strategy, see Matt Witt and Rand Wilson, "Part-Time America Won't Work: The Teamsters Fight for Good Jobs at UPS," in *Not Your Father's Union Movement: Inside the AFL-CIO*, ed. Jo-Ann Mort (London: Verso, 1998).

13. Lawrence B. Glickman, *A Living Wage: American Workers and the Making of Consumer Society* (Ithaca: Cornell University Press, 1997). Glickman explains that early proponents of the living wage in the post–Civil War era defined the wage as one that provides "the ability to support families, to maintain self-respect, and to have both the means and the leisure to participate in the civic life of the nation" (p. 3). Glickman argues that the family wage is a subset of the living wage.

14. West, "Big Win at UPS!" 14.

15. Langer, "Poll: Keep Clinton Out," 1.

16. See, e.g., David Gartman, *Auto Slavery: The Labor Process in the American Automobile Industry, 1987–1950* (New Brunswick: Rutgers University Press, 1986), 203–14.

17. See David Kusnet, "The 'America Needs a Raise' Campaign," in *Not Your Father's Union Movement: Inside the AFL-CIO*, ed. Jo-Ann Mort (London: Verso, 1998), 167–78.

18. Jarol B. Manheim, *The Death of a Thousand Cuts: Corporate Campaigns and the Attack on the Corporation* (Mahwah, N.J.: Lawrence Erlbaum, 2001), 337.

19. Jane Slaughter, "Teamsters May Strike UPS for Full-Time Jobs," *Labor Notes* (August 1997): 1, 14.

20. For an example of Sonnenfeld as pro-UPS commentator, see Allen Myerson, "Fracturing U.P.S. Image of Labor Peace," *New York Times*, 10 August 1997, p. A16. According to the *Augusta Chronicle Online*, "senior executives would pay up to $2,500 apiece to attend [Sonnenfeld's] conferences at Emory." See Associated Press, "Star Business Professor Falls Amid Vandalism Allegations," *Augusta Chronicle Online*, 23 December 1997, http://www.augustachronicle.com/stories/122397/bizdean .shtml (15 March 1998).

21. Deepa Kumar makes a similar conclusion in her analysis of newspaper cover-

age of the UPS strike: "For a brief period, organized labor demonstrated its ability to galvanize public opinion in the form of an emergent class identity and class consciousness." See Deepa Kumar, "Mass Media, Class, and Democracy: The Struggle over Newspaper Representation of the UPS Strike," *Critical Studies in Media Communication* 18, no. 3 (2001): 298.

22. "UPS Strike Starts," *ABC News.com*, 4 August 1997, http://more.abcnews.go .com/sections/world/1997/97_ups.html (4 August 1997).

23. See "The UPS Story," UPS, 25 March 2002, http://www.ups.com/about/ story.html.

24. Greenhouse, "Strikers at U.P.S. Backed," p. A16.

25. For an overview of the major arguments against the WTO and other international economic agencies, see Michael Albert, "A Q&A on the WTO, IMF, World Bank, and Activism," *Z Magazine* (January 2000): 24–29.

26. From the Preamble of the WTO Agreement (April 15, 1994), in John H. Jackson, *The World Trade Organization: Constitution and Jurisprudence* (London: Royal Institute of International Affairs, 1998), 133.

27. Based on the review of 167 dispute panel cases brought by 2000. See Lori Wallach and Michelle Sforza, *Whose Trade Organization?* (Washington, D.C.: Public Citizen, 1999). See also Silja J. A. Talvi, "World Trade or World Domination?" *MojoWire*, 24 November 1999, http://www.motherjones.com/wto/talvi.html (17 January 2000).

28. Public Law 162, 101st Cong., 1st sess., (21 November 1989).

29. World Trade Organization, *Annual Report 1999* (Geneva: WTO, 2000). See also Public Citizen/Global Trade Watch, *Testimony of Lori Wallach Regarding U.S. Preparations for the World Trade Organization's 1999 Ministerial Meeting*, 14 May 1999, http://www.tradewatch.org/gattwto/Testimonies%20&%20Comments/Testimon. htm (17 January 2000).

30. After the WTO appellate dispute panel's 1998 decision, the United States attempted to get section 609 of the Endangered Species Act in compliance with the WTO rules. As part of its more than year-long efforts to comply, the United States changed the Department of State guidelines for section 609; launched a new effort for negotiations on sea turtle conservation with governments in the Indian Ocean region; provided financial assistance to developing countries to attend those negotiations; and offered technical training and financial assistance on the design, construction, installation, and operation of turtle excluder devices. In October 2000, Malaysia was still unsatisfied and again requested a WTO dispute panel to investigate U.S. compliance with the 1998 appellate dispute panel's report. On 15 June 2001, a WTO dispute settlement panel ruled that the United States' new efforts had complied with the 1998 report and that the United States can refuse shrimp caught in a manner that is not turtle-safe. (Malaysia had ninety days to file an appeal, if it wished to do so.) The outcome was a rare case of an environmental rule ultimately surviving the WTO dispute settlement process. After years of environmentally unfavorable WTO decisions, U.S. Trade Representative Robert Zoellick was quick to proclaim that this case (along with a ruling in favor of a French ban on Canadian asbestos imports) proves the WTO is environmentally friendly: "this case follows the report in the recent asbestos case, which similarly confirms the WTO's sensitivity to health and safety concerns. These two cases show that the WTO rules are consistent with high levels of safety and environmental protection." See *U.S. Wins WTO Case on Sea Turtle Conservation*, Office of the United States Trade Representative, Press Release, 15 June 2001, http://www.ustr.gov/releases/2001/06/01–40.htm (8 August 2001). See also Cat Lazaroff, "WTO Upholds U.S. Right to Protect Sea Turtles," *Environment News Service*, http://ens.lycos.com/ens/jun2001/2001L-06–19–07.html (8 August 2001).

31. Brian Michael Goss, "'All Our Kids Get Better Jobs Tomorrow': The North American Free Trade Agreement in *The New York Times*," *Journalism & Communication Monographs* 3, no. 1 (2001).

32. Ibid., 29.

33. Jeff Faux, *Briefing Paper: NAFTA at Seven—Its Impact on Workers in All Three Nations,* (Washington, D.C.: Economic Policy Institute, April 2001), http://www.epinet.org/briefingpapers/nafta01/nafta-at-7.pdf, p. 1 (30 July 2001).

34. AFL-CIO, *NAFTA's Seven-Year Itch* (Washington, D.C.: AFL-CIO, 2001) http://www.aflcio.org/globaleconomy/nafta.pdf (30 July 2001).

35. Faux, *Briefing Paper: NAFTA*, 1.

36. David Glenn, "Fast Track Derailed," in *Not Your Father's Union Movement: Inside the AFL-CIO,* ed. Jo-Ann Mort (London: Verso, 1998), 189–99.

37. Ibid., 196.

38. Timothy Egan, "Free Trade Takes on Free Speech," *New York Times*, 5 December 1999, sec. 4, pp. 1, 5.

39. John J. Sweeney, "Making the Global Economy Work for Working Families: Beyond the WTO" (address to the National Press Club, Washington, D.C., 19 November 1999).

40. Jackie Calmes, "American Opinion—Despite Buoyant Economic Times Americans Don't Buy Free Trade," *Wall Street Journal*, 10 December 1998, p. A10.

41. Michael Medved, "Battle in Seattle: No, This Wasn't the '60s All Over Again," *USA Today*, 7 December 1999, p. 19A.

42. Thomas L. Friedman, "Senseless in Seattle," *New York Times*, 1 December 1999, p. A23.

43. Editorial, "Smashing Starbucks' Windows Won't Free World's Oppressed," *USA Today*, 2 December 1999, p. 14A.

44. Thomas Frank, *One Market Under God* (New York: Doubleday, 2000), 239.

45. Quoted in *This Is What Democracy Looks Like*, dir. Jill Freidberg and Rick Rowley (Seattle: Independent Media Center/Big Noise Films, 2000), 72 min.

46. Patrick McMahon, "Protestors Prepare to Make Views Known at Trade Summit; Billboards Go Up, Demonstrations Scheduled to Get Point Across," *USA Today*, 12 November 1999, p. 6A.

47. Ibid., p. 6A.

48. Joseph Kahn, "Global Trade Forum Reflects a Burst of Conflict and Hope," *New York Times*, 28 November 1999, sec. 1, p. 1.

49. Steven Greenhouse, "A Carnival of Derision to Greet the Princes of Global Trade," *New York Times*, 29 November 1999, p. A12.

50. Seth Ackerman, "Prattle in Seattle: Media Coverage Misrepresented Protests," in *Globalize This!* ed. Kevin Danaher and Roger Burbach (Monroe, Maine: Common Courage Press), 61.

51. See Paul Hawken, "Skeleton Woman Visits Seattle," in *Globalize This!* ed. Kevin Danaher and Roger Burbach (Monroe, Maine: Common Courage Press), 14–34.

52. Greenhouse, "A Carnival of Derision," p. A12.

53. Sam Howe Verhovek and Steven Greenhouse, "National Guard Is Called to Quell Trade-Talk Protests; Seattle Is Under Curfew after Disruptions," *New York Times*, 1 December 1999, p. A1.

54. Patrick McMahon and James Cox, "Seattle Tension Mounts," *USA Today*, 1 December 1999, P. 1A.

55. Friedman, "Senseless," p. A23.

56. Editorial, "Smashing Starbucks' Windows," p. 14A.

57. Seattle City Council, Report of the WTO Accountability Review Committee, 14

September 2000, p. 5, http://www.cityofseattle.net/wtocommittee/arcfinal.doc (23 May 2001). See also ACLU Washington, "Out of Control: Seattle's Flawed Response to Protests Against the World Trade Organization," July 2000, http://www.aclu-wa.org/ISSUES/police/WTO-Report.html (23 May 2001).

58. See the Independent Media Center, http://www.indymedia.org. The Independent Media Center was established in 1999 to create global, grassroots coverage on the WTO protests in Seattle. Allied independent media include Free Speech TV (http://www.freespeech.org) and Corporate Watch (http://www.corpwatch.org). The Independent Media Center film *This Is What Democracy Looks Like* (dir. Jill Freidberg and Rick Rowley, Independent Media Center/Big Noise Films, 72 min, 2000) visually documents the protests from a grassroots level and illustrates what the mainstream news didn't cover.

59. David E. Sanger and Joseph Kahn, "A Chaotic Intersection of Tear Gas and Trade Talks," *New York Times*, 1 December 1999, p. A14.

60. Sarah Lyall, "Talks and Turmoil: The Reaction; Internationally, Embarrassment for the U.S.," *New York Times*, 2 December 1999, p. A17.

61. Andrew Kohut, "Globalization and the Wage Gap," *New York Times*, 3 December 1999, p. A31.

62. Michelle Conlin, "Most Americans Feel the Business Boom Has Left Them Out in the Cold," *Business Week*, 27 December 1999, 52. Seven percent of survey respondents answered "Don't Know," and 2 percent refused to answer. The poll was conducted December 9–11, 1999, by Harris Interactive for *Business Week*.

63. Kevin Michael DeLuca and Jennifer Peeples argue that in today's "public screen" of the media, images, distraction, and dissent are valid forms of communication as well. They suggest that the anarchists' vandalism resulted in more news coverage about the protesters and helped to ultimately make the protests a more successful criticism of the WTO and the global economic order. See Kevin Michael DeLuca and Jennifer Peeples, "From Public Sphere to Public Screen: Democracy, Activism, and the 'Violence' of Seattle, *Critical Studies in Media Communication* 19, no. 2 (2002): 125–51.

64. Clinton quoted in *CBS Evening News*, John Roberts, rept., 2 December 1999.

65. Joseph E. Stiglitz, *Globalization and Its Discontents* (New York: W. W. Norton, 2002).

66. James Cox, "WTO Meeting Shrinks Amid Attack Fears, Feuds," *USA Today*, 7 November 2001, p. 1B.

67. Glickman, *A Living Wage*.

68. See Living Wage Resource Center, http://www.livingwagecampaign.org/.

69. See Thomas Frank, *The Conquest of Cool: Business Culture, Counterculture, and the Rise of Hip Consumerism* (Chicago: University of Chicago Press, 1997); David Brooks, *Bobos in Paradise: The New Upper Class and How They Got There* (New York: Simon & Schuster, 2000). See also the excellent documentary broadcast on PBS' *Frontline* in February 2001: *Merchants of Cool* (dir. Barak Goodman, prod. Barak Goodman and Rachel Dretzin, 60 min, 2001).

70. See Douglas Rushkoff, *Coercion: Why We Listen to What "They" Say* (New York: Riverhead Books, 1999).

71. Starhawk, "How We Really Shut Down the WTO," in *Globalize This!* ed. Kevin Danaher and Roger Burbach (Monroe, Maine: Common Courage Press), 35–40.

72. Howard Kimeldorf, *Battling for American Labor* (Berkeley: University of California Press, 1999). For more on corporate campaigns, see Manheim, *The Death of a Thousand Cuts*. Manheim's book has an excellent compendium of corporate campaigns, but he seems to be under the impression that they are unfairly wielded against cor-

porations. For an alternative opinion on corporate campaigns, see Brian Michael Goss, review of *The Death of a Thousand Cuts: Corporate Campaigns and the Attack on the Corporation,* by Jarol B. Manheim, *Journal of Communication Inquiry* 26, no. 1 (2002): 102–6.

73. Tom Juravich and Kate Bronfenbrenner, *Ravenswood: The Steelworkers' Victory and the Revival of American Labor* (Ithaca: Cornell University Press, 1999), xi.

74. Sam Pizzigatti and Fred J. Solowey, ed., *The New Labor Press: Journalism for a Changing Union Movement* (Ithaca: Cornell University Press, 1992).

75. NUA Internet, "How Many Online?" http://www.nua.ie/surveys/how_many_online/index.html (10 May 2003).

76. Douglas Gomery, "The FCC's Newspaper-Broadcast Cross-Ownership Rule: An Analysis" (Washington, D.C.: Economic Policy Institute), 6 June 2002, http://reclaimthemedia.org/stories.php?story=02/06/06/7369127 (11 June 2002).

77. Jonathan Lawson, "Media Politics: The Urge to Merge and Converge," Reclaimthemedia.org, 6 June 2002, http://www.reclaimthemedia.org/stories.php?story=02/06/06/9495929 (11 June 2002). See also "Now CanWest Is Censoring the News, Too," The Newspaper Guild, 22 March 2002, http://newsguild.org/gr/gr_display.php?storyID=701 (11 June 2002).

78. See CanWest Global—Vision's web site, http://www.canwestglobal.com/vision.html (11 June 2002).

INDEX